米国法適用下における
商取引契約書

瀬川 一真

Explanations of
Commercial Contracts
under U.S. law

大学教育出版

はじめに

　筆者は，日本に居住していたころから米国法を基礎とする「米国法契約書」を取り扱う機会も少なくはなく，また，それにあたって格別の不都合を感じてはいなかった．しかし，それが大きな誤りであることを悟ったのは渡米して間もないころである．

　そのことを顕著に感じたのは契約交渉の場であった．ビジネスのスピードを重視する米国においては，ある契約に関する交渉が難航してくると，それらを一気に解決するべく，双方の弁護士が面と向かって，あるいは，電話を通じて，直接の交渉を行うことも少なくない．そのような場面においては，自己の案の相当性に関する説明のみならず，相手方の反応および契約書全体の内容を踏まえつつ，即座に代替案を提示できる能力が求められる．それらを実践するためには，英語力は言うまでもなく，対象取引または対象製品に関する理解のほか，米国法に関する深い理解が強く期待されるのである．

　本書は，その後，筆者が行った，米国ロースクールにおける契約法を中心とした研究，ならびに，実務における契約交渉の準備または契約交渉の振り返りに際して行った調査および検討の結果を共有させていただくものである．契約書のサンプルには米国契約法の重要項目を広範にわたって見渡すことができる製品売買契約を用いることとし，そのうえで各条項について，その趣旨，米国法との関係，ならびに，最新の動向および実務上の取り扱いについて紹介している．ただし，米国において契約法はとりわけ州法が中心となる領域

であるところ，50州すべてについての解説を行うことは現実的ではない．そこで，本書は多数説と思われるものを中心とした解説を行っている．したがって，実務においては，各州法の確認が必要となることにご留意いただきたい．また，本書の性質上，契約書のサンプル条文の掲載は必要限度にとどめている．もっとも，サンプル条文の紹介に関してはすでに多くの優秀な文献があると思われるため，それらに譲らせていただくことに問題はないはずである．

　さて，実のところ，筆者も米国法契約書に関するプロフェッショナルとなることをひとつの目標とし，日々多くのことを学び続けている最中である．したがって本書も万能とは言えないかもしれないが，紙面の許す限り，筆者の持つ米国法契約書に関する理解と実務に関する見識を詰め込むべく全力を注いだことは紛れもない事実である．また，内容の正確性を担保する意味で，または，読者の方々のさらなる学習もしくは研究に資する目的で，参考文献に関する充実度および透明性を高めるように努めたことは，本書の特徴のひとつといえるのではないかと思う．もしも本書が筆者と同じような志をお持ちの方の一助となることができたならば，それはこの上ない喜びである．

　2019年2月

筆者

米国法適用下における商取引契約書
Explanations of Commercial Contracts under U.S. law

目 次

はじめに ……………………………………………………………… i

凡　例 ………………………………………………………………… viii

CHAPTER 1 / INTRODUCTORY PROVISIONS …… 1
  1.1 Preamble …………………………………………………… 1
  1.2 Recitals ……………………………………………………… 6
  1.3 Words of Agreement ……………………………………… 8

CHAPTER 2 / DEFINITIONS PROVISIONS ………… 10
  2.1 Definitions Provisionsの意義 …………………………… 14
  2.2 Definitionの配置箇所 …………………………………… 14

CHAPTER 3 / ACTION PROVISIONS ………………… 16
  3.1 U.C.C.の適用 ……………………………………………… 16
  3.2 Statute of Frauds ………………………………………… 17
  3.3 Installment Contract ……………………………………… 18
  3.4 Order of Precedence Clause …………………………… 20
  3.5 Forecasts Clause ………………………………………… 21
  3.6 Offerと Acceptance ……………………………………… 23
  3.7 Individual Transactionsに関する解約権 ……………… 26
  3.8 Individual Transactionsに関する解約権行使の効果 … 26
  3.9 Purchase Ordersの変更 ………………………………… 28
  3.10 Time is of the Essence Clause ………………………… 30
  3.11 欠陥品または数量超過品の提供 ……………………… 32
  3.12 Title Transfer Clause …………………………………… 37
  3.13 Risk of Loss Clause …………………………………… 39

3.14 製品の Price ……………………………………… *40*

3.15 Most Favored Nation Clause ……………………… *42*

3.16 Payment Terms ……………………………………… *44*

3.17 Setoff Clause ………………………………………… *45*

3.18 Setoff と倒産手続きとの関係 ……………………… *48*

3.19 製品を使用するためのライセンス権 ……………… *51*

3.20 製品を製造するためのライセンス権 ……………… *53*

3.21 知的財産権に関する所有権の帰属 ………………… *54*

3.22 著作権に関する所有権の帰属 ……………………… *58*

3.23 Warranty Clause …………………………………… *60*

3.24 Statute of Limitations との関係 …………………… *62*

3.25 Warranty 責任の否定または制限 …………………… *63*

3.26 契約違反と Warranty 違反………………………… *65*

3.27 Product Recall Clause ……………………………… *66*

3.28 Indemnification ……………………………………… *67*

3.29 Indemnification Clause……………………………… *72*

3.30 First Party Indemnification ………………………… *79*

3.31 Indemnification Clause に基づく義務からの免責 … *82*

3.32 Intellectual Property Indemnification Clause ……… *84*

3.33 Intellectual Property Indemnification Clause に基づく
　　 義務からの免責……………………………………… *85*

3.34 Exclusive Remedy Clause …………………………… *86*

3.35 Representation and Warranty Clause ……………… *89*

3.36 Covenant ……………………………………………… *91*

3.37 Dodd-Frank Act……………………………………… *93*

CHAPTER 4 / ENDGAME PROVISIONS …………………… 95

4.1 契約期間 ……………………………………………… *95*

4.2 Evergreen Clause ... *96*
4.3 契約の解除 ... *99*
4.4 Survival Clause ... *107*

CHAPTER 5 / OTHER SUBSTANTIVE PROVISIONS ... *109*

5.1 Confidentiality Clause ... *109*
5.2 Confidential Informationである旨の表示 ... *111*
5.3 秘密保持義務の不発生 ... *112*
5.4 秘密保持義務の継続期間 ... *116*
5.5 契約書の準備段階における条項の削除 ... *118*
5.6 Limitation of Liability Clause ... *119*
5.7 Insurance Clause ... *122*
5.8 Insurance Clauseに関する制限 ... *125*
5.9 保険契約に関する要求 ... *126*

CHAPTER 6 / GENERAL PROVISIONS ... *130*

6.1 Further Assurance Clause ... *130*
6.2 Cumulative Remedies Clause ... *132*
6.3 Irreparable Harm Clause ... *134*
6.4 Non-Waiver Clause ... *136*
6.5 Force Majeure Clause ... *139*
6.6 Entire Agreement Clause ... *141*
6.7 Notices Clause ... *143*
6.8 Headings Clause ... *144*
6.9 Severability Clause ... *145*
6.10 Non-Modification Clause ... *146*
6.11 Counterparts Clause ... *148*
6.12 Independent Contractor Clause ... *149*

6.13 Assignment and Delegation Clause ……………… *151*
6.14 Third Party Beneficiaries Clause ……………… *155*
6.15 Dispute Resolution Clause ……………… *157*
6.16 Choice of Law Clause ……………… *160*
6.17 CISG Clause ……………… *164*
6.18 Choice of Forum Clause ……………… *166*
6.19 Waiver of Jury Trial Clause ……………… *170*
6.20 Language Clause ……………… *171*

CHAPTER 7 / SIGNATURE LINES ……………… *172*

7.1 Testimonium Clause ……………… *172*
7.2 Signature Block ……………… *174*
7.3 電子署名 ……………… *176*
7.4 イニシャルの利用 ……………… *177*

CHAPTER 8 / ANCILLARY DOCUMENTS ……………… *178*

8.1 Ancillary Documents ……………… *178*

おわりに ……………… *180*

凡　例

1. サンプル契約書（General Purchase Agreement）
- Thomson Reuters のサンプル契約書[1]を基礎としつつ，筆者が本書の内容に応じた変更を加えている．

2. 説　明
- 文中において「●条」と言及している場合，それはサンプル契約書の条文番号を指す（例として，29 ページにおける，「5.5 条のように」）．

- 各項目における見出し記号については，a, i, (a), (i) の順序で使用している．なお，丸囲み数字については，法律上の効果の発生要件を示すために使用している．

- 鍵括弧または括弧については，以下のとおり，読み手の理解を補助する目的で使用している．したがって，同じ単語でも鍵括弧または括弧を伴う場合とそうでない場合とがありうるが，それはその単語の意味を異ならせる意図によるものではない．

    (1) 初出のキーワード，または，再出のキーワードであるものの再度強調すべきと思われる場合（例として，25 ページにおける，「Merchant」，または，31 ページにおける，（General Time is of the Essence Clause という））．

---

[1] Thomson Reuters, *Sale of Goods Agreement (Pro-Buyer)*, Practical Law Commercial Transaction, https://1.next.westlaw.com/Document/Ia09864cd7bd811e38578f7ccc38dcbee/View/FullText.html?navigationPath=Search%2Fv1%2Fresults%2Fnavigation%2Fi0ad7403600000164f0d1b62eb869676d%3FNav%3DKNOWHOW%26fragmentIdentifier%3DIa09864cd7bd811e38578f7ccc38dcbee%26startIndex%3D1%26contextData%3D%2528sc.Default%2529%26transitionType%3DSearchItem&listSource=Search&listPageSource=82f169ab5f367defad0110d20408429d&list=KNOWHOW&rank=2&sessionScopeId=939cfb40d31f9c49a64ad22c644442af88eb8f82e6c289b578a85a8e70ae5cf1&originationContext=Search%20Result&transitionType=SearchItem&contextData=%28sc.Default%29 (last visited Jul. 31, 2018).

(2) キーワードではないものの，専門用語として参考になると思われる場合（例として，50 ページにおける，「secured creditor」）．

(3) 定義づけを行いたい場合（例として，27 ページにおける，(以下，CISG という)）．

- 下線については，読み手が着目すべき箇所またはその他の事項と比較の対象となる箇所などに付している．

3. 脚注
- 参考文献については，筆者の判断のもと，その内容について，有用であること，かつ，信頼がおけるものであることを条件として，法令，判例，およびロースクール紀要といった伝統的な文献に限ることなく，例えば実務家（米国弁護士）のインターネット上の見解などについても幅広く紹介することとしている．

- 引用については，The Bluebook A Uniform System of Citation[2]に拠っている．そのうちの一部について紹介すると，*Id.* は，直前の脚注における文献と同じ文献を引用している場合において使用する[3]．*Supra* は，直前ではないもののすでに脚注で紹介した文献と同じ文献を引用している場合において使用する[4]．

4. 訳
- 参考文献などはすべて英語によるものを対象としているところ，それらの翻訳はすべて筆者による．

---

[2] The Bluebook A Uniform System of Citation (20th ed. 2015).
[3] *Id.* rule 4.1.
[4] *Id.* rule 4.2.

CHAPTER 1 / INTRODUCTORY PROVISIONS

Introductory Provisions は，Preamble，Recitals，および Words of Agreement から構成され，契約書の読み手に契約に関する基本情報を提供する[1]。

GENERAL PURCHASE AGREEMENT

This General Purchase Agreement (this "Agreement"), entered into as of March 31, 2015 (the "Effective Date"), is entered into between Buckeyes corporation, an Ohio corporation, having its principal place of business at 1000 Union Square Blvd., Dublin, OH 43016 ("Buyer") and Spartans LLC., a Michigan limited liability company, having its principal place of business at 1000 Goldrush Blvd., Rochester Hills, MI 48307 ("Seller"). Buyer and Seller may collectively be referred to herein as the "Parties", or individually as a "Party".

1.1 Preamble

「契約書の前文」を意味する[2]「Preamble」は契約書の対象を特定する目的のもと，契約書の名称，契約当事者，および契約締結日などを記載する。

　a. 契約書の名称
契約書の名称は，それ自体も契約書の内容の解釈の一資料となりうることなどをふまえると[3]，契約の内容と合致したものを適切に選択すべきである。また，例えば，「Agreement」など，あまりに簡略な契約書の名称は，同一の契約当事者間で複数の契約書を締結した場合における混乱などを避ける意味でも控えるべきである[4]。

---

[1] Tina L. Stark, Drafting Contracts How and Why Lawyers Do What They Do 4 (2d ed. 2013).
[2] *Black's Law Dictionary: Pocket Edition* 585 (4th ed. 2011).
[3] *See generally* Neece v. A.A.A. Realty Co., 159 Tex. 403, 9-20 (Sup.Ct. Tex. 1959) (quoting Bailey v. Mullens, 313 S.W. 2d 99, 103 (Civ. App. Tex. 1958) (契約の解釈にあたっては契約書本文の内容を重視するものの，契約書の表題についても一資料とはなる旨を示した) ("While in certain cases, one must consider captions in order to ascertain the meaning and nature of a written instrument, it has been held that the greater weight must be given to the operative contractual clauses of the agreement, for 'An instrument is that which its language shows it to be, without regard to what it is labelled.'").
[4] Kenneth A. Adams, A Manual of Style for Contract Drafting 2 (4th ed. 2017) (契約書の名称を単に「Agreement」とすることは，契約対象がまれなものである，または，契約内容が複数の種類の取引に関する規定を含むものであるなど，より適切な名称が見当たらない場合に限るべきであるとする)。

i. Agreement と Contract との区分

本契約書の名称は、「(General Purchase) Agreement」としているが、一般には契約書を Contract と呼ぶこともある。しかし、契約法[5]においては「Agreement」と「Contract」とは同義ではなく、次のように区分される。

(a) Agreement の意義

「Agreement」とは、権利および義務に関する契約当事者間における合意を指し[6]、一方契約当事者から提示された契約関係に入る意思表示(Offer[7]という)と他方契約当事者による Offer に同意する旨の意思表示(Acceptance[8]という)とが合致した場合に認められる[9]。

したがって、両当事者がそもそも取引自体に合意していない場合[10]、または、両当事者ともに取引自体には合意したつもりであったものの、取引対象に関する理解に大きな齟齬があった場合[11]などにおいては「Agreement」は成立していないことになる。

(b) Contract の意義

「Contract」とは、「Agreement」のうち執行力のあるものをいう[12]。「Contract」が成立するためには、①Offer、②Acceptance、および、③各契約当事者から他方契約当事者への Consideration の提供が必要である[13]。

したがって、「Agreement」と「Contract」との区分は「Consideration」の存在が認められるか否かによるといえる。

---

[5] 本書においては Common Law (主として判例が集積して形成される法) および制定法 (Uniform Commercial Code などを参考として制定された州法を含む) などを総称して「契約法」という。
[6] Black's Law Dictionary: Pocket Edition 29 (4th ed. 2011) ("A mutual understanding between two or more persons about their relative rights and duties regarding past or future performances; a manifestation of mutual assent by two or more persons.").
[7] Restatement (Second) of Contracts § 24 (Am. Law Inst. 1981).
[8] Id. § 50(1).
[9] Id. § 17(1).
[10] See id. § 174 cmt. (a) (一方契約当事者が他方契約当事者の脅迫によって契約を締結した場合、その契約は無効である).
[11] See id. § 152(1) (契約の基本条件たる事実について両契約当事者に誤解があった場合、その契約は無効としている)。
[12] See Black's Law Dictionary: Pocket Edition 158 (4th ed. 2011) ("An agreement between two or more parties creating obligations that are enforceable or otherwise recognizable at law.").
[13] See, e.g., Sauner v. Public Service Authority of South Carolina, 354 S.C. 397, 406 (Sup. Ct. S.C. 2003) ("The necessary elements of a contract are an offer, acceptance, and valuable consideration.").

ii.「Consideration」

「Consideration」の有無がどのように判断されるかは契約の執行力に関わる重大な問題である。例えば、旧型のヘッドフォンの在庫を大量に抱えた Seller が、Buyer にそれらを無償で譲渡する旨打診し、Buyer が合意したとする。後日、気が変わった Seller が旧型のヘッドフォンの引渡しを拒絶した場合、Buyer はたとえ旧型のヘッドフォンに関する譲渡契約書を保有していたとしてもそれを根拠としてそれらの引渡しを強制することはできない。旧型のヘッドフォンに関する譲渡契約には Buyer から Seller への「Consideration」の提供がないためである。

もっとも、Consideration は比較的容易に認められる傾向にあり[14]、契約当事者の間で何らかを交換したといえる状況にあれば足りるとされる[15]。Consideration は必ずしも等価値である必要はなく[16]、また、他方契約当事者のために交付される必要もない[17]。一方で、契約当事者の間で何らかの交換があったように見える場合であっても、Consideration とは認められない場合[18]もある。

このような「Agreement」と「Contract」の意義をふまえると、契約書の名称は「(General Purchase) Contract」とすべきようにも思われる。しかし、実務上は「Agreement」が用いられることの方が多いようである[19]。

---

[14] さらに「Goods」に関する取引を規定する契約内容を変更する場合 (つまりその契約が Uniform Commercial Code Article 2 の適用対象である場合)、Consideration が必要とされない場合もある。U.C.C. § 2-209(1) (Am. Law. Inst. & Unif. Law. Comm'n 2002). *See infra* note 88.
[15] このような Consideration に関する理解を Bargain theory という。*See* Restatement (Second) of Contracts § 71(2) (Am. Law. Inst. 1981). これに対して、Consideration は契約当事者に何らかの利益または不利益を与えるものであるとの理解もあり、このような理解を Benefit-detriment theory という。*See, e.g.*, Hollander v. Lipman, 885 N.Y.S.2d 354, 355 (App. Div. N.Y. 2009) (quoting Weiner v McGraw-Hill, Inc., 57 NY2d 458, 464 (App. Ct. N.Y. 1982)) ("'Consideration' to support an agreement exists where there is 'either a benefit to the promisor or a detriment to the promisee.'"). 近年は Bargain theory が多数説であるといわれているが、Bargain theory または Benefit-detriment theory のいずれに拠るかを明確にしないまま判断を示す事案も見受けられる。
[16] Restatement (Second) of Contracts § 79(b) (Am. Law. Inst. 1981).
[17] *Id.* § 79(c).
[18] Sham Consideration (例えばジェット機の対価として$1 を支払うといったように、形式的には Consideration が提供されているものの実質的には Consideration であるとは評価できない場合)、または、Past Consideration (対象契約とは関係なくすでに提供されていた価値を対象契約の Consideration に設定した場合) などが挙げられる。*See generally id.* § 87 cmt. b (Am. Law. Inst. 1981).
[19] もっとも実務家が実質的な理由に基づいて契約書の名称に「Agreement」を選択しているかについては定かでない。*See* Adams, *supra* note 4, at 12 (「Contract」よりも「Agreement」のほうが洗練された響きを有す

b. 契約当事者に関する基本情報

契約当事者が法人である場合、Preamble においてはその登記場所および会社住所を記載することが多い。このうち、会社の登記場所を「Registered Place」という。多くの米国企業は Delaware 州を設立地として選択しているため[20]、それらの会社の Registered Place も Delaware 州であることが少なくない。

会社住所との関係では「Principal Place of Business」の記載を求められることが多い。「Principal Place of Business」とは、会社の経営陣が所在し、会社をコントロールしている事業地を指す。その会社が米国内に複数のオフィスを持つ場合はいわゆる本社がこれに該当する[21]。

c. 契約の効力発生日

Preamble においては、本契約のように、契約の効力発生日を「Effective Date」として明示することが多い。「Effective Date」の設定に関しては両契約当事者に裁量が認められており、その契約書に対する実際の署名がたとえ「Effective Date」と異なる日に行われたとしてもその事実はその契約書の有効性には影響を及ぼさないのが原則である[22]。

これに対して「Effective Date」の明示がない場合、その契約の効力発生日は契約書を完成させるために必要となる署名のうち、最後の署名が行われた日となる[23]。最後に行われた署名に署名日が付されていない場合、その契約の効力発生日はその者による署名が行われた後、契約書がその者の手を離れ

るためではないかと推察する）。

[20] *See generally* Harvard Business Services, Inc., *Why Form a Delaware Corporation?*, https://www.delawareinc.com/corporation/ (last visited Mar. 26, 2018) (Fortune 500 に位置づけられる企業のうち実に 65％の企業が Delaware 州で設立された企業である旨言及する)。

[21] *See, e.g.*, Hertz Corp. v. Friend, 559 U.S. 77, 80-81 (U.S. 2010) (internal citation omitted) ("[W]e conclude that the phrase 'principal place of business' refers to the place where the corporation's high level officers direct, control, and coordinate the corporation's activities. Lower federal courts have often metaphorically called that place the corporation's 'nerve center.' We believe that the 'nerve center' will typically be found at a corporation's headquarters.") (民事訴訟の personal jurisdiction に関する連邦法 (28 U.S.C. § 1332(c)(1)) における「Principal Place of Business」(ある裁判所がその訴訟当事者に対して裁判を行う権利を有するかどうかに関する判断基準) の解釈を示した）。契約当事者を特定する目的のもと記載を求められる Preamble における「Principal Place of Business」についても同様に解釈する傾向にあると思われる。*See generally* Michael Ray Smith, *Common Elements of Business Contracts, Part1: Preamble to the Contract*, Smith Rayl Law Office, LLC (Aug. 19, 2011), https://businesslaw.smithrayl.com/common-elements-of-business-contracts-part1-preamble-to-the-cont.html (last visited Jun. 11, 2018)。

[22] Backdating および Predating に関する問題については後述する。

[23] Vinay Jain, *When Does a Contract Take Effect?*, Shake by LegalShield (Nov. 19, 2013), http://www.shakelaw.com/blog/when-does-a-contract-take-effect/#fn-1566-1 (last visited Apr. 25, 2018)。

時点である[24].

・Backdating および Predating

両契約当事者の間におけるビジネス自体はすでに開始しているものの，契約書の整備が間に合わなかった場合など，必ずしもビジネスと契約書の進捗が一致しない場合も少なくない．このような場合においては，契約の効力発生日を実際に契約が締結された日よりも以前（Backdating）または以後（Predating）に設定したいと考えることもあろう．

Backdating および Predating 自体は許容されており，契約を直ちに無効とするようなものではないが[25]，実際に契約を締結していない日をもってその契約が締結されたかのような誤解を与える記載は避けるべきである[26]．また，Backdating を選択した場合，Backdating によって遡及する過去の契約効力発生日から現在の契約締結日までの間についても契約上の義務を遵守していたといえるかについて確認が必要となりうることにも注意する必要がある[27]．Backdating または Predating を租税回避などの不当な目的で利用することが許されない[28]ことはいうまでもない．

[WITNESSETH Clause]

WITNESSETH:

WHEREAS, Buyer is in the business of selling laptop and desktop

---

[24] *See* Restatement (Second) of Contracts § 63(1) (Am. Law Inst. 1981).

[25] *See* Colello v. Colello, 9 A.D.3d 855, 857-58 (Sup. Ct. N.Y. 2004) (quoting Matthews v Jeremiah Burns, Inc., 205 Misc. 1006, 1013 (Sup. Ct. N.Y. 1954) (Backdating の有効性を示した) ("'It is fundamental that where parties to an agreement expressly provide that a written contract be entered into 'as of' 'an earlier date than that on which it was executed, the agreement is effective retroactively 'as of' the earlier date and the parties are bound thereby accordingly.'"); *see* Jain, *supra* note 23 (Predating の有効性について言及する).

[26] Richard Lionberger, *Backdating the Contract Effective Date; Pitfalls and Practices*, JS Supra, LLC (Jun. 26, 2013), 3, https://www.jdsupra.com/legalnews/backdating-the-contract-effective-date-61443/ (last visited 8 Feb. 2018)（例えば，実際に両契約当事者による契約書の署名が実施された日は2013年6月1日であるものの，契約の効力発生日については2013年1月1日であるとする場合，「entered into on January 1, 2013 (the "Effective Date")」と規定することは，あたかも2013年1月1日に契約の締結自体が行われたかのような誤解を与えるため避けるべきであり，「entered into June 1, 2013 to be effective as of January 1, 2013 (the "Effective Date")」と規定し，事実を正確に示すべきである旨推奨する).

[27] *Id.* at 1.

[28] *See, e.g.*, United States v. Bourgeois, 950 F.2d 980 (Partnership agreement に起因する損失を特定年度に計上することで税金の払い戻しを得る目的のもと，被告がその partnership agreement の修正契約の成立日を Backdating させたことに対して詐欺罪が問われた事案); *see generally* 18 U.S.C. § 371 (1994).

computers at its retail stores;

WHEREAS, Seller is in the business of manufacturing and selling the memory and the hard drive for laptop and desktop computers; and

WHEREAS, Buyer desires to purchase from Seller, and Seller desires to sell to Buyer the Products (as defined in Section 1.22).

[Background Clause]

BACKGROUND

Buyer is in the business of selling laptop and desktop computers at its retail stores.

Seller is in the business of manufacturing and selling the memory and the hard drive for laptop and desktop computers.

Buyer desires to purchase the Products (as defined in Section 1.22) from the Seller, and the Seller desires to sell to Buyer the Products.

1.2 Recitals

　Recitals においては，契約締結に至るまでの事実および背景，ならびに，両契約当事者が契約締結を決断した理由[29]などが説明される[30]．なお，契約締結にいたる背景を端的に説明するという Recitals の趣旨からして，例えば Definitions Clause などを参照しなければ理解できないような単語などはできる限り使用しないほうが得策である．

---

[29] *See* Union Pac. Resources Co. v. Texaco, 882 P.2d 212, 222 (Sup. Ct. Wyo. 1994) (quoting Wells-Stewart Const. Co. v. Martin Marietta Corp., 103 Ariz. 375, 442 (Sup. Ct. Ariz. 1968)) ("A 'recital' is a formal statement in a document of some matter of fact 'to explain the *reasons* for the transaction.'").

[30] Recitals が両契約当事者が契約締結をすでに決断していることを前提としたものであることとの関係から，Recitals においては「intends」(ある行為を為すかどうかについて当事者の自由意志に委ねる旨を示唆する単語とされる) の使用は控えるべきであるとの指摘もある．この見解に従う場合，本契約においては，「Buyer <u>intends</u> to purchase from Seller, and Seller <u>intends</u> to sell to Buyer the Products.」とはすべきでないことになる．*See generally* Kenneth A. Adams, *Using "Intend" in Recitals*, Adams on Contract Drafting (Oct. 26, 2014), http://www.adamsdrafting.com/using-intend-in-recitals/ (last visited Feb. 8, 2018).

a. Recitals の書式

Recitals においては，「WITNESSETH」の表題から始まる書式（以下，WITNESSETH Clause という）または「BACKGROUNDS」もしくは「RECITALS」の表題から始まる書式（以下，Background Clause という）を用いることが多い．

WITNESSETH Clause は，「対象契約書は両契約当事者の合意内容を証明するものであり，契約署名者はその証人として署名を行う」[31]という伝統的な契約書式をとるうえで必要とされ，現代においても多用されている．ここに「WITNESSETH」は「this agreement witnesseth that …」を短縮したものであり[32]，「WHEREAS」は「considering that」または「that being the case」を意味する[33]．

これに対して Background Clause (Recitals Clause ともいう) は WITNESSETH Clause の現代版ともいえる書式である[34]．

b. Recitals の意義

Recitals の内容は法的拘束力を有するものではないとされるが[35]，以下のような意義が認められる．

i. 契約の本旨の説明

その契約がどのような目的で作成されたものであるかについて，契約書の読み手が容易に把握することを可能にする．ただし，Recitals に記載する内容が事実およびその契約書の本文と矛盾など生じないように注意しなければならない[36]．

---

[31] The Law Dictionary, *What is IN WITNESS WHEREOF?*, http://thelawdictionary.org/in-witness-whereof-2/ (last visited Feb. 8, 2018).

[32] Brian A. Garner, *Ax these terms from your legal writing*, ABA Journal (Apr. 2014), http://www.abajournal.com/magazine/article/ax_these_terms_from_your_legal_writing/ (last visited Feb. 8, 2018).

[33] Farlex, Inc., *Whereas.*, TheFreeDictionary.com., http://legal-dictionary.thefreedictionary.com/Whereas (last visited Feb. 8, 2018).

[34] Adams, *supra* note 4, at 32.

[35] *See, e.g.*, Choquette v. City of New York, 839 F. Supp. 2d 692, 701 (S.D.N.Y. 2012) (quoting Abraham Zion Corp. v. Lebow, 761 F.2d 93, 103–04 (2d Cir. 1985)) (Although a statement in a 'whereas' clause may be useful in interpreting an ambiguous contract, it cannot create any right beyond those arising from the operative terms of the document.").

[36] *See generally* United Pac. Ins. Co. v. Roche, 401 F.3d 1362 (Fed. Cir. 2005) (米国空軍基地の補修工事に関する事案．米国空軍と Castle 社とは工事契約を締結し，米国空軍から Castle 社に工事費用の支払いが行われた．その後，米国空軍は Castle 社の契約不履行を理由として契約を解除したうえで，工事業務の承継者となる United 社との間で Takeover Agreement を締結した．Takeover Agreement の Recitals においては (上記の米国空軍から Castle 社への支払い金額を少なく勘定してしまったことから)，United 社の工事金額が過大に記載されていたため，その金額の当否に関する争いが生じた)．

ii. 特定の権利行使に関する補強
　ある事項がその契約の中でもとりわけ重要な位置づけを持つ場合，Recitals においてその旨を示すことは，対象事項に関して争いが生じた場合の裁判所による救済を促進する可能性がある．例えば，Seller による特定の期日までの製品の Delivery が Buyer にとって必須である場合などにおいてはその旨[37]とその理由[38]を Recitals において示すことが考えられる．

[Sample Clause 1]

NOW, THEREFORE, in consideration of the premises and mutual covenants set forth herein and for other good and valuable consideration, the Parties hereto hereby agree as follows:

[Sample Clause 2]

Accordingly, in consideration of the mutual covenants and for other good and valuable consideration stated in this Agreement, the Parties agree as follows:

1.3 Words of Agreement
　Words of Agreement (Statement of Consideration ともいう) は，契約当事者間において Consideration の交換が行われたこと，および，両契約当事者が契約本文の内容について合意したことを示す．

　a. Words of Agreement の書式
　　Words of Agreement の書式は，Recitals の書式に応じたものとなる．すなわち，Recitals において WITNESSETH Clause を用いた場合，Sample Clause 1

---

[37] *See, e.g.*, Union Pac. Resources Co. v. Texaco, 882 P.2d 212, 222 (Sup. Ct. Wyo. 1994) (Recitals が重要な事実に関して言及している場合，その Recitals は特に Estoppel (ある者が自己の以前の言動と異なる主張を行うことを認めないとする原則) との関係において大きな意義を有することとなる旨を示した) ("In the law of estoppel, a particular and definite recital provides conclusive evidence of the material facts stated.").
[38] *See, e.g.*, Detroit Grand Park Corp. v. Turner, 25 N.W.2d 184, 188 (Sup. Ct. Mich. 1946) (Recitals の意義が詳細な事実の描写がされている場合にいっそう大きなものとなる旨を示した) ("[W]e held that particular recitals in a contract involving a statement of fact are as a rule to be treated as conclusive evidence of the fact stated, while general recitals may not be.").

のように,「NOW, THEREFORE」から始まる一節を用いることになる[39]. また, この場合, 契約書全体にわたって契約書式を統一するべく,「IN WITNESS WHEREOF」[40] から始まる一節を, 契約本文の末尾に置く Testimonium Clause に用いることになる[41].

これに対して, Recitals において Background Clause を用いた場合, Words of Agreement においては Sample Clause 2 のように規定することで足りる. Testimonium Clause においても特定の形式が要求されるようなことはない.

b. Words of Agreement の意義

ある契約が執行力を有するといえるためには「Consideration」が必要となるのが原則であるところ, 契約書における Consideration に関する言及は, Consideration が有効に提供されたと推定させる機能を有する[42]. そこで, 例えば, Consideration が何であるのかの理解が容易でない契約などにおいては, Words of Agreement において,「in consideration of the mutual covenants and other good and valuable consideration」の一節のように, 契約当事者間において Consideration の交換が行われたことを示すことも有用である[43].

また, Words of Agreement における「the Parties hereto hereby agree as follows:」との規定は, 文字通り, 契約当事者の契約内容に関する合意を明らかにするものとして, 有用である[44].

---

[39] 一節の中に含まれる「premises」は,「which came before」(the information provided in the recitals) を意味する. Stark, *supra* note 1, at 85.

[40] *See generally* The Law Dictionary, *What is IN WITNESS WHEREOF?*, http://thelawdictionary.org/in-witness-whereof-2/ (last visited Feb. 8, 2018) (「IN WITNESS WHEREOF」は,「parties have hereunto set their hands」を意味すると説明する).

[41] Kenneth A. Adams, *The New Rules of Drafting (Part Two)*, 81, The Michigan Bar Journal, 40-41 (2002), https://www.michbar.org/file/generalinfo/plainenglish/pdfs/02_aug.pdf (last visited Feb. 8, 2018).

[42] *See, e.g.,* TIE Communications, Inc. v. Kopp, 218 Conn. 281, 292 (Sup. Ct. Conn. 1991) (internal citation omitted) ("It is simply prima facie evidence, shifting the burden of proof to the party disputing the consideration."). ただし, あくまで Consideration が現実に提供されていることが前提であることに注意が必要である. Recitals に Consideration の存在を記載したことのみをもって絶対的に Consideration の存在が認められるわけではない. *See, e.g., TIE Communications, Inc*, 218 Conn., 292 (Consideration に関する言及によって生じる Consideration の存在に関する推定は反証可能である旨を示した) ("A recitation of consideration received does not prevent proof that there was no such consideration.").

[43] *But see* Kenneth A. Adams, *Drafting a New Day Who needs that 'recital of consideration'?*, 12 ABA Bus. L. Sec. (2003), https://www.americanbar.org/content/dam/aba/publications/blt/2003/03/drafting-a-new-day-200303.authcheckdam.pdf (last visited Feb. 8, 2018) (Consideration の現実の提供が認められない場合などにおいては「in consideration of the mutual covenants and other good and valuable consideration」のような一節は無意味であり, むしろ使用すべきでない旨を指摘する).

[44] Stark, *supra* note 1, at 85.

CHAPTER 2 / DEFINITIONS PROVISIONS

Definitions Provisions は対象契約における単語の意味を設定するものである.

ARTICLE 1
DEFINITIONS

For purposes of this Agreement, capitalized terms have the meanings set forth or referred to in this Article 1.

1.1 "Action" means any claim, action, cause of action, demand, lawsuit, arbitration, inquiry, audit, notice of violation, proceeding, litigation, citation, summons, subpoena or investigation of any nature, civil, criminal, administrative, regulatory, or otherwise, whether at law, in equity, or otherwise.

1.2 "Affiliate" of a Person means any other Person that directly or indirectly, through one or more intermediaries, Controls, is Controlled by, or is under common Control with, such Person.

1.3 "Basic Purchase Order Terms" means any one or more of the following terms specified by Buyer in a Purchase Order pursuant to Section 2.1: (a) the Products to be purchased; (b) the quantity of each of the Products ordered; (c) the delivery date; (d) the unit Price for each of the Products to be purchased; (e) the billing address; and (f) the delivery location; in each case, including all terms and conditions attached to, or incorporated into, such Purchase Order.

1.4 "Business Day" means any day other than Saturday, Sunday, or a federal or Ohio state holiday.

1.5 "Claim" means any Action brought against a Person entitled to indemnification under Article 11.

1.6 "Control" (and with correlative meanings, the terms "Controlled by" and "under common Control with") means, with respect to any

Person, the possession, directly or indirectly, of the power to direct or cause the direction of the management or policies of another Person, whether through the ownership of voting securities, by contract, or otherwise.

1.7 "Defective" means not conforming to the warranties in Section 10.1.

1.8 "Defective Products" means Products shipped by Seller to Buyer pursuant to this Agreement that are Defective.

1.9 "EDI" means the electronic data interchange technology agreed on by the Parties for use under this Agreement.

1.10 "Encumbrance" means any charge, claim, community property interest, pledge, condition, equitable interest, lien (statutory or other), option, security interest, mortgage, easement, encroachment, right of way, right of first refusal, or restriction of any kind, including any restriction on use, voting, transfer, receipt of income, or exercise of any other attribute of ownership.

1.11 "Excess Products" means Products that, when counted together with all other Products having the same model number and received by Buyer under the same Purchase Order, are in excess of the quantities of the Products ordered under that Purchase Order.

1.12 "Forecast" means, regarding any three (3) month period, a good faith projection or estimate of Buyer's requirements for Products during each calendar month during the period, which approximates, as nearly as possible, based on information available at the time to Buyer, the quantity of Products that Buyer may order for each such month.

1.13 "Governmental Authority" means any federal, state, local, or foreign government or political subdivision thereof, or any agency or instrumentality of such government or political subdivision, or any self-regulated organization, or other non-governmental regulatory authority or quasi-governmental authority (to the extent that the rules, regulations, or orders of such organization or authority have the force of Law), or any arbitrator, court, or tribunal of competent jurisdiction.

1.14 "Governmental Order" means any order, writ, judgment, injunction, decree, stipulation, award, or determination entered by or with any Governmental Authority.

1.15 "Individual Transaction" means an individual transaction under this Agreement that is governed by the terms and conditions of a Purchase Order that has been accepted by Seller pursuant to Section 5.2 and that incorporates by reference the terms and conditions of this Agreement.

1.16 "Intellectual Property Rights" means all industrial and other intellectual property rights comprising or relating to: (i) Patents; (ii) Trademarks; (iii) internet domain names, whether or not Trademarks, registered by any authorized private registrar or Governmental Authority, web addresses, web pages, websites, and URLs; (iv) works of authorship, expressions, designs, and design registrations, whether or not copyrightable, including copyrights and copyrightable works, software and firmware, application programming interfaces, architecture, files, records, schematics, data, data files, and databases and other specifications and documentation; (v) Trade Secrets; (vi) semiconductor chips, mask works, and the like; and (vii) all industrial and other intellectual property rights, and all rights, interests, and protections that are associated with, equivalent or similar to, or required for the exercise of, any of the foregoing, however arising, in each case whether registered or unregistered and including all registrations and applications for, and renewals or extensions of, such rights or forms of protection pursuant to the Laws of any jurisdiction throughout in any part of the world.

1.17 "Law" means any statute, law, ordinance, regulation, rule, code, constitution, treaty, common law, Governmental Order, or other requirement or rule of law of any Governmental Authority.

1.18 "Nonconforming Products" means any Products received by Buyer from Seller that: (i) do not conform to the model number listed in the applicable Purchase Order; or (ii) on visual inspection, Buyer reasonably determines are otherwise Defective. Where the context requires, Nonconforming Products are deemed to be Products for the purposes of this Agreement.

1.19 "Patents" means all patents (including all reissues, divisionals, provisionals, continuations, and continuations-in-part, re-examinations, renewals, substitutions, and extensions thereof), patent applications, and other patent rights and any other Governmental Authority-issued indicia of invention ownership (including inventor's certificates, petty patents, and patent utility models).

1.20 "Person" means any individual, partnership, corporation, trust, limited liability entity, unincorporated organization, association, Governmental Authority, or any other entity.

1.21 "Personnel" means agents, employees, or subcontractors engaged or appointed by Seller or Buyer.

1.22 "Products" means the Products set forth in Schedule I.

1.23 "Purchase Order" means Buyer's purchase order issued to Seller hereunder, including all terms and conditions attached to, or incorporated into, such purchase order.

1.24 "Representatives" means a Party's Affiliates, and each of their respective Personnel, officers, directors, partners, shareholders, agents, attorneys, third-party advisors, successors, and permitted assigns.

1.25 "Specifications" means the specifications for the Products attached hereto as Schedule II.

1.26 "Taxes" means any and all sales, use, gross receipts, environmental, ad valorem, or excise tax or any other similar taxes, fees, duties, or charges of any kind imposed by any Governmental Authority on any amounts payable by Buyer under this Agreement; exclusive, however, of any taxes, assessments, or other levies imposed on Seller's income or capital (including leased or purchased property, equipment, or software), any franchise taxes, any taxes in lieu of net income taxes, and any other direct taxes imposed on Seller.

1.27 "Trademarks" means all rights in and to US and foreign

> trademarks, service marks, trade dress, trade names, brand names, logos, trade dress, corporate names, and domain names, and other similar designations of source, sponsorship, association, or origin, together with the goodwill symbolized by any of the foregoing, in each case whether registered or unregistered and including all registrations and applications for, and renewals and extensions of, such rights and all similar or equivalent rights or forms of protection in any part of the world.
>
> 1.28 "Trade Secrets" means all inventions, discoveries, trade secrets, business, and technical information and know-how, databases, data collections, patent disclosures, and other confidential and proprietary information and all rights therein.

2.1 Definitions Provisions の意義

Definition は，契約内容の理解および把握の容易化，ならびに，定義の曖昧さからくる論争の防止といった機能を有する[45]．特にある単語が多義的な意味を持っている場合，その契約上の意味をめぐって紛争が発生する可能性もあるため[46]，とりわけ注意を払い明確な定義を試みることが望ましい．

2.2 Definition の配置箇所

Definition を契約上どのようにして規定するかについては，主として以下の形式が挙げられる．

　a. Definitions Provisions を設置する場合
　1 条のように Definitions Provisions を独立して設置し，そのもとで

---

[45] Stark, *supra* note 1, at 95.
[46] *See generally*, Ellington v. EMI Music, Inc. 24 N.Y.3d 239, 246 (Ct. App. N.Y. 2014) (quoting VKK Corp. v. National Football League, 244 F.3d 114, 130–31 (2d Cir. 2011)) (「Affiliate」の定義に関して，契約締結時点で契約当事者の affiliate であった会社のみを指すのか，または，契約締結後に契約当事者の affiliate となった会社も含むのかについて争われたところ，契約上「Affiliate」についての特段の定義がない場合，「Affiliate」とは契約締結時に存在する契約当事者の affiliate を指すと示した) ("Absent explicit language demonstrating the parties' intent to bind future affiliates of the contracting parties, the term 'affiliate' includes only those affiliates in existence at the time that the contract was executed."); *contra*. Ciment v SpanTran, Inc., 2017 N.Y. Misc. LEXIS 82 (Sup. Ct. N.Y. 2017) (契約締結時の両契約当事者の「Affiliate」に関する理解が将来的に設立される会社も含むものであったとして，「Affiliate」は契約締結時に存在する契約当事者の affiliate に限られない旨を示した).

Definition を用意する[47]．この場合，閲覧の容易性を考慮して，各単語をアルファベット順に列挙することが多いようである．

　もっとも Definitions Provisions において単語の定義づけを行うことが必ずしも得策というわけではない．例えば契約を通して一度しか使用しない単語については，その単語が使用される条項内において Definition を設ければ十分ともいえる[48]．

　b. Action Provisions などを活用する場合
　例えば 15.1 条における「Disclosing Party」および「Receiving Party」のように，その単語が使用される条項内において Definition を適宜設ける形式もとりうる．Definitions Provisions を設置した場合，その Definition が使用される条項を閲読する際にその都度 Definitions Provisions を参照しなければならないという手間が発生するが，この形式であればそのような手間は発生せず，契約内容の理解がいっそう容易となりうる．

　もっとも，この形式によった場合，ある単語の Definition が明確にならない場合が想定されるという問題がある[49]．

---

[47] Stark, *supra* note 1, at 98.
[48] *Id.* at 101.
[49] *See generally* G. Golden Assocs. v. Arnold Foods Co., 870 F. Supp. 472 (E.D.N.Y. 1994) (食料品の製造技術などを有する者 (以下，Seller という) が製造技術などを譲受人 (以下，Buyer という) に譲渡するに際して締結した契約に関する事案．製造技術などの譲渡契約において Buyer は「Product」の売上額の一部を Commission として Seller に支払うこととなっていたところ，「Product」は次のように定義されていた．「WHEREAS, Seller possesses technical information and know-how (the "Technical Information") relating to the production and manufacture of <u>food products which look similar to the thin, crispy crust of 'french bread' from which the dough has been removed</u> (the "Products") and is the sole owner and proprietor of the trademarks "La Crunch Une" and "La Crunch" which it has used in connection with sales of the Products.」．Buyer は「Products」は Seller の技術情報に関係するものに限られると主張したのに対し，Seller は「Products」は下線部分で定義されているとおりであり，Buyer の Commission 支払い対象となる「Products」は Seller の技術情報に関係するかどうかとは関係がないと主張した).

CHAPTER 3 / ACTION PROVISIONS

　Action Provisions においては，契約当事者の権利および義務ならびに契約に違反した場合の取り扱いなどについて規定する．

ARTICLE 2
PURCHASE AND SALE

Section 2.1 Purchase and Sale.

Subject to the terms and conditions of this Agreement, during the Term of this Agreement, Buyer shall purchase the Products from Seller, and Seller shall manufacture and sell the Products to Buyer, at the prices and in the quantities set forth on the Purchase Order.

The Purchase Order may contain: (a) a description of the Product's number of Seller; (b) the purchase price for the Products; (c) the quantity of the Products; and (d) the delivery date. The Parties shall, from time to time, amend the Purchase Order to reflect any agreed revisions to any of the terms described in the foregoing clauses (a)-(d); provided that no such revisions will modify this Agreement or be binding on the Parties unless such revisions have been fully approved in a signed writing by authorized Representatives of both Parties.

3.1 U.C.C.の適用

　契約法の内容は各州が自己の権限のもと規定することができるのが原則である[50]．しかし，州をまたぐ取引が当然となっている現代において，各州がまったく別の契約法を持っていたのでは，取引の予見性や効率性を著しく損なうことになりかねない．そこで，商取引に関する州法の標準化を目的として用意さ

---

[50] Brian H. Bix, *Theories of Contract Law and Enforcing Promissory Morality: Comments on Charles Fried*, 45 Suffolk U. L. Rev. 719 (2012), 720, http://scholarship.law.umn.edu/faculty_articles/204. ただし，州法に連邦法の規定と相反する部分がある場合は連邦法が優先する．U.S. Const. art. 6, cl.2.

れたのが Uniform Commercial Code（以下，U.C.C.という）である[51]．ある取引が U.C.C.の適用対象であるかどうかは，例えば製品に対する保証内容[52]などとの関係で大きな影響を及ぼす．

U.C.C.のうち，本契約にも大きく関係してくる Article 2 は，とりわけ「Goods」[53]の取引に関する契約を適用対象とする[54]．もっとも，例えばあるソフトウェアライセンス契約がソフトウェアの売買とそのソフトウェアサポートサービスから成る場合のように，ある契約が製品の売買取引に関する部分とそれ以外の取引に関する部分の双方を含む場合もある．このような場合，U.C.C.の適用の有無は，対象契約の主目的が製品の売買であるのかどうかによって決定される[55]．

本契約の場合，取引対象は「memory and hard drive for laptop and desktop computers」という「Goods」であるから U.C.C.（Article 2）が適用されることになる．

3.2 Statute of Frauds

Statute of Frauds は，口頭契約に伴う偽証などのリスクを回避するために設けられた要件である．特定の契約[56]については文書による締結を要求し，その契

---

[51] Jesse M. Brush, *"Mixed Contracts and the U.C.C.: A Proposal for a Uniform Penalty Default to Protect Consumers"* (2007), Student Scholarship Papers. Paper 47, at 2, http://digitalcommons.law.yale.edu/student_papers/47 (last visited April 26, 2018). なお，現在U.C.C.は全50州で採択されているが，それら50州が必ずしもすべての規定を同内容で採択しているわけではない．例えばLouisiana州はU.C.C.のうちArticle 2を採択していない．US Legal, Inc., *Louisiana*, https://uniformcommercialcode.uslegal.com/states-adopting-the-ucc/louisiana/ (last visited April 26, 2018).

[52] *See, e.g.*, Brush, *supra* note 51, at 5 n.27 (quoting Bruce A. Singal, *Extending Implied Warranties Beyond Products: Equal Protection for Consumers of Services*, 12 New Eng. L. Rev. 859, 931 (1977)) ("Buyers seek Article 2 coverage for mixed transactions because state common law generally does not contain implied warranties.").

[53] U.C.C. § 2-105(1) (Am. Law Inst. & Unif. Law Comm'n 2002) (「Goods」とは，売買契約の対象として特定された時点において動産といえるもの全般をいう) ("'Goods' means all things (including specially manufactured goods) which are movable at the time of identification to the contract for sale other than the money in which the price is to be paid, investment securities (Article 8) and things in action. 'Goods' also includes the unborn young of animals and growing crops and other identified things attached to realty as described in the section on goods to be severed from realty (Section 2-107)").

[54] *Id.* § 2-102. これに対して，「Goods」以外の取引に関する契約 (例えば典型的なソフトウェアライセンス契約) はいわゆるCommon Lawの適用対象である．Brush, *supra* note 51, at 3.

[55] これをPredominant purpose testといい，多数説である．*See, e.g.*, Yorke v. B.F. Goodrich Co., 474 N.E.2d 20, 22 (App. Ct. Ill. 1985) ("The test of the applicability of the Uniform Commercial Code to the instant transaction is whether the predominant purpose of the contract is for services or for the sale of goods.").

[56] Restatement (Second) of Contracts § 110(1) (Am. Law Inst. 1981) ("(a) a contract of an executor or administrator to answer for a duty of his decedent (the executor administrator provision); (b) a contract to answer for the duty of another (the suretyship provision); (c) a contract made upon consideration of marriage (the marriage provision); (d) a contract for the sale of an interest in land (the land contract provision); (e) a contract that is not to be performed within one year from the making thereof (the one-year provision).").

約に署名をしていない契約当事者に対してはその契約を執行することができないという効果を持つ[57].

・U.C.C.における Statute of Frauds

U.C.C.においては,「Goods」の取引額が$500 を超える契約に Statute of Frauds を適用している[58]. そのような契約の執行は, ①相手方契約当事者の署名がある場合に, ②その契約書に具体的に記載されている取引数量の範囲内[59]において認められる[60].

本契約の場合, 本契約自体には具体的な製品の注文数量は明示されておらず, それは 5.1 条および 1.3 条のもと Purchase Order に記載されることになっている. したがって, 上記要件②との関係から, 本契約締結時点においては, 原則として, Buyer も Seller も他方契約当事者に対して本契約の執行を求める権利を有していないことを理解しておくべきである.

3.3 Installment Contract

本契約は Seller と Buyer との間で行われる継続的な取引のために用意されるものである. すなわち, 5.1 条のもと, Buyer は自己の Offer を Purchase Order として提示し, 5.2 条のもと, Seller がそれを Accept することをもって個別の Individual Transaction に関する契約が成立することを予定している.

さて, Buyer は, Purchase Order において, 対象製品を複数回に分けて発送してほしい旨 Offer することもある. このような要求を Seller が Accept した場合

---

[57] ただし, Statute of Frauds の適用を受ける契約であっても例外的にその契約に署名をしていない契約当事者に対して契約を執行できる場合がある. 例えば, 3 年間にわたってビルを建築する契約 (1 年以内に契約を履行できない契約) について建築業者の署名がなかったとしても, ビル建築の委託者が建築委託費を全額支払った場合, もはやその契約は Statute of Frauds の対象とはならず, 委託者はビル建築業者に契約上の義務の履行を求めることができる. See id. § 130(2).
[58] U.C.C. § 2-201(1) (Am. Law Inst. & Unif. Law Comm'n 2002).
[59] Statute of Frauds との関係で要求される取引条件に関する記載は,「取引数量」に関するもののみである. See, e.g., Koenen v. Royal Buick Co., 162 Ariz. 376, 380 (Ariz. Ct. App. 1989) (quoting U.C.C. § 2-201, cmt. 1 (Am. Law Inst. & Unif. Law Comm'n 2002)) ("The only term which must appear is the quantity term which need not be accurately stated but recovery is limited to the amount stated. The price, time and place of payment or delivery, the general quality of the goods, or any particular warranties may all be omitted.").
[60] U.C.C. § 2-201(1) (Am. Law Inst. & Unif. Law Comm'n 2002) ("A writing is not insufficient because it omits or incorrectly states a term agreed upon but the contract is not enforceable under this paragraph beyond the quantity of goods shown in such writing."); but see, id. § 2-201(3)(a) (「Goods」が Buyer のために特別に用意されるものであって, すでに Seller がその製造のために重要な工程に取り掛かっているような場合においては, これら要件を満たさない場合においても, Seller はその範囲で Buyer に対して契約を執行できる.

に成立する Individual Transaction に関する契約を Installment Contract という[61]。

U.C.C.は Installment Contract について，(1) 製品の出荷，(2) 製品の受領，(3) 製品の受領拒絶，および (4) 欠陥ある製品が納入された場合の取り扱いとの関係で，通常の売買契約と取り扱いを異にしている[62]。

例えば Installment Contract のもと Seller から Buyer に向けて対象製品が出荷されたところ，その製品に欠陥があったとする。この場合，Buyer がその製品の受領を拒否できるのは，①その欠陥がその製品の価値を大きく損なうものであり，かつ，②Seller がその欠陥を治癒することも，その欠陥の治癒に関する保証を提供することもできない場合に限定されるのである[63]。

ARTICLE 3
ORDER OF PRECENDENCE

Section 3.1 Order of Precedence.

The Parties intend for the express terms and conditions contained in this Agreement (including any Schedules and Exhibits hereto) and in any Purchase Order that are consistent with the terms and conditions of this Agreement to exclusively govern and control each of the Parties' respective rights and obligations regarding the manufacture, purchase and sale of the Products, and the Parties' agreement is expressly limited to such terms and conditions.

Notwithstanding the foregoing, if any terms and conditions contained in a Purchase Order supplement or conflict with any terms and conditions contained in this Agreement, the applicable term or condition of this Agreement will prevail and such additional, contrary or different terms will have no force or effect.

---

[61] *Id.* § 2-612(1).
[62] Thomson Reuters, *Installment Contracts for the Sale of Products Under the Uniform Commercial Code*, Practical Law Commercial Transactions, https://uk.practicallaw.thomsonreuters.com/1-584-2948?transitionType=Default&contextData=(sc.Default)&firstPage=true&comp=pluk&bhcp=1&OWSessionId=10fb2923bc054d07a6a8edf448110512&skipAnonymous=true (last visited April 26, 2018).
[63] U.C.C. § 2-612(2) (Am. Law Inst. & Unif. Law Comm'n 2002); *cf. id.* § 2-601 (対象契約が Installment Contract に該当しない場合においては，対象製品に契約条件と合致しない欠陥がわずかでも認められる限り，Buyer はその製品の受領を拒否することができる)。

> Except for such additional and contrary terms, the terms and conditions of all Purchase Orders are incorporated by reference into this Agreement for all applicable purposes hereunder. Without limitation of anything contained in this Section 3.1, any additional, contrary or different terms contained in any Confirmation (as defined in Section 5.2) or any of Seller's invoices or other communications, and any other attempt to modify, supersede, supplement or otherwise alter this Agreement, are deemed rejected by Buyer and will not modify this Agreement or be binding on the Parties unless such terms have been fully approved in a signed writing by authorized Representatives of both Parties.

3.4 Order of Precedence Clause

　ある取引を遂行するにあたっては，さまざまな段階で複数の書面が取り交わされることが予想される．例えば本契約の場合，Buyer による製品の注文は 5.1 条のもと発行される Purchase Order によるものとなっているから，本取引に関しては少なくとも本契約書と Purchase Order という 2 種類の書面の取り交わしが予定されている．ここで問題となりうるのは，契約書と Purchase Order の双方に取引条件が記載されており，それらの間に齟齬がある場合である．Order of Precedence Clause（Conflict or Inconsistency Clause などともいう）は，このような場合における書面の優先関係を明確にするものである[64]．

　Order of Precedence Clause においてどの書面を優先的地位に置くかについては，実際のビジネス上の運用もふまえる必要があるものの，実際に内容を確認する機会のある書面をそうでないもの[65]よりも優先させることが原則となる．

---

[64] *See also* Silver Bow Constr. v. State, 2016 Alas. LEXIS 53, 31-32 (Sup. Ct. Alaska 2016) (quoting Lakloey, Inc. v. University of Alaska, 2002 Alas. LEXIS 174, 14 (Sup. Ct. Alaska 2002)) ("Construction contracts usually contain an order of precedence provision stating that conflicting language between the various contract documents will be resolved by giving preference to one document over another. 'The order of precedence clause should be used only where the performance called for by the contract cannot be determined by reviewing all the provisions of the contract.'"); *see also generally* Hensel Phelps Construction Co., Appellant, v. U.S., 886 F.2d 1296 (Fed. Cir. 1989) (工場の建設契約において，建設業者は specification 所定の業務に基づいた落札を行ったところ，注文主は建設業者に対して specification よりも業務量の多い drawing にも基づいた対応を要求した．対象契約には「specification」と「drawing」との間に齟齬がある場合は specification が優先する旨の Order of Precedence Clause があることを理由として，建設業者が specification の業務量に基づいた落札を行ったことを正当化し，注文主が drawing に基づいた対応を建設業者に要求する場合には追加の費用を支払うべきである旨を示した)．

[65] 例えば Purchase Order にはその対象取引に関する取引条件（Terms and Conditions などという）が添付

ARTICLE 4
NON-BINDING FORECASTS

Section 4.1 Provision of Forecasts.

From time-to-time, Buyer may, but shall not be required to, provide Seller with the Forecasts.

Section 4.2 Forecasts are Non-Binding.

The Forecasts are for information purposes only. Any product quantities cited in or pursuant to this Agreement, except for quantities cited in a Purchase Order as firm, are preliminary and non-binding only. Buyer makes no representation or warranty as to the quantity of products that it will purchase, if any.

3.5 Forecasts Clause

　Forecast は多義的な単語である．すなわち，Forecast には例えば Seller から Buyer に製品発送に関する予定などを知らせるものである Delivery Forecast があるが[66]，本契約における「Forecast」は，1.12 条のもと，Buyer から Seller に対して製品注文に関する予定などを知らせるものである Order Forecast を意図している．Order Forecast は，一般に契約当事者の便宜のために提供されるものであると理解される．つまり，Seller は Forecast を製品の製造に必要な材料の仕入れなどの参考とできるし，Buyer はその結果として Seller による製品の予定通りの製造を期待できるのである．
　しかし，両契約当事者にとって Forecast に関わる責任範囲が関心の対象となることも少なくない．例えば Seller が Buyer から発行された Forecast を信頼し

されていることが多いが，Purchase Order 自体は専ら Sales Department によって取り扱われる結果として，その Terms and Conditions の内容について精査されないことが多いものと思われる．

[66] The Law Dictionary, *Black's Law Dictionary: Free Online Edition (2nd ed.)*, https://thelawdictionary.org/delivery-forecast/ (last visited Apr. 30, 2018).

て製品製造の準備を開始したところ，後日発行された Purchase Order に記載された製品注文数量が Forecast よりも少なかった場合，その数量差分についてどのように取り扱うべきかという問題が生じるためである．

　この点については，特段の慣習[67]または契約上の規定がない限り，Forecast の提供のみをもって Buyer に製品の購入義務を認めることは困難であると思われる[68]．もっとも，Buyer に契約上の義務が発生していない場合においても，Buyer が Seller から，Forecast に寄せた信頼などを根拠として，別の請求原因に基づいた請求を受けることも否定できない[69]．そこで，Buyer としては，Forecast は Seller に対してなんらの義務を発生させるものではない旨を明示することが得策である[70]．これに対して Seller としては，自己の製品製造に関するリスクを低減する意味でも，一定の範囲で Buyer に製品購入の義務を生じさせたいところであろう[71]．特に Forecast に基づいて特定の材料を事前に調達する必要がある場合などは，少なくともその材料については Buyer の引き取り義務を規定するよう試みるべきである[72]．

---

[67] 特段の慣習の例として，(1) Course of Performance (契約当事者が契約の対象となる取引に関して反復継続して行った振る舞いに基づいて想定される行為をいう．U.C.C. § 1-303(a) (Am. Law Inst. & Unif. Law Comm'n 2002))，(2) Course of Dealing (契約当事者が以前に (本契約とは別の) 特定の取引に関して反復継続して行った振る舞いが合理的に本取引にも該当するといえる場合にその振る舞いに基づいて想定される行為をいう．Id. § 1-303(b))，または (3) Usage of Trade (そのビジネス業界における慣行に基づいて想定される行為をいう．Id. § 1-303(c)) が挙げられ，これらは対象取引の条件または履行に関する解釈の指標となる場合がある．Id. § 1-303(d)．

[68] See generally Ariens Co. v. WEC Co., 2006 U.S. Dist. LEXIS 6894, 9-10 (E.D. Wis. 2006) ("Whereas the forecasts are merely advisory and for the parties' 'convenience', 'purchase orders are not nearly so ephemeral'").

[69] See, e.g., Logger Head Tools, LLC v. Sears Holding Corporation 19 F.Supp.3d 775 (N.D. Ill 2013) (Buyer が Seller に対して発行した Forecast に記載の注文予定数量がその後大幅に減少したことに関して，Seller から Buyer に対する詐欺的行為などの主張に基づく損害の請求が行われた)．

[70] もっとも，そのような規定があったとしても万全とはいえないことに注意が必要である．See, e.g., Druckzentrum Harry Jung GmbH & Co. KG v. Motorola, Inc., 2010 U.S. Dist. LEXIS 66043 (N.D. Ill 2010) (対象契約において Forecast には契約上の拘束力はない旨が規定されていたにもかかわらず，そのような規定は相手方契約当事者による Forecast が詐欺的行為に基づいて提供された場合においては，その Forecast によって被った損害の請求を行うことまでをも妨げるものではない旨を示した)．

[71] 例えば，次のような規定を設けることになる．「On or before the first day of each calendar month, Purchaser shall furnish to Seller a written twelve (12) months rolling forecast of the quantities of the Product that Purchaser intends to order from Seller ("Rolling Forecast"). The first three (3) months of such Rolling Forecast shall constitute a binding and irrevocable order for the quantities of Product specified therein and the following nine (9) months of the Rolling Forecast shall be non-binding and good faith estimates.」．

[72] この場合，次のような規定を設けることになる．「In the event Buyer purchases less than the amount stated in the Forecast, Buyer shall be liable for raw materials. Seller shall use reasonable efforts to reschedule those materials for production and delivery in subsequent months.」．

CHAPTER 3 / ACTION PROVISIONS   23

ARTICLE 5
ORDER PROCEDURE

Section 5.1 Purchase Orders.

Buyer shall issue Purchase Orders to Seller in written form or by using EDI.

Section 5.2 Acceptance and Rejection of Purchase Orders.

Seller shall confirm to Buyer the receipt of each Order issued (each, a "Confirmation") within three (3) Business Days following Seller's receipt by notice. Each Confirmation must reference Buyer's Purchase Order number, confirm acceptance of the Purchase Order or, advise Buyer of Seller's rejection of such Purchase Order, the date of acceptance or rejection, and the basis for rejection, if applicable.

If Seller fails to issue a Confirmation within the time set forth in the first sentence of this Section 5.2, or otherwise commences performance under such Purchase Order, Seller will be deemed to have accepted the Purchase Order. Buyer may withdraw any Purchase Order prior to Seller's acceptance or deemed acceptance.

3.6 Offer と Acceptance

本契約においては，別途発行される Purchase Order に従って Individual Transaction に関する契約の成立が予定されていることについてはすでに紹介した．すなわち，5.1 条のもと Buyer（Offeror となる）が Seller に向けて発する Purchase Order が Offer を構成し，5.2 条のもと Seller（Offeree となる）が Buyer に向けて発する Confirmation または契約上の義務の履行開始が Acceptance を構成することになり，それらの結果として Buyer と Seller との間で Individual Transaction に関する「Agreement」が成立するのである．

・Offer と Acceptance との間に齟齬がある場合

それでは Buyer が発する Order と Seller が発する Confirmation との間に隔たりが認められる場合はどうなるのであろうか．例えば Buyer が Seller の製品 100 個について製品到着から 10 日以内に代金を支払うという条件で Purchase Order を発行したところ，Seller が製品発送前に Buyer が代金を支払うという条件であれば取引を行いたい旨を Buyer に返信したとする[73]．

この場合，(1) そもそも製品 100 個の売買契約は成立したといえるのであろうか．そして，(2) 仮に製品 100 個の売買契約が成立している場合，支払い条件はどのように設定されるのであろうか．これらについては，対象契約が Common Law または U.C.C.のいずれに依拠するものであるかが大きく影響を及ぼす．

i. Common Law における取り扱い

取引対象が「Goods」以外である場合（U.C.C.の適用を受けない場合），Offer と Acceptance との間には完全な一致が要求される（Mirror Image Rule という）[74]．したがって，「Agreement」を形成するためには，両契約当事者は，契約条件に関して完全な合意に至ったといえる状況になるまで契約交渉を継続する必要がある．

もっとも，Acceptance は，Offeree による契約上の義務の履行によっても認められる[75]．したがって，契約当事者間に契約条件に関する完全な合意がなかったとしても，例えば Seller が製品を Buyer に発送するなど，一方契約当事者が契約上の義務を履行したことをもって，その履行の直前に他方契約当事者から提示されていた契約内容に基づく合意が認められることになる[76]．

ii. U.C.C. における取り扱い

取引の円滑化を図る U.C.C.においては Mirror Image Rule が排除されている[77]．すなわち，Offer と完全には一致しない Acceptance が行われた場合に

---

[73] このように両契約当事者が自己の契約条件に従った取引を進めるべく，契約案を提示し，その応酬が繰り広げられる状況を Battle of the Forms という．*See generally Black's Law Dictionary: Pocket Edition* 69 (4th ed. 2011).

[74] *See, e.g.*, Restatement (Second) of Contracts § 59 (Am. Law Inst. 1981); *see generally Black's Law Dictionary: Pocket Edition* 487 (4th ed. 2011).

[75] *See, e.g.*, Restatement (Second) of Contracts § 54(1) (Am. Law Inst. 1981).

[76] このように契約上の義務の履行の直前に提示された契約がその取引内容の条件となるとする原則を Last Shot Rule という．*See* Leslie Marell, *Mirra Image Rule vs. Last Shot Rule* (Jun. 12, 2015), http://marell-lawfirm.com/mirror-image-rule-vs-last-shot-rule/. (last visited April 30, 2018).

[77] U.C.C. § 2-207 (1) (Am. Law Inst. & Unif. Law Comm'n 2002).

おいても Agreement の成立を認めたうえで，その契約条件については Offer と Acceptance の不一致の内容および程度[78]に応じて定めることとしている．

このうち，両契約当事者が「Merchant」[79]である場合においては，Acceptance に含まれる (Offer と一致しない) 契約条件は Agreement の一部となるのが原則である．例外は，(1) Offer において Offeree との契約は Offer の内容のとおりでのみ成立する旨を明示している場合，(2) Acceptance に含まれる契約条件が Offer を「Materially」[80]に変更することになる場合，または，(3) Offeror から Offeree に向けて Acceptance に含まれる契約条件には従えない旨の通知がすでに提示されている場合，もしくは，Acceptance に含まれる契約条件を受領してから合理的期間内に提示された場合である．

Section 5.3 Buyer's Right to Terminate Individual Transactions.

In addition to its rights under Section 14.3 to terminate all Individual Transactions in connection with the termination of this Agreement, Buyer may, in its sole discretion, on notice to Seller, without liability or penalty, terminate any Individual Transaction with or without cause effective immediately or otherwise as specified in such notice.

---

[78] Id. § 2-207 ("(1) A definite and seasonable expression of acceptance or a written confirmation which is sent within a reasonable time operates as an acceptance even though it states terms additional to or different from those offered or agreed upon, unless acceptance is expressly made conditional on assent to the additional or different terms. (2) The additional terms are to be construed as proposals for addition to the contract. Between merchants such terms become part of the contract unless: (a) the offer expressly limits acceptance to the terms of the offer; (b) they materially alter it; or (c) notification of objection to them has already been given or is given within a reasonable time after notice of them is received. (3) Conduct by both parties which recognizes the existence of a contract is sufficient to establish a contract for sale although the writings of the parties do not otherwise establish a contract. In such case the terms of the particular contract consist of those terms on which the writings of the parties agree, together with any supplementary terms incorporated under any other provisions of this Act.").

[79] 「Merchant」とは，対象製品を自己の業務として取り扱っている者をいう．Id. § 2-104 ("Merchant means a person who deals in Products of the kind or otherwise by his occupation holds himself out as having knowledge or skill peculiar to the practices or Products involved in the transaction or to whom such knowledge or skill may be attributed by his employment of an agent or broker or other intermediary who by his occupation holds himself out as having such knowledge or skill.").

[80] Id. § 2-207(2)(b). (ある契約条件が Offer を「Materially」に変更することになるかどうかについては，そのような契約条件への変更を認めることが相手方契約当事者にとって予期しないものであるのか，または，相手方契約当事者に困難を生じさせるものであるかによって判断することになる．例えば，一般的な製品の品質保証を否定するような契約条件は Offer を「Materially」に変更するものであると思われる．Id. § 2-207 cmt.4.).

3.7 Individual Transactions に関する解約権

5.3 条は，Buyer に，無条件で Purchase Orders のもと合意に至った Individual Transactions を解約する権利を規定している（これに対して 14.3 条は所定の条件のもとで，Buyer に本契約自体を解約する権利を認めている）．

Offeror は，いったん Offeree から Acceptance の意思が発信されると，もはや自己の発した Offer を撤回できなくなるのが契約法上の原則である[81]．したがって，5.3 条はそれと相反した，Buyer に解約に関する強力な権利を付与するものである．Seller としては自己の契約上の地位を安定させる意味でも，(1) Buyer にそもそもこのような解約権を認めない，または，(2) Buyer による解約権行使の場合においてはそれに伴う損害の補償義務を負わせるといった対応が必要となる．

Section 5.4 Effect of Termination of Individual Transactions.

If any Individual Transaction is terminated under this Article 5 or Article 14, in accordance with Buyer's written direction, Seller shall immediately:

(a) cease work and purchasing materials relating to fulfilling the Individual Transaction, subject to the terms and conditions of this Section 5.4; and

(b) deliver to Buyer on request all or any portion of Products under the relevant Individual Transaction at the Prices.

3.8 Individual Transactions に関する解約権行使の効果

5.4 条は，Buyer が 5.3 条または 14.3 条に基づいて Individual Transaction の撤回を行った場合における Seller の義務を規定する．そのうち 5.4 条(a) は Seller に製品の製造を中止する義務を負わせている．これは Seller が Buyer による Individual Transaction の解約後もなお漫然と製品の製造を継続し，その後，その

---

[81] 格別の規定がない限り，Acceptance は Offeree からの発信をもって効力を有する (Mailbox Rule という). See, e.g., Rosenthal v. Walker, 111 U.S. 185, 193 (U.S. 1884) ("[I]f a letter properly directed is proved to have been either put into the post office or delivered to the postman, it is presumed, from the known course of business in the post office department, that it reached its destination at the regular time, and was received by the person to whom it was addressed."); see generally Black's Law Dictionary: Pocket Edition 469 (4th ed. 2011).

費用を Individual Transaction の解約に基づく損害の請求に含めるといった事態を予防する意義を持つ．

・Duty to Mitigate

仮に 5.4 条(a)のような規定を欠いていたとしても，Seller は Buyer による Individual Transaction の撤回に伴う自己の損害の軽減に努めることをまったく要求されないわけではない．契約法においても，契約違反または不法行為によって損害を被った者は，その損害の軽減に向けて合理的に行動する義務を負うこととされているためである[82]．このような被害者の義務を「Duty to Mitigate」（Doctrine of Avoidable Consequence ともいう）という．Duty to Mitigate は，経済的損失の予防による公共の利益の確保を趣旨とする[83]．Duty to Mitigate に違反したと認められた場合，被害者の加害者に対する損害の請求は，その軽減が可能であった範囲で縮減される．その一方，Duty to Mitigate を尽くした被害者は，そのために要した費用について加害者に請求することができる[84]．

Duty to Mitigate の懈怠に関する立証責任は加害者が負う[85]．すなわち，加害者は，①自己の損害を軽減するために合理的な手段を講じることについての被害者の懈怠，および，②その結果として拡大した被害者の損害額を証明する必要がある．もっとも，Duty to Mitigate は被害者にその損害を軽減するためにあらゆる手段を講じることを要求するようなものではないし[86]，その

---

[82] See, e.g., Restatement (Second) of Contracts § 350(1) (Am. Law Inst. 1981); see also, e.g., U.C.C. § 2-712(2) (Am. Law Inst. & Unif. Law Comm'n 2002) (Buyer に対する Duty to Mitigate を要求する); see also, e.g., id. § 2-709(1)(b) (Seller に対する Duty to Mitigate を要求する); なお，Duty to Mitigate は The United Nations Convention on Contracts for the International Sale of Products (52 Fed. Reg. 6262, 6275 (Mar. 2, 1987). 以下，CISG という）においても要求されている (CISG art. 77)．

[83] Jason T. Strickland, *Leaving the Apples to Rot: The Duty of a Wronged Party to Mitigate its Damages and its Potential Waiver in Commercial Contracts*, Ward and Smith, P.A. (Mar. 27, 2013), https://www.wardandsmith.com/articles/the-duty-of-a-wronged-party-to-mitigate-its-damages-in-commercial-contracts (last visited Apr. 30, 2018).

[84] Coutney D. Tedrowe, interviewed by Chelan David, *Mitigation of damages How to take reasonable actions to limit damages in a lawsuit*, Smart Business Network Inc., http://www.novackmacey.com/files/5514/6229/8859/Courtney-Tedrowe-Interview-in-Smart-Business-Dec-2011.pdf (last visited Feb. 22, 2018).

[85] *Id.*

[86] *See, e.g.,* USGen New Eng., Inc. v. TransCanada Pipelines, Ltd. (In re USGen New Eng., Inc.), 429 B.R. 437, 460 n.8 (Bakr. Md. 2010) ("[T]he duty to mitigate is not a 'duty' in the strict sense. However, since a number of cases refer to the obligation of a plaintiff to take reasonable steps to avoid damages as a duty to mitigate, it will be referred here either as the duty to mitigate or the obligation to take reasonable steps to mitigate damages."). 被害者の損害の軽減に向けた対応として期待される程度を理解するうえでは，次の例が参考となる．映像編集業者が映画制作会社から 1 年にわたってコメディ映画の編集作業を $60,000 で行うサービス契約を締結したが，映画制作会社は映像編集業者に 1 か月分の業務に関する $5,000 を支払っ

手段が功を奏する必要はないとされるなど，上記要件①の証明がいかなる場合において認められるのかについて明らかでない面も多い．5.4 条(a)のように被害者に対して具体的な損害軽減に向けた措置を義務付けることは，このような問題を解決しようとするものであると評価できる．

Section 5.5 Buyer's Right to Request Amendments to Purchase Orders.

Buyer may, on notice to Seller, request changes to a Purchase Order. On or before the thirty (30) Business Day after receiving the request, Seller shall submit to Buyer its good faith description of the impact of such changes on the Basic Purchase Order Terms. Buyer may then submit an amended Purchase Order reflecting all Buyer-accepted changes.

3.9 Purchase Orders の変更

5.5 条においては Buyer に Purchase Order の変更に関する権利を認めている．先に紹介したとおり，「Agreement」は Offer と Acceptance の一致があった時点で成立しているから，その後の一方的な Agreement の変更（Modification という）は認められないのが原則である．したがって，5.5 条は契約法よりも Buyer に有利な内容を規定したものといえる．

・Modification

契約の Modification が有効に認められるための要件は契約の成立要件と同じであり[87]，原則として，①Offer，②Acceptance，および③Consideration が要求される[88]．Modification は新たな契約を創出するに等しいため[89]，

たところで，その契約を解約した．その後まもなく，映像編集業者は第三者から，バスルームの清掃業務 ($40,000)，および，スリラー映画の編集作業 ($30,000)の依頼を受けたがこれらを拒否した．この場合，映画制作会社の契約違反に関して，映像編集業者の損害として認容されうる金額は，$25,000 ($60,000-$5,000-$30,000) である．Legal Info. Inst., *Duty to mitigate example*, https://www.law.cornell.edu/wex/example/%5Bfield_short_title-raw%5D_33 (last visited Feb. 22, 2018).

[87] *See, e.g.*, Beacon Terminal Corp. v. Chemprene, Inc., 75 A.D.2d 350, 354 (Sup. Ct. N.Y. 1980) ("Fundamental to the establishment of a contract modification is proof of each element requisite to the formulation of a contract, including mutual assent to its terms".).

[88] *But see* U.C.C. § 2-209 cmt. 2 (Am. Law Inst. & Unif. Law Comm'n 2002) (U.C.C.においては Modification に Consideration は不要である旨規定しつつ，Consideration なくしての Modification はそれが「good faith」に行われる場合に限って認められるとする). Modification が「good faith」なものであるかについて

Consideration はもともとの契約で提供された Consideration とは別のものである必要がある．例外的に新たな Consideration なくしての Modification も認められるのは，その Modification を正当化するような事情が認められる場合に限られる[90]．

5.5 条のように Buyer に Purchase Order に関する自由な Modification を認めた場合の問題としては，例えば Buyer による対象製品のデザイン変更に関する要求の結果，追加のコスト負担を Seller が余儀なくされることになった場合が想定できるところ，このような Modification が常に正当化されるべきとはいえない．そこで，5.5 条は，Buyer による Purchase Order の変更要求に伴う追加のコストについては，Seller が別途 Buyer に開示し，Buyer はそれを受け入れてでも Purchase Order を変更するかについて別途の決断を行うものとしている．

ARTICLE 6
SHIPMENT AND DELIVERY

Section 6.1 Shipment and Delivery Requirements.

Subject to Section 18.5, time, quantity, and delivery to the delivery location are of the essence under this Agreement. Seller shall assemble, pack, mark, and ship Products strictly in the quantities, by the methods,

---

は，その Modification がビジネス上合理的なものといえるかどうかによって判断されるものと思われる．例えば，契約上の義務の履行が一方契約当事者に損失を生じさせることになった場合においてそれを改善するための Modification も「ビジネス上合理的な modification」といいうる．See id.

[89] See, e.g., Beacon Terminal Corp., 75 A.D.2d, at 354 (citing Becker v Faber, 280 NY 146 (Ct. App. N.Y. 1939)) ("The modification of a contract results in the establishment of a new agreement between the parties which pro tanto supplants the affected provisions of the original agreement.").

[90] Restatement (Second) of Contracts § 89 (a) cmt. b. illus. 1 (Am. Law Inst. 1981) (新たな Consideration なくしての Modification が認められる例として，掘削工事の請負契約を締結したところ，工事対象の土地に思いもよらぬ強固な石が潜んでいたため，工事金額を当初の工事金額の9倍にあたる金額に Modification することに合意した場合を挙げる); see, e.g., Herron v. Wells Fargo Fin., Inc., 2006 U.S. Dist. LEXIS 63319, 52 (D. Ore. 2006) ("Under the RESTATEMENT (SECOND) OF CONTRACTS § 89, a promise modifying a duty under a contract not fully performed on either side is binding, even if the promise is without new consideration, if: '(a) the modification is fair and equitable in view of circumstances not anticipated by the parties when the contract was made; or (b) to the extent provided by statute; or (c) to the extent that justice requires enforcement in view of material change of position in reliance on the promise.'").

to the delivery locations, and by the delivery dates, specified in this Agreement. Delivery times will be measured to the time that Products are actually received at the delivery location.

If Seller does not comply with any of its delivery obligations under this Section 6.1, without limiting Buyer's other rights under this Agreement or applicable Law, Buyer may, in Buyer's sole discretion and at Seller's sole cost and expense:

(a) approve a revised delivery date; or

(b) require expedited or premium shipment.

Unless otherwise expressly agreed to by the Parties in writing, Seller may not make partial shipments of Products to Buyer.

3.10 Time is of the Essence Clause

例えば製品の代金支払日や製品の引渡し日など，特定の期日までに特定の契約上の義務の履行を要求する場合も少なくない．しかしながら，一方契約当事者がこれに違反した場合において，裁判所が直ちにそれを契約違反であるとして他方契約当事者による損害の請求や契約の解除を認めるかというとそうとは限らない．特にCommon Lawにおいて一方契約当事者による契約の解除が認められるためには他方契約当事者に「Material Breach」[91]が認められる必要があるが[92]，実際には，ある義務の不履行についてMaterial Breachを構成しないと判断される例も少なくないようである[93]．

---

[91] See, e.g., Restatement (Second) of Contracts § 241 (Am. Law Inst. 1981) (ある事象が「Material Breach」を構成するかについては次の要素を考慮して決定するべきとする．"(a) the extent to which the injured party will be deprived of the benefit which he reasonably expected; (b) the extent to which the injured party can be adequately compensated for the part of that benefit of which he will be deprived; (c) the extent to which the party failing to perform or to offer to perform will suffer forfeiture; (d) the likelihood that the party failing to perform or to offer to perform will cure his failure, taking account of all the circumstances including any reasonable assurances; (e) the extent to which the behavior of the party failing to perform or to offer to perform comports with standards of good faith and fair dealing.").

[92] Triple J Saipan, Inc. v. Agulto, 2002 MP 11, P9 (Sup. Ct. N. Mal. I. 2002) ("The material breach of an 'entire' contract by one party justifies termination by the nonbreaching party.").「Material Breach」の詳細については4.3（契約の解除）において紹介する．

[93] See, e.g., Coddon v. Youngkrantz, 562 N.W.2d 39, 42, 43 (Ct. App. Minn. 1997) (一方契約当事者による一度の支払い遅延は他方契約当事者による対象契約の解除を認める根拠とはなりえない旨を示した) ("Only a material breach or a substantial failure in performance gives the seller a right to terminate a contract for

CHAPTER 3 / ACTION PROVISIONS　　31

　そこで，契約上，特定の期日までの契約上の義務の履行が重要（「Time is of the Essence」）である旨を強調し，その不履行があった場合において救済を得られる可能性を高めようとすることが考えられる．このような趣旨のもと用意された規定を Time is of the Essence Clause という．

・Time is of the Essence Clause の非絶対性
　ある契約において Time is of the Essence Clause を用意した場合であっても，それのみをもってあらゆる遅延について規定のとおりの効果が認められるわけではない[94]．特に契約当事者がどの契約上の履行義務に関して「Time is of the Essence」であると認識しているかに関する明示のない Time is of the Essence Clause (General Time is of the Essence Clause という)[95] は機能しないことが多い[96]．これに対して，①契約当事者が「Time is of the Essence」であると理解する契約上の履行義務が特定されており，かつ，②その義務に不履行があった場合の他方契約当事者に対する救済手段が明示されている場合[97]（Specific Time is of the Essence Clause という）には，その規定のとおりの効果が認められやすい傾向にある[98]．
　なお，Recitals において，特定の義務の履行について「Times of the Essence」である旨を強調しておくことが有用であることは先に紹介したとおりである．

---

deed.... This seven-day delay in making a single installment payment can not be the basis of default.").

[94] *See, e.g.,* Restatement (Second) of Contracts § 242, cmt. d. (Am. Law Inst. 1981) (一方契約当事者にある義務の不履行があったとしても，対象契約書に典型的な「time is of the essence」の語句が規定されていることをもって他方契約当事者による契約解除を直ちに認めるべきではなく，その義務の不履行が事実上も他方契約当事者に重大な影響を与えている場合にこそ契約の解除を認めるべきであると指摘する); *see also, e.g.,* 17 W. 127th St. Partners LLC v Baruch Realty, LLC, 2016 N.Y. Misc. LEXIS 3040, 9 (Sup. Ct. N.Y. 2016) (quoting ADC Orange, Inc. v. Coyote Acres, Inc., 7 N.Y.3d 484, 489 (Ct. App. N.Y. 2006)) ("As we have long held, 'the mere designation of a particular date upon which a thing is to be done does not result in making that date the essence of the contract.'").

[95] 例えば次のような規定をいう．「Time shall be of the essence with regard to all obligations under this Agreement.」．

[96] Thomson Reuters, General Contract Clauses: *Time of the Essence*, Practical Law Commercial Transactions, https://1.next.westlaw.com/Document/I0f9fe588ef0811e28578f7ccc38dcbee/View/FullText.html?contextData=(sc.Default)&transitionType=Default&firstPage=true&bhcp=1&OWSessionId=4c79304c26b74cfa948c72cdd4aacecf&isplcus=true&fromAnonymous=true (last visited May 1, 2018).

[97] *See generally* Jeffery S. Ammon, *Time Is of the Essence (to Banish That Phrase from Your Contracts)!,* Mich. B. J. (2016), https://www.michbar.org/file/barjournal/article/documents/pdf4article2814.pdf (last visited May 1, 2018) (実務上，Time is of the Essence Clause において，対象義務の不履行があった場合における相手方契約当事者の救済手段が明示されていることはまれであると指摘する).

[98] Thomson Reuters, *supra* note 96.

Section 6.2 Acceptance of Products.

If Buyer determines, in its sole discretion, that Products delivered under this Agreement are Nonconforming Products or Excess Products, Buyer may, at its option:

(a) if such Products are Nonconforming Products, either:

 (i) reject Nonconforming Products (including entire lots of Products) for a refund plus any inspection, test, shipping, handling, and transportation charges paid by Buyer; or

 (ii) require prompt correction or replacement of such Products on Buyer's written instruction,

(b) if such Products are Excess Products, reject such Excess Products for a refund, plus any inspection, test, shipping, handling, and transportation charges paid by Buyer; or

(c) in either case, retain such Products.

In each case the exercise by Buyer of any other rights available to Buyer under this Agreement or pursuant to applicable Law shall not be limited.

Buyer shall ship from any location, at Seller's expense and risk of loss, the Nonconforming Products or Excess Products to the nearest authorized Seller location. If Buyer exercises its option to replace Nonconforming Products, Seller shall, after receiving Buyer's shipment of Nonconforming Products, ship to Buyer, at Seller's expense and risk of loss, the replaced Products to the delivery location in a timely manner.

3.11 欠陥品または数量超過品の提供

 6.2 条は，Seller から提供された製品が欠陥品または数量超過品であった場合において，Buyer にその救済手段に関する選択権を認めるものである．

a. 救済手段の選択権

6.2 条においては，Buyer はその自由裁量（「in its sole discretion」）によって欠陥品または数量超過品の提供に関する対応を決定できる旨を規定している．Seller としてはそのような広汎な裁量を認めずにすむよう Buyer との契約交渉に臨むこととなるが，仮に契約上「in its sole discretion」の語句が残ることとなってしまったとしても，Buyer による裁量の行使について何らの異議も唱えることができないわけではない．契約法上，一般に契約当事者は「duty of good faith and fair dealing[99]」の理念のもと，契約に基づく取引関係を誠実に進めていくことが要求されているためである[100]．

b. U.C.C.における取り扱い

U.C.C.においては「Perfect Tender Rule」のもと，Seller は Buyer と合意した製品に関するすべての仕様（品質，配送，および配送形態などを含む）を満たす責任[101]を負う．この Seller の責任に反する製品が Buyer に届けられた場合，Buyer の Seller に対する責任追及，および，それに対する Seller の対応などについては次のとおりとなる．

i. Buyer の対応
(a) Seller に対する通知義務
Buyer は，Buyer が欠陥品に関する Seller の責任を追及する前提として，

---

[99] See generally U.C.C. § 1-201(20) (Am. Law Inst. & Unif. Law Comm'n 2002) (「[G]ood faith」を「honesty in fact in the observance of reasonable commercial standards of fair dealing.」と定義する).

[100] See, e.g., Wilson v. Amerada Hess Corp., 773 A.2d 1121, 1130 (Sup. Ct. N.J.) (ガソリンの供給業者と Distributor との間におけるガソリン供給契約において，ガソリン供給事業者にガソリンの供給価格に関する自由裁量を認めている (「subject to change at any time without notice」) 場合に関する事案. 一方契約当事者の有する自由裁量については相手方契約当事者が対象契約のもと享受できるものと合理的に期待していた利益を奪う目的では行使されるべきでなく，それは「duty of good faith and fair dealing」に反すると示した) ("[A] party exercising its right to use discretion in setting price under a contract breaches the duty of good faith and fair dealing if that party exercises its discretionary authority arbitrarily, unreasonably, or capriciously, with the objective of preventing the other party from receiving its reasonably expected fruits under the contract."); see also, e.g., Restatement (Second) of Contracts § 205 (Am. Law Inst. 1981) ("Every contract imposes upon each party a duty of good faith and fair dealing in its performance and its enforcement."); see also, e.g., U.C.C. § 1-304 (Am. Law Inst. & Unif. Law Comm'n 2001) ("Every contract or duty within [the Unifrom Commercial Code] imposes an obligation of good faith in its performance and enforcement.").

[101] See, e.g., Midwest Mobile Diagnostic Imaging, L.L.C. v. Dynamics Corp. of America, 965 F. Supp. 1003, 1011 (W.D. Mich. 1997) (ある製品について欠陥が認められる場合，それがいかに些細な欠陥であってもそれは Perfect Tender Rule に反する旨を示した) ("Known as the 'perfect tender' rule, this standard requires a very high level of conformity. Under this rule, the buyer may reject a seller's tender for any trivial defect, whether it be in the quality of the goods, the timing of performance, or the manner of delivery.").

その欠陥を発見した後「合理的期間内」に Seller に対する通知を行わなければならない[102]。

(i)「合理的期間内」
欠陥品である旨の通知が「合理的期間内」に Buyer から Seller に行われたといえるかどうかについては個別の判断によることとなるものの，例えば Buyer が Seller への通知前に代替品を購入したような場合においては，たとえその後に Seller に通知が行われたとしても，それはもはや「合理的期間内」の通知には該当しないものと思われる[103]。

(ii) Buyer から Seller に対する通知の内容
Buyer から Seller に対する通知の内容については，単に製品に関して問題が発生したことの通知で足りるとする見解と，製品の瑕疵が Seller に起因するものであり契約違反を構成する旨の通知を要するとする見解[104]とに分かれる．したがって対象契約の適用法がいずれの見解をとるか明確でない場合などにおいては後者の要件を満たすよう配慮して対応すべきである[105]。

(iii) Buyer が Seller に対する通知を欠いた場合
Buyer が Seller に対する通知を欠いた場合，Buyer はあらゆる救済措置を受けることができないとされる[106]。

---

[102] U.C.C. § 2-607(3) (Am. Law Inst. & Unif. Law Comm'n 2002); *see generally* Am. Bumper & Mfg. Co. v. Transtechnology Corp., 252 Mich. App. 340, 346-47 (Ct. App. Mich. 2002) (Buyer から Seller に対する通知を要求する趣旨について次のとおり示した) ("The purposes of the UCC's notice requirement are (1) to prevent surprise and allow the seller the opportunity to make recommendations how to cure the nonconformance, (2) to allow the seller the fair opportunity to investigate and prepare for litigation, (3) to open the way for settlement of claims through negotiation, and (4) to protect the seller from stale claims and provide certainty in contractual arrangements.").

[103] John B. Bursch, *The Importance of Complying With the Uniform Commercial Code's "Notice" Requirement When a Supplier Provides Defective Goods*, The Mich. Bus. L. J. (2002), https://www.wnj.com/Publications/The-Importance-of-Complying-With-the-Uniform- (last visited Feb. 12, 2018).

[104] *See, e.g., Am. Bumper & Mfg. Co.*, 252 Mich. App., at 347 (Ct. App. Mich. 2002) (first citing Aqualon Co. v. Mac Equip., 149 F.3d 262, 266-67 (4th Cir. 1998); and then citing K & M Joint Venture v. Smith International, Inc., 669 F.2d 1106, 1113 (6th Cir. 1982)) ("Some courts have made clear that it is not enough for the buyer to only notify the seller that it is having difficulty with the goods.").

[105] Bursch, *supra* note 103.

[106] U.C.C. § 2-607(3)(a) (Am. Law Inst. & Unif. Law Comm'n 2002) (Buyer が Seller に対する通知を欠いた場合には「remedy」を受けられない旨を規定する); *id.* § 1-201(32) (「[R]emedy」について，「any remedial right to which an aggrieved party is entitled with or without resort to a tribunal」と定義する); *see, e.g., Am. Bumper & Mfg. Co.*, 252 Mich. App., at 348 ("To the extent that plaintiff argues that the 'any remedy' language

(b) Seller に対する責任追及

　例えば Buyer が Seller に対して青色のボールペン 100 個を 3 月 31 日までに配送する条件で注文したところ，Seller から黄色のボールペン 100 個が届けられたとする．この場合，Buyer は，(1-a) 黄色のボールペン 100 個の受領を拒否する[107]，(1-b) 黄色のボールペン 100 個をそのまま受領する[108]，または (1-c) 黄色のボールペン 100 個のうち，いくつかは受領し，残りについては受領を拒否する[109]といった手段をとることが可能である．

　また，Buyer は，これらいずれの場合であっても，(2) 別途黄色のボールペン 100 個が配送された結果生じた損害の賠償を Seller に対して請求できる[110]．

ii. Seller の対応

　Buyer から Seller に対して欠陥品に関する通知があった場合，Seller としては取引に関する信頼を維持する目的，および，損害賠償の義務を軽減する目的などのため，すぐさま欠陥のない製品を代替品として納入したいと考える場合もあろう．U.C.C.はこのような Seller の欠陥品の対応を「Cure」と呼称する．

　「Cure」に関しては，欠陥品がいつ Seller から Buyer に納入されたのか（本来予定されていた製品の納入予定日（契約上の義務履行日）よりも以前に納入されているのかどうか）が重要な指標となる．例えば Buyer が Seller に対して，青色のボールペン 100 個を 3 月 31 日までに配送する条件で注文したところ，Seller から黄色のボールペン 100 個が届けられたとする．U.C.C.はこの黄色のボールペンの配送が 3 月 31 日よりも以前であった場合と 3 月 31 日を徒過している場合とで「Cure」に関する取り扱いを異にするのである．

---

applies only to any remedy under the UCC and does not include its claims of express and implied indemnification, we disagree. MCL 440.1201(34) broadly defines 'remedy' as 'any remedial right to which an aggrieved party is entitled with or without resort to a tribunal.' Further, MCL 440.2607(3)(a) also clearly states that if notice of the breach is not given within a reasonable time, the buyer is 'barred from any remedy.' It does not state "any remedy under the UCC" as plaintiff contends. Here, the statute plainly and unambiguously states that notice must be given or the buyer is barred from *any* remedy.").

[107] U.C.C. § 2-601(a) (Am. Law Inst. & Unif. Law Comm'n 2002).
[108] *Id.* § 2-601(b).
[109] *Id.* § 2-601(c).
[110] *Id.* § 2-714; *id.* § 2-715.

(a) 欠陥品の納入日が契約上の義務履行日よりも以前である場合

Seller は契約上の義務履行日までに欠陥のない製品の出荷を行うという「Cure」する権利を有する[111]。ここに，「Cure」はあくまで Seller の権利であって，Buyer が Seller に対してその実行を強制できるものではない[112]。

(b) 欠陥品の納入日が契約上の義務履行日を徒過している場合

原則として Seller は「Cure」する権利を有さない。例外的に Seller に「Cure」する権利が認められるのは，Seller がその欠陥品が Buyer によって受領されるであろうと信じるに合理的な根拠を持っていた場合である[113]。

先の例（Buyer が Seller に対して青色のボールペン 100 個を 3 月 31 日までに配送する条件で注文したところ，Seller から黄色のボールペン 100 個が届けられた）の場合，青色のボールペンの注文を行ったにもかかわらず Seller から届けられたのは黄色のボールペンであったという状況が以前に幾度もあったところ，Buyer は常に黄色のボールペンを受領していたような場合において，Seller は「Cure」する権利を有するといいうる。

---

[111] *Id.* § 2-508(1).

[112] 6.2(a)(ii)条においては，「(Buyer may) require prompt correction or replacement of such Products on Buyer's written instruction」としており，あくまで Buyer が「Cure」に相当する行為を Seller に対して要求することを認めている。これに対して，Seller に「Cure」する権利を許容する趣旨で起案する場合には，「[i]f any Products delivered under this Agreement are Nonconforming Products, Seller may seasonably notify the Buyer of his intention to cure and may then make a conforming delivery.」などと規定することになる。ただし，契約上 Seller に「Cure」を認める趣旨の規定を設けていたとしてもそれが絶対ではないことを留意しなければならない。*See* Larken, Inc. v. Larken Iowa City Ltd. P'ship., 589 N.W.2d 700 (Sup Ct. Iowa 1998) (quoting 6 Lawrence A. Cunningham & Arthur J. Jacobson, *Corbin on Contracts* § 1266, at 23 (1997 Supp.)) (ある契約において「Cure」の権利がある旨を規定していたとしても，一方契約当事者による契約不履行が対象契約の目的を損なうようなものである場合，他方契約当事者は相手方契約当事者に「Cure」の権利行使の機会を付与することなく対象契約を解除することができる旨を示した) ("'There was a *frustration of purpose* when a breach involving fundamental dishonesty by one party occurred, because no amount of payment for past thefts by Central could ever restore the business trust and confidence which Olin wanted to have in its distributors. . . . Under the circumstances, then, Central's breach was a *vital* breach, it would have been sufficient to allow Olin to rescind the contract even if the contract had been in terms an absolute one for a fixed term with *no right of termination at all*; it seems strange to suggest that the right of immediate termination is lost because the parties expressly provided a means of terminating for lesser, curable breaches.'").

[113] U.C.C. § 2-508(2) (Am. Law Inst. & Unif. Law Comm'n 2002).

ARTICLE 7
TITLE AND RISK OF LOSS

Section 7.1 Title.

Title to Products shipped under any Individual Transaction passes to Buyer upon the earliest to occur of (a) delivery of the Products to Buyer, (b) payment of any portion of the Price for such Products by Buyer, (c) Buyer's acceptance of the Products, or (d) Seller's tender of the Products to the carrier. Title will transfer to Buyer even if Seller has not been paid for such Products, provided that Buyer will not be relieved of its obligation to pay for Products in accordance with the terms hereof.

3.12 Title Transfer Clause

7.1条は、対象製品の所有権がSellerからBuyerに移転する時期を規定する。所有権の移転時期は契約当事者の合意によって自由に設定できるところ、7.1条はBuyerからSellerへの製品代金の支払いが完了するかどうかにかかわらず、Buyerが製品の所有権を取得することを許容している。

 a. Romalpa Clause

例えばBuyerの支払い能力に疑義がある場合など、Sellerとしては自己のBuyerに対する債権の安全性を確保したい場合もある。そこで、SellerからBuyerへの所有権の移転は、その製品代金の支払いが行われてはじめて発生するものとすることが考えられる[114]。このような規定[115]をRomalpa Clauseという(Retention of Title Clauseともいう)[116]。Romalpa Clauseは欧州においては

---

[114] この場合、たとえBuyerが倒産したとしても、その製品はBuyerの債権者に対する配当原資とはならない。11 U.S.C. § 541(a)(1) (2010).

[115] この場合、次のような規定を設けることになる。「Title to Products will not transfer to Buyer until the Price has been fully paid.」。

[116] より正確には、Romalpa Clauseは、①製品の所有権のSellerへの留保、および、②Trust provision (Buyerが製品代金支払い前に製品を使用し第三者に販売するなどした場合において、Buyerはその第三者から受領した代金をSellerに対する代金支払いのために保管することを義務付ける規定)によって構成される。*Romalpa Clause*, Academic Dictionaries and Encyclopedias, https://law.academic.ru/6368/Romalpa_clause. (last visited May 2, 2018).

一般的であるものの[117]，北米においてはそうとはいえないようである[118]。

b. U.C.C.における取り扱い

契約当事者間で格別の合意がない場合においては，U.C.C.が所有権の移転時期を各取引内容に応じて規定しているため，それらが参考になる．例えば Seller が特定の場所への製品の配送を要求されている場合，製品の所有権はその配送先において Buyer に移転する[119]。

c. Incoterms との関係

契約が国際取引に関するものである場合，7.1 条および 7.2 条に関する条項においては，International Commercial Terms（Incoterms という）が用いられることも少なくない．ここに Incoterms とは国際的な合意に基づいて作成された商業用語集をいい，それらは International Commercial Chamber of Commerce によって公表されている[120]．しかし，Incoterms はあくまで対象製品の滅失などに関するリスク，および，製品の輸送に関する費用の負担に関するものであり，製品の所有権移転時期に関して定めるものではない．したがって，7.1 条のような製品の所有権の移転時期に関する規定は，たとえその契約が Incoterms を用いていたとしても必要となる．

Section 7.2 Risk of Loss.

Notwithstanding any agreement between Buyer and Seller concerning transfer of title or responsibility for shipping costs, risk of loss to Products shipped under any Individual Transaction passes to Buyer upon receipt and acceptance by Buyer at the delivery location, and Seller will bear all risk of loss or damage regarding Products until Buyer's receipt and acceptance of such Products in accordance with the terms hereof.

---

[117] Romalpa Clause は AluminiumIndustrie Vassen BV v. Romalpa Aluminium [1976] 1 WLR 676 (Eng.) において認められた規定を起源とする．Id.
[118] US Legal, Inc., *Romalpa Clause Law and Legal Definition*, https://definitions.uslegal.com/r/romalpa-clause/ (last visited May 2, 2018).
[119] U.C.C. § 2-401(2)(b) (Am. Law Inst. & Unif. Law Comm'n 2002).
[120] International Chamber of Commerce, *Incoterms rules 2010*, https://iccwbo.org/resources-for-business/incoterms-rules/incoterms-rules-2010/ (last visited Jun. 12, 2018).

3.13 Risk of Loss Clause

7.2条は，SellerがBuyerに向けて発送した製品がその輸送過程で損傷，滅失，または紛失などした場合のリスク（Risk of Lossという）をBuyerまたはSellerのいずれが負担するか[121]について規定するものである．

a. U.C.C.における取り扱い

U.C.C.は，(1) SellerによるBuyerへの対象製品の発送に関して，運送業者の利用が許容されている場合，(2) 対象製品は受寄者によって保管されることとなっている（そしてその後のBuyerによる受寄者からの製品の受け取りが予定されている）場合，または(3) これらのいずれの場合にも該当しない場合，に分類した上でBuyerまたはSellerのいずれに「Risk of Loss」が所在するかを規定している[122]．

b. Incotermsにおける取り扱い

契約が国際取引に関するものである場合，Risk of Loss ClauseにおいてはIncotermsが使用されることも少なくないことについては先に紹介したとおりである[123]．その場合，そのIncotermsと矛盾する取引条件が他の契約条項に規定されていないよう確認すべきである．

ARTICLE 8
PRICE AND PAYMENT

Section 8.1 Price.

Subject to Section 8.2, Seller shall provide Products to Buyer for the prices set forth on Schedule I attached hereto ("Prices"). All Prices include, and Seller is solely responsible for, all costs and expenses relating to packing, crating, boxing, transporting, loading and unloading, customs, Taxes, tariffs and duties, insurance, and any other similar financial contributions or obligations relating to the production,

---

[121] *See generally Black's Law Dictionary: Pocket Edition* 661 (4th ed. 2011).
[122] U.C.C. § 2-509 (Am. Law Inst. & Unif. Law Comm'n 2002).
[123] この場合，次のような規定を設けることになる．「Terms of delivery shall be [Free On Board (FOB) Seller's port] as that term is defined in INCOTERMS 2010, or any subsequent revision of the INCOTERMS.」．

manufacture, sale, and delivery of the Products.

All Prices are firm and are not subject to increase for any reason, including changes in market conditions, increases in raw material, component, labor or overhead costs, or because of labor disruptions, changes in program timing or length, or fluctuations in production volumes.

3.14 製品の Price
8.1 条においては対象製品の「Price」に関する定義および「Price」に含まれる費用などを明示している．

a. U.C.C.における取り扱い
　契約当事者としては，取引内容によっては製品の「Price」の決定は留保しつつ，先に契約を締結してしまおうと考える場合もあろう（Open Price という）[124]．取引の促進を図る U.C.C.においては，たとえ「Price」が定まっていない契約であっても，次のいずれかに該当する場合にはその契約の成立を認める．

　i. 両契約当事者が（「Price」は決定されていないものの）その契約に拘束される意思のもとで契約を締結している場合
　(1) 何ら「Price」について定めるものがない場合，(2) 契約当事者間で「Price」を別途決定することとしていたものの結局その決定がなかった場合，または (3) 契約当事者間で「Price」を特定の市場価格または基準に基づいて決定することとしていたものの，結局その決定がなかった場合のいずれかに該当する場合，契約の成立が認められる．これらの場合における「Price」は，対象製品の Delivery 時点における「Reasonable Price」[125]となる．

---

[124] Jason Klinowski, *The Law does not recognize "Price After Sale" Terms…* (Apr. 2, 2012), https://freshfactsblog.wordpress.com/2012/04/02/the-law-does-not-recognize-price-after-sale-terms/ (last visited May 3, 2018).
[125] U.C.C. § 2-305(1) (Am. Law Inst. & Unif. Law Comm'n 2002); *see generally* Weisberg v. Handy & Harman, 747 F.2d 416 (7th Cir. 1984) (「Reasonable Price」について，Seller から Buyer に対象製品が配送されるまでの期間における市場価格を参考として決定した); *cf.* U.C.C. § 2-305(4) (Am. Law Inst. & Unif. Law Comm'n 2002) (契約当事者が，「Price」の確定または合意に至るまでは契約に拘束されない旨の意思を有する場合，契約は成立していないものとする).

ii. 契約上，Buyer または Seller によって「Price」が決定されることとしている場合

  この場合，「Price」はその決定権者（Buyer または Seller）が「in good faith」[126]に決定するものを指すと理解したうえで契約の成立が認められる．

 b. Firm Fixed Price Clause
「Price」について契約当事者間で合意に至った場合であっても，例えば原材料価格が高騰したなど，その後の予期せぬ事情により，一方契約当事者が「Price」の変更を希望する場合がある．合意済みの「Price」を変更し，新たな「Price」での取引を進めるためには，「Price」の変更に関する両契約当事者の合意が必要となる[127]．

  Firm Fixed Price Clause は，これとは反対に，契約締結後どのような予期せぬ事情が発生したとしても「Price」の変更を認めないとするものである．Firm Fixed Price Clause は Seller に製品納入に関するコストのあらゆるリスクを負わせることで，効率的な製品生産活動を促すことを趣旨とするが，Seller としては少なくとも Buyer の都合から生じたコストの変動などについてはその対象から除外したいところであり，契約交渉の対象事項の一つとなると思われる．

Section 8.2 Most Favored Nation.

Seller represents and warrants that each of the Prices set forth on Schedule I is at least as low as the price charged by Seller to other

---

[126] 「Price」が「in good faith」に決定されたといえるかどうかの判断については，その「Price」が，(1) 客観的に商業上合理的なものであるのかという観点に着目して行う州と，(2) 客観的観点に加えて，「Price」を決定した契約当事者に他方契約当事者に損害を与えるような目的が認められるかといった主観的観点も考慮して行う州とに分かれる．Robert LeVine, *No Price? - No Problem* (Jan. 29, 2016), http://ucc-madeeasy.blogspot.com/2016/06/no-priceno-problem.html (last visited May 3, 2018); *see, e.g.*, Tom-Lin Enters. v. Sunoco, Inc., 349 F.3d 277, 281-82 (6th Cir. 2003) (客観的な観点に着目する旨を示した) ("[U]nder Ohio law, to show that a merchant-seller lacks good faith in fixing a price pursuant to a contract with an open price term, it must be shown that the price was not fixed in a commercially reasonable manner and, moreover, that the pricing was commercially unjustifiable. These are two distinct issues, and both involve an *objective* analysis of the merchant-seller's conduct."); *see, e.g.*, Mathis v. Exxon Corp., 302 F.3d 448, 456 (5th Cir. 2002) (客観的な観点に加えて主観的な観点についても考慮する旨を示した) ("(Tex. Com. & Bus. Code Ann. § 2.305 cmt. 3) embraces both the objective (commercial reasonableness) and subjective (honesty in fact) senses of good faith; objective good faith is satisfied by a 'price in effect' as long as there is honesty in fact.")
[127] すなわち契約の Modification が必要となる．Modification については 3.9 (Purchase Orders の変更) において紹介した．

> buyers for similar volumes of the same Products or similar Products.
>
> If, at any time during the Term, Seller charges any other buyer a lower price for the same Products or similar Products, Seller shall apply that price to all same or similar Products under this Agreement. If Seller fails to meet the lower price, Buyer may, at its option, in addition to all of its other rights under this Agreement or at Law, terminate this Agreement without liability pursuant to Section 14.3.
>
> The Parties shall reflect any adjustment to pricing under this Section 8.2 in an amendment to Schedule I; provided, however, that, notwithstanding anything to the contrary contained in Section 2.1, the execution and delivery of any such amendment by each of the Parties will not be a condition to the effectiveness of such Price adjustment.

3.15 Most Favored Nation Clause

　Most Favored Nation Clause（または Most Favored Customer Clause ともいう）は Buyer に有益な規定である．すなわち，Buyer は，対象契約の条件は Seller が他の取引先との間で有する条件よりも劣るものではない旨の確約を Seller から得ることで，対象製品市場における自社の優位性の確保を試みるのである．

　・独占禁止法との関係

　Most Favored Nation Clause に関しては独占禁止法との関係に注意が必要となる[128]．つまり，Most Favored Nation Clause は，(1) Seller と Seller の競合事業者との間での製品価格を下げない旨の合意形成を助長する，または，そのような競合事業者との合意形成がない場合においても Seller の製品価格の低減に向ける意欲を損なわせ，製品価格の維持を助長する[129]，(2) Buyer が Seller に対して優越的な地位にある場合にはその地位の利用を助長する[130]，ならびに (3) Seller が Buyer と Buyer の競争事業者とに提供する製品価格に不当な差別が生じうる[131]といった問題を有するとされるのである[132]．

---

[128] *See generally* Fiona Scott-Morton, *Contracts that Reference Rivals*, U.S. Dep't of Just. (Apr. 5, 2012), https://www.justice.gov/atr/file/518971/download (last visited Feb. 14, 2018) (Most Favored Nation Clause の製品価格の高止まりに関する影響などについて指摘する).

[129] *See generally* 15 U.S.C. § 1 (2004).

[130] *See generally id.* § 2.

[131] *See generally id.* § 13.

[132] Steve Cernak & Tal Chaiken, *Most Favored Nation Clauses*, Practical Law Publishing Limited & Practical

CHAPTER 3 / ACTION PROVISIONS   43

したがって，Most Favored Nation Clause を設定する場合においては，自社の業界における立場，相手方契約当事者の業界シェア[133]，および Most Favored Nation Clause を正当化する事情の有無などについて十分に検討すべきである。

なお，独占禁止法に関しては Federal Trade Commission および U.S. Department of Justice Antitrust Division が執行権限を有する[134]。Most Favored Nation Clause との関係においてこれら機関がこれまでに着目してきたのはヘルスケア業界のようである[135]。これに対し，私人が Most Favored Nation Clause の独占禁止法違反を問う訴訟については，ヘルスケア業界に限られることなく見受けられる[136]。

Section 8.3 Invoices.

Seller shall issue a monthly invoice to Buyer for all Products ordered in the previous month. Each invoice for Products must set forth in reasonable detail the amounts payable by Buyer under this Agreement and contain the following information, as applicable: a reference to this Agreement; Purchase Order number, amendment number, and line-item number; Seller's name; Seller's identification number; carrier name; ship-to address; weight of shipment; quantity of Products shipped; number of cartons or containers in shipment; bill of lading number; country of origin and any other information necessary for identification and control of the Products.

---

law, 1-2, https://www.schiffhardin.com/Templates/media/files/publications/PDF/Cernak_Chaiken_Most-Favored-Nation-Clauses_20130311.pdf (last visited Oct. 25, 2017).

[133] *Id.* at 6 (同種の製品を取り扱う複数の事業者と同種の Most Favored Nation Clause を締結する場合においては，それら事業者の業界シェア総計の考慮も必要となりうる旨を指摘する)。

[134] Federal Trade Commission, *The Enforcers*, https://www.ftc.gov/tips-advice/competition-guidance/guide-antitrust-laws/enforcers (last visited Feb. 14, 2018).

[135] Cernak, *supra* note 132, at 3; *see, e.g.*, United States v. Blue Cross Blue Shield, 809 F. Supp. 2d 665 (E.D. Mich 2011) (保険契約を提供する事業者が被保険者となる病院に対して自社に対する保険金請求額は他の保険契約提供事業者に対する請求額を下回ることなどを含む Most Favored Nation Clause を含んだ契約を締結していた場合において，連邦政府および Michigan 州から独占禁止法違反を問われた事案)。

[136] Cernak, *supra* note 132, at 5; *see, e.g.*, In re On-Line Co., 908 F. Supp. 2d 1369 (J.P.M.L.) (宿泊予約事業者に関する事案); *see also, e.g.*, Starr v. Sony BMG Music Entm't, 592 F.3d 314 2d Cir. 2010) (音楽配信事業者に関する事案)。

Buyer reserves the right to return and withhold payment for any invoices or related documents that are inaccurate or incorrectly submitted to Buyer.

Section 8.4 Payment Terms.

Except for any amounts disputed by Buyer in good faith, Buyer shall pay all invoiced amounts due to Seller within thirty (30) days following the later of (a) Buyer's receipt of Seller's invoice or (b) Buyer's receipt of applicable Products.

Payment of invoices will not be deemed acceptance of the Products or waive Buyer's right to inspect, but rather such Products will be subject to acceptance under Section 6.2. Buyer is entitled to any discounts allowable by Seller if its failure to make timely payment is due to Seller's actions or other circumstances or events beyond Buyer's reasonable control.

Buyer shall make all payments in US dollars by check, wire transfer, or automated clearing house, in accordance with the following wire instructions:

ABA Number:

Account Number:

Bank Address:

Attn:

3.16 Payment Terms
　8.4 条は格別の法律問題を含むものではなく，規定内容が予定する取引条件と整合しているかを確認することが中心となる．この確認作業との兼ね合いから 8.4 条において使用されている各用語について理解しておくことは有用である．

a. Wire transfer と Automated Clearing House

Wire transfer とは，銀行間で特定の通信手段を用いて行われる送金をいい[137]，主に大口決済や海外送金で利用されている．Wire transfer は即座の送金が可能である一方，個別の手続きを要するため費用も割高になりがちである．これに対して Automated Clearing House (ACH) とは，ACH と呼ばれるネットワークを利用して行われる送金をいう[138]．ACH は，給与振込，公共料金の引き落とし，または PayPal の決済などで広く利用され，小切手に替わる小口決済の主要手段となりつつある．ACH は一定の詐欺的行為からの保護が図られているほか[139]，Wire transfer よりも低額で利用できるものの，送金に時間を要する．

b. ABA number

ABA number (Routing number ともいう) は 9 桁の数字から成り，特定の米国の銀行を指す．銀行との間での送金または受金などを実施するうえで必要となる．

Section 8.5 Setoff Permitted.

Notwithstanding anything to the contrary in this Agreement, and without prejudice to any other right or remedy it has or may have, Buyer may, with three (3) Business Days' prior notice to Seller, set off or recoup any liability it owes to Seller against any liability for which Buyer determines in good faith Seller is liable to Buyer or its Affiliates, whether either liability is matured or unmatured, is liquidated or unliquidated, or arises under this Agreement.

3.17 Setoff Clause

Setoff[140] とは，一方当事者が他方当事者に対して有する債権の範囲で他方当事者に対して負う債務を減殺する権利をいう[141]．

---

[137] Miranda Marquit, *Difference Between Wire Transfer and ACH*, https://www.depositaccounts.com/blog/difference-between-wire-transfer-and-ach.html (last visited Nov. 20, 2017).
[138] *Id.*
[139] *See generally* Federal Reserve Bank of Minneapolis, *Payments Fraud Liability Matrix* (Apr. 2015), https://www.minneapolisfed.org/~/media/files/about/what-we-do/payments-fraud-liability-matrix.pdf?la=en (last visited May 3, 2018).
[140] いわゆる相殺については「Setoff」または「Offset」が適切な単語の候補となりうるところ，「Offset」は

a. Common Law Setoff
　i. 権利行使の要件
　一般に Setoff は（契約上の規定を待つまでもなく）当事者が Common Law 上有する権利であると認識されている[142]．Common Law 上の権利としての Setoff を実行するうえで必要となる要件は，①Setoff 被実行者が Setoff 実行者に対して有効な債務を有すること，②Setoff の実行者が Setoff 被実行者に対して有効な債務を有すること，および③両当事者の債務が「Mutual」であることである[143]．

　・「両当事者の債務が『Mutual』であること」
　上記要件③を満たすうえにおいて，Buyer と Seller が相互に負う債務は必ずしも同一の取引から発生する必要はないが[144]，各当事者はそれぞれ，①他方当事者に対して，②無条件の債務を負っているといえる必要がある．
　したがって，例えば Buyer が Seller に対して負う製品代金の支払い債務について，Seller の Affiliate が Buyer に対して負う債務と Setoff すること[145]は認められない．Seller と Seller の Affiliate は異なる法人である以上，

状態動詞として用いることは適切である一方，動態動詞として用いることは不適当であるため「Setoff」がより適切である旨を指摘する見解がある. Kenneth A. Adams, *"Setoff" and "Offset" - Adams on Contract Drafting*, Adams on Contract Drafting (Feb. 9, 2014), http://www.adamsdrafting.com/setoff-and-offset/ (last visited Oct. 27, 2017).

[141] *See, e.g.*, Keegan v. Estate of Keegan, 179 N.J. Super. 242, 246 (Super. Ct. N.J. 1981) (quoting John Wills, Inc. v. Citizens Nat'l Bank of Netcong, 125 N.J.L. 546, 548 (Ct. Err. & App. 1940)) ("[A] set-off is: That right which exists between two parties each of whom under an independent contract owes *an ascertained amount* to the other to set-off his respective debts by way of a mutual deduction so that in any action brought for the larger debt, the residue only, after such deduction, shall be recovered"); *see also* Black's Law Dictionary: Pocket Edition 686 (4th ed. 2011).

[142] *See generally* Bruce Nathan & Scott Cargill, *Got Setoff Rights? Think Again Contractual Provision Allowing Triangular Setoff is Unenforceable in Bankruptcy*, International Association of Credit Management (Mar. 2012), 3, https://www.lowenstein.com/files/publication/30c4461e-c296-46c3-8a8f-d2e5dc6c6d4b/presentation/publicationattachment/87ff39dd-5243-4aad-8cbe-db9dda3debbd/got%20setoff%20rights%20think%20again.pdf (last visited Feb. 14, 2018).

[143] David N. Crapo, *Basics of Setoff under New Jersey Law*, Gibbons P.C. (May 26, 2005), https://www.gibbonslaw.com/basics-of-setoff-under-new-jersey-law-05-26-2005/ (last visited May 4, 2018) ("There are three requirements for effectuating a setoff: (a) the person against whom the setoff is being effectuated must be indebted to the person effectuating the setoff; (b) the person effectuating the setoff must be indebted to the person against whom it is being effectuated; and (c) the obligations of the two parties must be mutual.").

[144] *See, e.g.*, Guarantee Co. of North America v. Tandy & Allen Constr. Co., 66 N.J. Super. 285, 289 (Super. Ct. N.J. Law Div. 1961) ("A setoff is an offsetting claim arising out of a completely independent and unrelated transaction.").

[145] このように一方当事者Ａが他方当事者Ｂに負う債務について，第三者ＣがＡに対して負う債務と

Buyer は他方当事者である Seller に対して債務を負っているとはいえないためである。次に，例えば Buyer が Seller に対して負う製品代金の支払い債務について，Buyer が Seller による欠陥品の提供の結果被った旨を一方的に主張する損害額と Setoff することも認められない。Seller は Buyer に対して無条件の債務を負っているわけではないためである。

ii. 権利行使の方法

Setoff は Setoff を実行する意図のもとで Setoff の実効履歴を記録することをもって行使される[146]。Setoff の実効履歴の記録は公的な手続きが要求されるものではないが，書面を残すべきである[147]。

b. Statutory Setoff

Setoff はその権利が州法などによって認められている場合もある[148]。

c. Contractual Setoff

Setoff は Common Law または州法上の権利であるが，権利内容を明確化する，または，それらによっては認められていない Setoff（例えば Triangular Setoff）を実効できるようにするといった趣旨から，あらためて契約上 Setoff Clause を設けることも少なくない。なお，Setoff Clause においては契約当事者が Setoff の権利を放棄[149]する旨を規定することも認められる[150]。

の間で行う Setoff を Triangular Setoff という。Charles M. Oellermann & Mark G. Douglas, *Another Blow to Triangular Setoff in Bankruptcy: "Synthetic Mutuality" No Substitute for the Real Thing* (Nov. and Dec. 2011), Jones Day, http://www.jonesday.com/Another-Blow-to-Triangular-Setoff-in-Bankruptcy-Synthetic-Mutuality-No-Substitute-for-the-Real-Thing-12-01-2011/ (last visited May 7, 2018).

[146] *See, e.g.*, In re Czyzk, 297 B.R. 406, 408 (Ct. Err. & App. N.J. 1948) ("A set off occurs where a creditor takes three steps: (1) it decides to exercise the right of set off, (2) it takes some action to accomplish the set off, and (3) it makes a record that evidences that the right to set off has been exercised").

[147] David A. Murdoch et al., *Bankruptcy Getting to Know your two Best Friends: The Rights of Setoff and Recoupment*, at 1, Kirkpatrick & Lockhart Nicholson Graham LLP (Dec. 2005), http://www.klgates.com/files/Publication/56da8ca6-ba6a-4973-8fa4-3b2d8aaf05a5/Presentation/PublicationAttachment/77554d2e-5845-481f-9f1c-4f3a7f161e4d/ba1205.pdf (last visited Nov. 14, 2017).

[148] *E.g.*, N.Y. Debt. & Cred. Law § 151; *see*, *e.g.*, U.C.C. § 2-717 (Am. Law Inst. & Unif. Law Comm'n 2002).

[149] Setoff の権利は契約当事者の作為または不作為によって，明示または黙示に放棄することも可能である。Murdoch, *supra* note 147, at 4.

[150] この場合，次のような規定を設けることになる。「Each Party shall perform its obligations under this Agreement without setoff, deduction, recoupment, or withholding of any kind for amounts owed or payable by the other Party whether under this Agreement, applicable law, or otherwise and whether relating to the other Party's breach, bankruptcy, or otherwise.」. Thomson Reuters, *General Contract Clauses: No Setoff*, Practical Law Commercial Transactions, https://1.next.westlaw.com/Document/I5d8c7fd8642611e38578f7ccc38dcbee/View/FullText.html?originationContext=document&transitionType=DocumentItem&contextData=(sc.DocLink)&firstPage=true (last visited May 4, 2018).

48

3.18 Setoff と倒産手続きとの関係
　Setoff の実行は，それが Common Law，州法など，または Setoff Clause に基づくものであるかにかかわらず，倒産法による制約を受けうる[151]。

　a. Setoff が倒産手続き申し立て前に実行された場合
　一方契約当事者による Setoff が他方契約当事者に対する倒産手続き開始日より<u>前</u>に実行された場合，原則としてその Setoff は有効である[152]。しかし，次のいずれかに該当する場合，破産財団の管財人はその Setoff に対して否認権などを行使することができる[153]。

　　i. Acquired Claim Setoff
　Acquired Claim Setoff は，① Setoff 被実行者の倒産手続き開始日からさかのぼって 90 日内の間に，② Setoff 被実行者が債務超過の状態において，③ Setoff 実行者が第三者の有する Setoff 被実行者に対する<u>債権</u>をその第三者から譲り受けた場合を対象とした問題である。この場合，Setoff 実行者が（第三者から譲り受けた）Setoff 被実行者に対する債権と Setoff 実行者が Setoff

---

[151] 倒産手続きにおける債権保護手段として Setoff と同じく有力な手段として挙げられるのが Recoupment である。Recoupment は，破産財団が債権者に対して債務の支払いを要求した場合において，債権者が自己の有する債権を理由としてその債務支払いを拒否する抗弁である。Recoupment は倒産法上の権利ではなく Common Law によって認められてきた衡平法上の権利 (equitable doctrine などという) である。Recoupment は債権と債務とが「same transaction」から生じる必要があるため (*see, e.g.*, In re B & L Oil Co., 782 F.2d 155, 157 (10th Cir. 1986) ("Under recoupment, a defendant could meet a plaintiff's claim with a countervailing claim that arose "out of the same transaction.")，Recoupment を主張できる場面は Setoff よりも限られる。一方，Recoupment は消滅時効の適用がない (*see, e.g.*, Harmer v. Hulsey, 321 Pa. Super. 11, 14 (Super. Ct. Pa. 1983)) ("[R]ecoupments have traditionally been permitted, even if raised after the limitations period has run, whereas set-offs will not be permitted if late")，および，Automatic Stay の適用を受けない (*see, e.g.*, In re Holford, 896 F.2d 176, 179 (5th Cir. 1990) (internal citation omitted) ("The trustee of a bankruptcy estate 'takes the property subject to rights of recoupment.' That is, 'to the extent the damages equal or exceed the funds withheld, the debtor has no interest in the funds and, therefore, the stay has not been violated.' Further, ... , the Tenth Circuit specifically allowed post-petition recoupment of damages against continuing payments.") といった Setoff よりも有用な面も持つ。

[152] *See, e.g.*, In re Czyzk, 297 B.R. 406, 409 ("In order to show that it is entitled to a set off, a creditor must establish that there is: 1) a debt owed by the creditor to the debtor which arose prior to the bankruptcy case; 2) a claim of the creditor against the debtor which arose prior to the bankruptcy case; 3) the debt and the claim are mutual obligations; and 4) applicable non-bankruptcy law permits a right to set off the debts.). なお，Setoff の対象となる債務と債権とは<u>ともに倒産手続き申し立てより前</u> (Pre-Petition)，または，<u>倒産手続き申し立てより以降</u> (Post-Petition) に発生したものでなければならない。すなわち，例えば，<u>Pre-Petition</u> で発生した債務と <u>Post-Petition</u> で発生した債権とを Setoff することはできない。Murdoch, *supra* note 147, at 2.

[153] *Id.* at 2 (裁判所は，これらの Setoff を preferential transfer (11 U.S.C. § 547(b)) または fraudulent transfer (11 U.S.C. § 548 (a)) として扱い，破産管財人による否認権の行使を許容することになると説明する)。

被実行者に対して負う債務とを Setoff することは認められない[154]．

ii. Acquired Debt Setoff

Acquired Debt Setoff は，① Setoff 被実行者の倒産手続き開始日からさかのぼって 90 日内の間に，② Setoff 被実行者が債務超過の状態において，③ Setoff 実行者が第三者の有する Setoff 被実行者に対する<u>債務</u>をその第三者から譲り受けた場合を対象とした問題である．この場合，Setoff 実行者が Setoff 被実行者に対して有する債権と Setoff 実行者が（第三者から譲り受けた）Setoff 被実行者に対して負う債務とを Setoff することは認められない[155]．

iii. Improvements in Position Setoff

Improvements in Position Setoff は，(1) Setoff 実行者が Setoff の実行によって得た利益と (2) Setoff 実行者が Setoff 被実行者の倒産手続き開始日からさかのぼって 90 日内の別の日に Setoff を実行していたと想定した場合に得られた利益とを比較し，(1) の方が (2) よりも大きい場合を対象とした問題である．この場合，破産財団の管財人はその差の範囲内で Setoff 実行者から財産を直接取り戻すことができる[156]．

b. Setoff が倒産手続き申し立て後に実行された場合

一方当事者が倒産手続き対象者となった場合，その倒産手続きの申し立て日以降，他方当事者は倒産手続き対象者に対して自己の債権の回収行為を行うことが許されない（Automatic Stay という）[157]．ここに禁止対象となる回収行為にはその倒産手続き申し立て日より前から存在していた債権および債務を対象とした Setoff も含まれる[158]．ただし，他方当事者が裁判所より

---

[154] 11 U.S.C. § 553(a)(2) (2015).
[155] Id. § 553(a)(3).
[156] Id. § 553(b). 例えば，Buyer が倒産手続きを申し立てた日からさかのぼって 90 日前の時点においては，Buyer が Seller に対して$100 の債務と$50 の債権を有していたとする．これに対して Buyer が倒産手続きを申し立てた日からさかのぼって 20 日前の時点において，Buyer が Seller に対して$100 の債務と$75 の債権を有しており，Seller の Buyer に対する Setoff の権利行使がこの時点で行われたとする．この場合，Seller は Setoff の権利行使日を調整することによって$25 分の利益を得ているとして，破産財団の管財人は Seller に対して$25 の返還を請求することができる．
[157] Id. § 362.
[158] Id. § 362(a)(7). 倒産手続き申し立て日より以降に発生した債権と債務とを対象とした Setoff についは (倒産法上明確な規定はないものの Common Law をふまえると) その実行が認められるものと理解される．Samuel R. Maizel, *65. Setoff and Recoupment in Bankruptcy -- Setoffs (cont'd), Recoupment*, Civ. Resource Manual (Jan. 26, 1996), U.S. Dep't of Just., https://www.justice.gov/usam/civil-resource-manual-65-setoff-and-recoupment-bankruptcy (last visited May 7, 2018).

Automatic Stay からの救済を得た場合[159]はその例外として，倒産手続き対象者に対する Setoff の実行が認められる．

・倒産手続きにおける取り扱い
先に紹介したとおり，一方当事者が倒産手続きを申し立てた後において，倒産手続き申し立て日より前から存在していた債権と債務とを対象とした他方当事者による Setoff の実行は許されないものの，他方当事者の債権については一定の範囲で倒産手続きによる保護を受ける．

(a) 優先弁済権の取得
一方当事者が倒産手続きに入らなければ Setoff が可能であった範囲（他方当事者が倒産手続き対象者に対して有する債権と他方当事者が倒産手続き対象者に対して負う債務のうち金額の重なり合う部分）において，他方当事者は担保債権者（secured creditor）として優先弁済を受けうる地位に置かれる[160]．これに対して，それ以外の範囲（他方当事者が倒産手続き対象者に対して有する債権のほうが他方当事者が倒産手続き対象者に対して負う債務よりも大きい場合においてその超過する部分）については，他方当事者は非担保債権者（unsecured creditor）として劣後弁済を受ける地位に置かれる．

(b) 破産管財人による財産保護
破産管財人は，他方当事者の有する債権が倒産手続きによって毀損されないよう適切な措置をとる義務を負う．破産管財人がこの義務を怠ったといえる場合，他方当事者は Automatic Stay からの救済を申し立てたうえで Setoff を実行しうる[161]．

c. Triangular Setoff
Common Law 上は認められていない Triangular Setoff についても，契約上，Setoff Clause においてそれを認める旨規定することが許容されうることについてはすでに紹介したとおりである．しかし，その場合であっても倒産手続き対

---

[159] これに対して，Automatic Stay からの救済なくして実施された Setoff は無効であるほか，Setoff 実行者は法廷侮辱罪（contempt of court）などを理由として罰金などを受ける可能性もある．Murdoch, *supra* note 147, at 2.
[160] 11 U.S.C. § 506(a)(i) (2005).
[161] *Id.* § 362(d).

象者との関係においては、Triangular Setoff を実行することは認められない[162]。

ARTICLE 9
INTELLECTUAL PROPERTY RIGHTS

9.1 Rights to Use for Buyer's Products.

For the purposes of the manufacture, assembly, distribution, and sale by Buyer of its products, parts and accessories and to the extent of necessary to use the Products for those products, Seller grants to Buyer, its Affiliates, and subcontractors irrevocable, nonexclusive, worldwide, and royalty free licenses under the Intellectual Property Rights to use, modify, or distribute the same, the Confidential Information, and any necessarily incidental right thereto.

3.19 製品を使用するためのライセンス権
　a. Free License Clause
　9.1 条においては、Buyer は Seller から、対象製品に関する知的財産権などの無償ライセンス権を確保している。Seller が対象取引の完了後に「対象製品の使用行為は Seller の知的財産権を侵害している」といった主張を Buyer に対して行うといった事態が発生することのないよう手当てしたものである[163]。
　もっとも、Seller としてはそもそもそのような主張を行う意図はなく[164]、

---

[162] *See* Sass v. Barclays Bank PLC (In re Am. Home Mortg., Holdings, Inc.), 501 B.R. 44, 56 (Bankr. D.Del. 2013). 倒産法上の「mutuality」(倒産手続き開始前から倒産手続き対象者に対して有する債権と債務との Setoff が倒産手続きとの関係においても有効なものといえるためには、それら債権と債務が「mutual」でなければならないとされる (11 U.S.C. § 553(a))) を契約上の規定によって満たすことは許容されない旨示した) ("Because of the mutuality requirement in section 553(a), courts have routinely held that triangular setoffs are impermissible in bankruptcy.").

[163] *See generally* Unarco Indus., Inc. v. Kelley Co., 465 F.2d 1303, 1307 (7 th Cir. 1972) (Non-Exclusive License は実質的に Licensor が Licensee に対する訴訟提起を禁じたものと同視できる旨評価した) ("We hold the nonexclusive license agreement which was, in fact, a forbearance of suit.").

[164] *But see* Quanta Computer, Inc. v. LG Electronics, Inc., 553 U.S. 617 (U.S. 2008) (Licensee が Licensor からライセンスした技術に基づいて製造した製品に関して、その後その製品を組み込む第三者の行為についてはライセンス契約の対象外であるとして第三者に対する royalty の請求が行われた事案。裁判所は Licensee である Intel Corporation から chip を購入した Quanta Computer, Inc.は、Licensor である LG Electronics. Inc.に対する royalty の支払い義務を負わない旨を示した)。

Free License Clause を受け入れることに問題はないと判断することも多いかと思われる[165]．しかしその場合においても，9.1 条の「to the extent of necessary to use the Products for those products」の一節のように，①無償ライセンス権の対象はあくまで Buyer が Seller から購入した製品との関係において，②Buyer に真に必要な限りにおいて認められる旨を明示し，いたずらにその対象が拡大しすぎないよう注意しなければならない．

b. Not to Sue Clause

Not to Sue Clause[166]は，Seller から，対象製品に関する特許権侵害などの訴訟を Buyer に対して提起しない旨の確約を取り付けるものであり，実質的に Free License Clause と同様の目的を達成する手段として用いることができる．もっとも，Not to Sue Clause は，以下の事項において Free License Clause よりもいっそうの注意を払う必要がある[167]．

i. 対象製品に権利未確定の知的財産権が利用されている場合

Not to Sue Clause は，Seller が Buyer に対して，Seller の有する「訴訟を起こす権利」の不行使を確約するものであると理解されうる[168]．この理解によると，Seller がその確約（covenant not to sue）を提供した時点において確定的に権利を保有しているわけではないもの（例えば知的財産権取得の申請手続き中の対象権利）については Not to Sue Clause の対象となりえないともいえるのである[169]．

---

[165] もっとも，Free License Clause の意義は，Patent Exhaustion Doctrine および Indemnification Clause の存在によってそれほど大きなものではなくなっているかと思われる．このうち，Patent Exhaustion Doctrine とは，ある特許権を使用した製品が有効な権限のもとでいったん販売された場合 (Authorized Sale という)，以降，特許権者は特許権を対象製品に対して行使できなくなるとする原則をいう (see, e.g., U.S. v. Univis Lens Co. 316 U.S. 241, 249 (U.S. 1942) ("An incident to the purchase of any article, whether patented or unpatented, is the right to use and sell it, and upon familiar principles the authorized sale of an article which is capable of use only in practicing the patent is a relinquishment of the patent monopoly with respect to the article sold.")．Indemnification Clause については 3.29 (Indemnification) 以降において紹介する．

[166] 例えば，次のような規定を設けることになる．「Seller hereby covenants that it shall not enforce, or permit or encourage the enforcement of, against Buyer, any of Buyer's respective Affiliates, sub-licensees, successors or assigns any Seller's Intellectual Properties in connection with the development or commercialization of any Products. In the event Seller transfers any right under such Seller's Intellectual Properties to a third party, Seller shall ensure that such covenant not to sue is binding upon such third party in writing.」

[167] Marc Malooley, *Patent Licenses Versus Covenants Not to Sue: What Are the Consequences?*, 1, https://www.brookskushman.com/wp-content/uploads/2015/06/131.pdf (last visited Feb. 14, 2018).

[168] *See, e.g.*, 3M Innovative Properties Co. v. Barton Nelson, Inc., 2003 U.S. Dist. LEXIS 22743, 6 (D.Minn. 2003) ("A covenant not to sue is a covenant by one party who, at the time the covenant was made, had a right of action against another party, by which the first party agrees not to sue to enforce such action.").

[169] Malooley, *supra* note 167, at 1-2.

ii.知的財産権が第三者に譲渡された場合

Not to Sue Clause の対象とする知的財産権がその後 Seller から 第三者に譲渡された場合，Seller の提供した covenant not to sue がその第三者を拘束するのか[170]明らかでないという問題がある[171]．

9.2 Right to use for Products.

Following the expiration or earlier termination of this Agreement, Seller grants, and agrees to grant, to Buyer, its affiliates, and subcontractors an irrevocable, non-exclusive, worldwide license to use any Intellectual Property Right that is used in the manufacture of the Products to make, have made, use and sell the Products.

This license may be exercised only upon the transfer of the supply of the Products from Seller to an alternate supplier or to Buyer and will be subject to Buyer's payment of a reasonable royalty with respect to any of Seller's patented intellectual property that is used in the manufacture of the Products. Upon Buyer's request, Seller agrees to provide all documents necessary for Buyer's use of such intellectual property.

3.20 製品を製造するためのライセンス権

9.2 条は，Buyer が本契約の対象製品と同種の製品を自己または第三者から調達することを決定した場合において，Seller から製品の製造に必要となる知的財産権などのライセンスを受ける権利を確保するものである．

しかし，このようなライセンス権は，例えば，Seller が一方的に製品の製造を中止した場合のように，Buyer 自身による製品の製造が必要となった理由が

---

[170] See generally GTE Wireless, Inc. v. Cellexis Intern., Inc. 341 F.3d 1 (1st Cir. 2003) (一方契約当事者の提供した covenant not to sue がその第三者を拘束するのかについて争われた事案 (ただし，契約内容の解釈が必要であるとして summary judgment の申し立てが却下されており，Not to Sue Clause の第三者に対する拘束力に関しては明確な判断が示されていない)).

[171] Cf. In re Singer Co., N.V., 262 B.R. 257, 265 (Bankr. S.D.N.Y. 2001) (ライセンス契約について，対象特許の譲受人に対する拘束力を有する旨を示した) ("It is well established that the federal law regarding the assignment of patents makes patent assignments subject to the conditions of any licenses, including implied licenses").

Sellerに起因するような場合に限って認めることが相当と思われる[172].
　したがって，Sellerとしては，(1)いかなる場合において Buyer に対してライセンス権の許諾義務を負うのか，および，(2)ライセンス権の許諾義務を負う場合それはどのような条件となるのかについて確認すべきである．

9.3 Intellectual Property Ownership.

Except as stated in this Section 9.3, each Party will retain ownership of their respective Intellectual Property Right relating to the Products (a) existing prior to the effective date of this Agreement or the commencement of any technical cooperation by the Parties relating to the Product, or (b) that each Party acquires or develops after these dates but in an independent manner and entirely outside of any work conducted under this Agreement.

If Seller creates or develops an invention, patentable discovery, improvement or process based on (a) the technical data, information, proposals or opinions provided by Buyer in connection with this Agreement, or (b) the development service fully funded by Buyer, Seller shall forthwith notify Buyer thereof and the Parties shall discuss in good faith and agree on the ownership of the Intellectual Property Rights subsisting or embodied therein.

3.21 知的財産権に関する所有権の帰属
　対象製品に関する知的財産権については，例えば製品の開発段階などにおける関心事となることが多いが，製品売買契約においてもその所有権の帰属に関する規定が散見される．Sellerとしては，Sellerが本契約関係に入る前から有していた知的財産権についてはもちろん，対象製品に関して本契約締結後に有するに至った知的財産権についても自己の権利として確保することにより，

---

[172] 例えば，次のような規定を設けることになる．「If this Agreement is terminated by Buyer pursuant to Section 14.3, Seller grants to Buyer a non-exclusive right and a free license to use Seller's Intellectual Property Rights to obtain from alternate sources products and services similar to the Products for use in the products covered by the terminated Purchase Orders and for the balance of the Purchase Orders at the date of the termination.」．(SellerからBuyerに対する無償のライセンス権は，①BuyerがSellerに重大な契約違反などがあったことを理由に契約を解除した場合において，②BuyerとSellerとの間で合意済みの Purchase Orders において注文済みの数量の範囲内においてのみ供与されることとしている).

Buyer がその他の seller から同種製品を調達するといった事象を可能な範囲で抑制したいところである．

もっとも，例えばその知的財産権が Buyer から提示された情報に基づく場合，または，Buyer から提供された開発資金に基づく場合など，Seller がその知的財産権を自己の権利として維持するだけの合理的根拠が見いだしがたい場合もある．9.3 条は，そのような場合においては，Seller から Buyer に知的財産権が生じた旨を通知したうえで，その所有権については別途の協議を行う旨規定している．

a. 知的財産権をめぐる雇用者と従業員との関係

9.3 条は，Buyer および Seller がその従業員によって創出された知的財産権を所有していることを前提として用意された規定である．しかし，従業員がある知的財産権を創出した場合，その知的財産権は雇用者ではなくその従業員に帰属するのが原則である[173]．したがって，雇用者が従業員の創出した知的財産権を所有するためには，次のいずれかによる適切な措置を講じる必要がある[174]．

---

[173] *See, e.g.*, Tees v. Chromalloy Gas Turbine Corp., 83 F.3d 403, 407 (Fed. Cir. 1996) ("Ownership springs from invention. The patent laws reward individuals for contributing to the progress of science and the useful arts. As part of that reward, an invention presumptively belongs to its creator."); *see also, e.g.*, Mainland Indus., Inc. v. Timberland Machines & Eng'g Corp., 58 Or. App. 585, 589 (Ct. App. Or. 1982) ("Absent an agreement to the contrary, when an employe is hired to invent, or is assigned the responsibility for solving a particular problem, any resulting invention belongs to the employer. When the employment relationship is general, an employe is entitled to retain any patent he procures, even though the patent relates to the employer's product line.").

[174] 雇用者が従業員の創出した知的財産権を所有するために適切な処置がとられているかどうかについては，一方契約当事者が他方契約当事者にその従業員により創出された知的財産権を譲渡などする旨を義務付けられている場合に特に問題となる．例えば次のような規定である．「9.5 Seller, on behalf of itself and Seller's Personnel, hereby grants, assigns and transfers, to Buyer all rights, title and interest to all Intellectual Property Rights, including any "moral rights," in the Products, free and clear of any and all claims for royalties or other compensation, unless otherwise limited by applicable law. Seller shall promptly disclose all inventions to Buyer, execute such documents and do such other acts as may be reasonably necessary to further evidence or effectuate Buyer's rights in and to the Products, and shall cause the Seller Personnel to do so. If and to the extent that any moral rights cannot be assigned to Buyer, then Seller will obtain such waivers, releases or consents as may be necessary or appropriate to ensure that Buyer's use, transfer, license, exploitation and alienation of the Products will not infringe or misappropriate the rights that cannot be assigned.」；「9.6 Seller shall acquire all inventor rights of Seller's Personnel required under applicable law to enable it to grant Buyer the rights under Section 9.5.」；「9.7 Seller shall assume full and sole responsibility for compensating Seller's Personnel for assigned work done in connection with this Agreement, including without limitation the remuneration of employees for inventions. Seller shall indemnify Buyer from and against all claims of Seller's Personnel for compensation for such work upon first demand and Seller shall be excluded from assertion of all defenses and objections.」．

i. 雇用契約

典型的な措置としては，従業員と締結する雇用契約において，その従業員の創出した知的財産権については雇用者に譲渡される旨を規定しておくことが挙げられる．この場合，従業員から雇用者への譲渡対象とする知的財産権の範囲についても注意を払ったうえで雇用契約を用意しなければならない[175]．

なお，雇用契約を締結した後，従業員の創出した知的財産権については雇用者に譲渡される旨の合意に至った場合，その知的財産権の譲渡に関する同意に対しては（雇用以外の）「Consideration」の提供が必要とされうる[176]．

ii. Hired to Invent Exception

Hired to Invent Exception は，知的財産権の創出者が知的財産権の創出のために特別に雇用されたとの事情が認められる場合において，その知的財産権の雇用者への譲渡を義務付けるものである[177]．もっともその従業員が「Hired to Invent」であるかどうかの判断は必ずしも容易ではないため[178]，雇用者はその旨を明示した雇用契約を用意することが推奨される．

これらは従業員が創出した知的財産権を雇用者が所有するうえで必要となる措置であるが，これとは別に，Common Law 上，雇用者には，従業員が雇用者の設備または資金などを用いて創出した知的財産権ならびに就業時間内

---

[175] 例えば California 州および Washington 州においては，従業員の就業時間外に従業員の費用のもとで雇用者のビジネスとは関係ない分野に関して創出された知的財産権についてまでを従業員から雇用者への譲渡対象として含むことを禁止している．Cal. Lab. § 2872 (1979); Wash. Rev. Code § 49.44.140 (1979).

[176] Thomson Reuters, *Employer Rights To Employees' Inventions*, FindLaw, http://smallbusiness.findlaw.com/intellectual-property/employer-rights-to-employees-inventions.html (last visited Mar. 2, 2018).

[177] *See, e.g.*, United States v. Dubilier Condenser Corp., 289 U.S. 178, 187 (U.S. 1933) (citing Standard Parts Co. v. Peck, 264 U.S. 52 (U.S. 1924)) ("One employed to make an invention, who succeeds, during his term of service, in accomplishing that task, is bound to assign to his employer any patent obtained. The reason is that he has only produced that which he was employed to invent. His invention is the precise subject of the contract of employment. A term of the agreement necessarily is that what he is paid to produce belongs to his paymaster."); *see* William C. Lewis, *Hey! You stole the invention I paid you to invent!*, Nexsen Pruet, LLC. (2011), https://www.lexology.com/library/detail.aspx?g=e09583fd-789b-48b7-a59b-6601b8b40313 (last visited Mar. 2, 2018).

[178] *Id.* (ある従業員が「Hired to Invent」であるかどうかについての判断要素として次を挙げる．"1. Whether or not there was a written employment agreement addressing patent rights, 2. Whether past employment agreements or policies addressed patent rights, 3. Whether the employment was in an inventive capacity, 4. Whether the contracted-for inventive work was performed by the employee, 5. Whether the inventive work was performed at the employer's facility, 6. Whether the employee permitted or refused to allow the employer to use the invention, 7. Whether the employer provided guidance and direction to the employee, and 8. Whether the employer's resources were used in development.").

に創出した知的財産権について，無期限，非独占，および譲渡不可能のライセンス権を有すること（Shop Right という）が認められている[179]．

b. Feedback Clause
Feedback Clause は，ある情報の受領者がその情報に基づいて知的財産権などを創出した場合に，情報開示者に向けてその知的財産権の権利譲渡またはライセンス権の供与を行う旨の規定をいい[180]，情報開示者が別途その Feedback に含まれる知的財産権に関する主張を情報受領者から受けるような事態を防止することを趣旨とする．

Seller としては，Seller が Feedback に貢献する程度などを予測しつつ Feedback Clause に合意するかどうかについて検討するほか，仮に Feedback Clause に合意する場合にはその Feedback に対する保証などを行うのかについても検討することになる[181]．

9.4 Software and Written Works Ownership.

All works of authorship, including without limitation, software, computer programs and databases (including object code, micro code, source code and data structures), and all enhancements, modifications and updates thereof and all other written work products or materials created by Seller or its Personnel, will be considered "works made for hire" and all copyrights for such work shall belong to Buyer to the extent that such works of authorship is ordered or commissioned by Buyer, or is a necessary part of the performance of Seller under the Purchase Order.

---

[179] *See, e.g., Dubilier Condenser Corp.*, 289 U.S., 188-89 ("Recognition of the nature of the act of invention also defines the limits of the so-called shop-right, which shortly stated, is that where a servant, during his hours of employment, working with his master's materials and appliances, conceives and perfects an invention for which he obtains a patent, he must accord his master a non-exclusive right to practice the invention."); *see* Sean M. O'Connor, *Hired to Invent vs. Work Made For Hire: Resolving the Inconsistency Among Rights of Corporate Personhood, Authorship, and Inventorship*, 35 Seattle U. L. Rev. 1227, 1240 (2012), https://digitalcommons.law.seattleu.edu/sulr/vol35/iss4/10/ (last visited May 10, 2018).

[180] Rahul Kapoor & Shokoh H. Yaghoubi, *IP Agreements: Don't Forget the Feedback Clause*, Morgan, Lewis & Bockius LLP. (Feb. 27, 2017), https://www.morganlewis.com/blogs/sourcingatmorganlewis/2017/02/ip-agreements-dont-forget-the-feedback-clause?p=1. (last visited Mar. 1, 2018).

[181] *See id.* (Feedback については，その提供自体に対する consideration が認められない限り，Warranty and Representation Clause または Indemnification Clause の対象とする根拠が見いだしがたい旨を指摘する）．

> To the extent that such works of authorship do not qualify under any applicable law as works made for hire, Seller hereby assigns to Buyer all right, title and interest in any copyrights in such works of authorship. If such assignment is not possible under any applicable law, Seller hereby grants an exclusive and royalty-free license to Buyer with respect to such works of authorship.

3.22 著作権に関する所有権の帰属

対象製品に関する著作権については，9.4 条のように，他の知的財産権とは別にその所有権の帰属に関する規定が置かれることもある．

・Work Made for Hire Doctrine

著作権については，著作権を創出する根拠となった業務に関して著作権の創出者に費用を拠出している者がある場合，その第三者が著作権者となるという原則があり，これを Work Made for Hire Doctrine という[182]。「Work Made for Hire」は，(1) 著作権創出者が雇用契約下の従業員である場合において，その著作権創出活動が雇用契約の範囲内で実施されたといえる場合，または，(2) ①第三者が著作権創出者に向けて著作権創出活動に関する指示または資金の提供を行っており，②著作権創出活動が著作権法所定の活動のいずれかに該当し[183]，③著作権創出者と第三者との間の契約において著作権創出者の活動は「Work Made for Hire」である旨明示されている場合において認められる．

---

[182] 17 U.S.C. § 101 (2010). これに対して，著作権以外の知的財産権についてはそれら知的財産権に関する Work Made for Hire Doctrine を意図して Hired to Invent Exception が認められているとされる．しかし，Hired to Invent Exception が適用される場合においてもその知的財産権の発明者は知的財産権創出者であってその雇用者ではない (Hired to Invent Exception は知的財産権創出者に対して雇用者への知的財産権の譲渡を義務付けるものにすぎない)．したがって，著作権者たる地位自体を著作権創出者ではなく雇用者とする Work Made for Hire Doctrine とは異なるものである．O'Connor, *supra* note 179, at 1240-41, https://digitalcommons.law.seattleu.edu/sulr/vol35/iss4/10/ (last visited May 10, 2018).

[183] 17 U.S.C. § 101(2) (2010) ("[A] work specially ordered or commissioned for use as a contribution to a collective work, as a part of a motion picture or other audiovisual work, as a translation, as a supplementary work, as a compilation, as an instructional text, as a test, as answer material for a test, or as an atlas, if the parties expressly agree in a written instrument signed by them that the work shall be considered a work made for hire. For the purpose of the foregoing sentence, a "supplementary work" is a work prepared for publication as a secondary adjunct to a work by another author for the purpose of introducing, concluding, illustrating, explaining, revising, commenting upon, or assisting in the use of the other work, such as forewords, afterwords, pictorial illustrations, maps, charts, tables, editorial notes, musical arrangements, answer material for tests, bibliographies, appendixes, and indexes, and an "instructional text" is a literary, pictorial, or graphic work prepared for publication and with the purpose of use in systematic instructional activities.").

本契約のように両契約当事者が雇用契約関係にはない場合，一方契約当事者は，上記 (2) の要件すべてを満たすことによって他方契約当事者の創出した著作権の所有を試みることになる．しかし，それら要件のうち，契約上直接的に対応できるのは要件③のみにすぎない[184]．そこで，この点について注意深い契約当事者は，仮に Work Made for Hire Doctrine の要件を満たさない場合においては他方契約当事者からの著作権の譲渡またはライセンス権の供与がある旨をあわせて規定するのである[185]．

ARTICLE 10
PRODUCT WARRANTIES

Section 10.1 Product Warranties.

Seller warrants to Buyer that:

(a) for the period of three (3) years from the date of shipment of the Products (the "Warranty Period"), the Products will;

　(i) conform, in all respects, to the Specifications, standards, drawings, samples, descriptions, quality requirements, performance requirements, statements of work, and fit, form and function requirements furnished, specified or approved by Buyer for the Products;

　(ii) conform with Buyer's quality standards;

---

[184] Owen, Wickersham & Erickson, P.C., *Legalities 4: What is Work Made For Hire?*, https://www.owe.com/resources/legalities/4-what-is-work-made-for-hire/ (last visited Mar. 1, 2018).

[185] このほか，契約上 Work Made for Hire Doctrine を利用するかどうかについては適用法も考慮しつつ検討すべきといえる．例えば California 州の場合，「Work Made for Hire」の条件のもと契約を締結している個人については，労働災害補償および失業保険との関係において，相手方契約当事者の従業員とみなされるのである．Cal. Unemp. Ins. § 686 (1982); Cal. Unemp. Ins. § 621(d) (1982); Cal. Lab. § 3351.5(c) (1989); *see, e.g.*, Elizabeth Russell, *Work for Hire + California = Employee* (Aug. 13, 2017), https://erklaw.com/work-for-hire-california-employee/ (last visited Mar. 2, 2018); *see also, e.g.*, Gordon Firemark, *Producer beware: "Work Made For Hire" agreement creates a "statutory employee" relationship* (Jul. 1, 2013), https://firemark.com/2013/07/01/producer-beware-work-made-for-hire-agreement-creates-a-statutory-employee-relationship/ (last visited Mar. 2, 2018).

> (iii) be merchantable and free from defects, latent or otherwise, in design, materials and workmanship;
>
> (iv) not infringe upon, violate or misappropriate the Intellectual Property Rights of any Person;
>
> (v) be fit and sufficient for the particular purpose intended by Buyer and its customers, of which the Seller is aware and Seller acknowledges that it knows of Buyer's intended use of the Products and that such Products have been selected, designed, manufactured or assembled by Seller based upon Buyer's stated use and will be fit and sufficient for the particular purposes intended by Buyer; and
>
> (vi) comply with all applicable Laws.
>
> (b) each of the Products will be new and conveyed by Seller to Buyer with good title, free and clear of all Encumbrances.

3.23 Warranty Clause

　Warranty Clause は Warranty の対象事項が真実であることを確約するものである．U.C.C.においては，Warranty を「Express Warranty」[186]と「Implied Warranty」[187]とに分類したうえで，それぞれの保証内容について規定している．

　a. Express Warranty
　「Express Warranty」は，10.1 条のように，Seller から Buyer に向けて提供された製品の品質および特徴などに関する確約である．例えば，Seller が Buyer に向けて，対象製品が防水機能を有する旨を表明した場合であり，その際において「Warranty」または「Guarantee」といった品質保証に直接関係する単語が用いられる必要はない．

　また，Express Warranty は品質に関する直接的な表明が行われた場合に限ることなく認められる．例えば Seller が Buyer にサンプル製品を提示した場合，Seller は対象製品がそのサンプルと同等のものである旨の Express

---

[186] U.C.C. § 2-313 (Am. Law Inst. & Unif. Law Comm'n 2002).
[187] *Id.* § 2-314; *id.* § 2-315.

Warranty を Buyer に向けて行ったものと理解される[188]。

・Express Warranty に関する違反
　一方契約当事者が Express Warranty に違反した場合，他方契約当事者は損害の賠償を請求することができる。この他方契約当事者による損害の請求は，たとえ他方契約当事者が Express Warranty を真実であると信じていなかったとしても認められうる[189]。

b. Implied Warranty
「Implied Warranty」は，取引関係に入ろうとする Buyer が対象製品の品質に関して寄せる期待を保護することによって取引の円滑化を図ったものである。したがって，Implied Warranty は，Seller から Buyer に対して具体的に何らかの保証が行われたかどうかを問うことなしに認められる。

　ただし，Implied Warranty はあくまで Seller が通常取引している製品との関係においてのみ認められるものであることに注意が必要である。例えば，カバン店を営んでいる Seller が Buyer に対してカバンを販売した場合，Seller にはカバンに関する Implied Warranty の提供が認められる。これに対して，Seller がそのカバン店で使用していた商品展示用の棚を店舗整理のため Buyer に販売した場合，Seller には棚に関する Implied Warranty の提供が認められない。

　Implied Warranty はその保証内容に基づいて，「Merchantability」[190] および「Fitness for Particular Purpose」[191] とに分類される。

　i. Merchantability
　ある製品が「Merchantability」を満たしているかについては，その業界にお

---

[188] Cadden & Fuller LLP., *Commercial Law: Express and Implied Warranties Under the Uniform Commercial Code.*, http://www.caddenfuller.com/Articles/Commercial-Law-Express-and-Implied-Warranties-Under-the-Uniform-Commercial-Code.shtml (last visited Nov. 15, 2017).
[189] *See, e.g.*, Norcold, Inc. v. Gateway Supply Co., 154 Ohio App. 3d 594, 623-24 (Ct. App. Ohio 2003) ("A decisive majority of courts that have considered this issue have reached the similar conclusion that reliance is not an element in a claim for breach of an express written warranty."); *see also, e.g.*, Power Soak Sys. v. EMCO Holdings, Inc., 482 F.Supp.2d 1125, 1134 (W.D. Mo. 2007) ("The modern trend is that a buyer need not rely on a seller's express warranty in order to recover for the seller's subsequent breach of the express warranty."); *but see* Hendricks v. Callahan, 972 F.2d 190 (8th Cir. 1992) (Express Warranty の被提供者が Express Warranty 提供者に対して Express Warranty 違反を問うにあたっては，Express Warranty の被提供者が Express Warranty について真実であると信じていたことを要件とした)。もっとも，この判決は強い批判を受けている。
[190] U.C.C. § 2-314 (Am. Law Inst. & Unif. Law Comm'n 2002).
[191] *Id.* § 2-315.

ける製品の品質に関する一般的な認識が重要な基準となるが[192]，U.C.C.は製品が最低限度満たすべきと考える事項を列挙している．これには例えば，その製品が通常の製品使用目的に適合していること[193]，および，製品の梱包またはラベルなどで表示されている保証内容を満たすこと[194]などが含まれる[195]．なお，「Merchantability」に関する Implied Warranty は「Merchant」[196]である Seller についてのみ，その提供が認められる．

ii. Fitness for Particular Purpose
対象製品が Buyer の特定の使用目的に適合していることの保証である．例えば，Buyer が庭に備え付けた柵の塗装に使う目的のもとペンキを Seller から買い求めたところ，翌日の雨ですぐにペンキの色が落ちてしまった場合，そのペンキは「Fitness for Particular Purpose」を満たしていないといえる．

「Fitness for Particular Purpose」に関する責任を追及するにあたって，Buyer は製品に瑕疵があることを証明する必要はなく，製品が Buyer の「特定の使用目的に適合していない」ことを証明すれば足りる[197]．この点，「特定の使用目的に適合していない」といえるための要件は，①実際に Seller が Buyer の特定の使用目的を知っていたこと，または，Seller が Buyer の特定の使用目的を知っているべきであったこと，および，② Buyer が Seller の製品に関する知見を信頼していたことである[198]．

3.24 Statute of Limitations との関係
相手方契約当事者に対する契約違反に関する請求権は時効（Statute of Limitations という）の対象となるところ，U.C.C.における売買契約に関する請求権の時効期間はその権利を取得したときから 4 年である[199]．

---

[192] *Id.* § 2-314 cmt. 2.
[193] *Id.* § 2-314(c).
[194] *Id.* § 2-314(f).
[195] Russelle E. Jumper et al., *Implied Warranty Under the UCC (TX)*, Thomson Reuters, http://m.grayreed.com/portalresource/Implied%20Warranties%20Under%20the%20UCC.pdf (last visited May 10, 2018).
[196] U.C.C. § 2-104 (Am. Law Inst. & Unif. Law Comm'n 2002). *See supra* note 79.
[197] Timothy Davis, *UCC Breach of Warranty and Contract Claims: Clarifying the Distinction*, 61 Baylor L. Rev. 783, 788 (2009), https://wakespace.lib.wfu.edu/bitstream/handle/10339/16048/Davis_UCC_Breach_of_Warranty_and_Contract_Claims.pdf (last visited Feb. 15, 2018).
[198] U.C.C. § 2-315 (Am. Law Inst. & Unif. Law Comm'n 2002). なお，「Fitness for Particular Purpose」に関する Implied Warranty は，Seller が「Merchant」ではない場合であっても認められうる．*Id.* § 2-315 cmt. 4.
[199] *Id.* § 2-725(1). 多くの州が U.C.C. § 2-725(1) をそのまま取り入れている．*E.g.*, Mich. Comp. Laws § 440.2725 (1964) (Michigan 州); *e.g.*, Ohio Rev. Code § 1302.98 (Ohio 州). なお，契約上の請求権に関する時効期間は契約当事者間で別に規定することもできるが，その場合の時効期間は権利を取得したときか

CHAPTER 3 / ACTION PROVISIONS   63

したがって，Buyer が Seller に対して Warranty に関する契約上の責任を追及しうる期間は，契約上合意した品質保証期間とその後の時効期間とを合算した期間ということになる[200]。

3.25 Warranty 責任の否定または制限

U.C.C.は，Seller が Express Warranty および Implied Warranty に関する責任を否定すること，または，責任を制限することを許容する[201]。しかし，厳密には，10.1 条のように契約上 Express Warranty が明確に提供されているといえる場合においては，Express Warranty に関する責任を否定したり，制限したりすることは認められない[202]。

したがって，契約上 Warranty 責任を否定または制限する規定を置く場合，それは Implied Warranty に関するものであるといえる。

・Implied Warranty 責任の否定または制限の方法

Implied Warranty に関する責任の否定または制限を行う[203]ためには次の要件

ら 1 年未満とはできず，また，4 年を超えるものとすることはできないとする。U.C.C. § 2-725(1) (Am. Law Inst. & Unif. Law Comm'n 2002); *id.* § 2-725(1) ("An action for breach of any contract for sale must be commenced within four years after the cause of action has accrued. By the original agreement the parties may reduce the period of limitation to not less than one year but may not extend it.").

[200] 時効期間内に訴訟による権利行使が行われなかった場合，以降，被告は原告が権利行使の権利を喪失した (Lapse of Time という) 旨主張しうることになる。なお，時効期間を停止 (Tolling the Statute of Limitations という) させることとの関係においては，いつの時点をもって訴訟が開始したといえるかが問題となりうるが，これについては連邦法または州法においてそれぞれの規定が用意されている。Fed. R. Civ. P. 3. (裁判所における訴状の提出をもって訴訟の開始を認める); *e.g.*, Or. Rev. Stat. § 12.020 (2017) (裁判所における訴状の提出のほか，被告に対する召喚状の送達を要求する)。

[201] U.C.C. § 2-316 (Am. Law Inst. & Unif. Law Comm'n 2002).

[202] *See id.* § 2-316(1); *see also* Kurt M. Saunders, *Can You Ever Disclaim an Express Warranty?*, 9 J. Bus. Entrepreneurship & L. 59, 61-64 (2016), http://digitalcommons.pepperdine.edu/jbel/vol9/iss1/3 (citing Husky Spray Serv., Inc. v. Patzer, 471 N.W.2d 146, 152 (Sup. Ct. S.D. 1991)) (この結論は対象契約が包括的に Warranty 責任を否定または制限する規定 (General Disclaimer という) をおいている場合であっても，または，特定の Warranty 責任を否定または制限する規定 (Specific Disclaimer という) をおいている場合であっても変わらない旨を指摘する)。

[203] 例えば，次のような規定を設けることとなる。「Disclaimer of Warranty. THE PRODUCTS ARE BEING SOLD "AS IS". EXCEPT FOR THE EXPRESS WARRANTIES SET FORTH IN THIS SECTION 10.1, SELLER MAKE NO REPRESENTATIONS AND GRANT NO WARRANTIES, EXPRESS OR IMPLIED, EITHER IN FACT OR BY OPERATION OF LAW, BY STATUTE OR OTHERWISE, AND SELLER SPECIFICALLY DISCLAIM ANY OTHER WARRANTIES, WHETHER WRITTEN OR ORAL, OR EXPRESS OR IMPLIED, INCLUDING ANY WARRANTY OF QUALITY, MERCHANTABILITY OR FITNESS FOR A PARTICULAR USE OR PURPOSE (OR ANY WARRANTY AS TO THE VALIDITY OF ANY PATENTS OR THE NON-INFRINGEMENT OF ANY INTELLECTUAL PROPERTY RIGHTS OF THIRD PARTY).」。

を満たす必要がある．

i. Merchantability
「Merchantability」に関する責任については，①責任の否定または責任の制限を行う旨を明示すること[204]，②責任の否定または責任の制限を「Conspicuous」に行うこと，および③責任の否定または責任の制限がMerchantabilityに関するものであることを明示すること[205]が要件となる．

ii. Fitness for Particular Purpose
「Fitness for Particular Purpose」に関する責任については，①責任の否定または責任の制限を行う旨を明示すること，および，②責任の否定または責任の制限を「Conspicuous」に行うことが要件となる．

「Merchantability」と「Fitness for Particular Purpose」とは，その責任の否定または制限を行うための要件①および②を同じくしている．要件①との関係では，対象条項において「as is」または「with all faults」などのような語句を用いることで，Buyerが対象条項を読んだ場合にその条項がSellerのWarranty責任の否定または責任の制限を行うものであることを明確に理解できるよう配慮することが要求される[206]．要件②との関係では，そもそもBuyerが対象契約にSellerの責任の否定または責任の制限に関する規定が含まれていることについて合理的に気付くことができるような配慮が要求される[207]．一般には，文字を他の条項よりも大きくする，文字の色を変える，大文字を使用する，イタリックを使用する，アンダーラインを引く，太文字にする[208]，または，責任否定もしくは責任制限に関する条項を他の規定から独立させて設けるといった方法が適切と考えられる．

---

[204] U.C.C. § 2-316(3) (Am. Law Inst. & Unif. Law Comm'n 2002).
[205] Id. § 2-316(2).
[206] Id. § 2-316(3)(a).
[207] See, e.g., FMC Finance Corp. v. Murphree, 632 F.2d 413, 418-19 (5th 1980) (first citing Alan Wood Steel Co. v. Capital Equipment Enterprises, Inc., 39 Ill.App.3d 48 (App. Ct. Ill 1976); and then citing U.C.C. § 1-201 cmt. 10 (Am. Law Inst. & Unif. Law Comm'n 2001)) ("Section 2-316(2) provides that for a written disclaimer of the implied warranties to be valid, the disclaimer language must be 'conspicuous.' Section 1-201(10) defines a conspicuous writing as one that a reasonable person against whom it is to operate ought to have noticed. It further provides that a printed heading in capitals is conspicuous, and that language in the body of a form is conspicuous if it is in larger or other contrasting type or color. The concept of conspicuousness is thus one of reasonable notice-whether the writing would have invited the attention of a reasonable person.").
[208] Contract Terms: Express and Implied Warranties, http://apps.americanbar.org/abastore/products/books/abstracts/5070449_SampleCh.pdf (last visited Feb. 22, 2018).

Section 10.2 Remedies for Breach of Warranties.

During the Warranty Period, if Products do not comply with the warranties in this Agreement, in addition to other remedies available at Law or in this Agreement, Seller shall, at Buyer's discretion:

(a) repair or replace such Defective Products; or

(b) credit or refund the Price of such Defective Products plus any inspection, test and transportation charges paid by Buyer, less any applicable discounts, rebates, or credits.

For such Products, Buyer shall ship, at Seller's expense and risk of loss, such allegedly Defective Products to the nearest authorized Seller location and Seller will, at Seller's expense and risk of loss, return any repaired or replaced Good to the address of delivery location in a timely manner.

3.26 契約違反と Warranty 違反

U.C.C.は対象製品が Seller によって提供された Warranty を満たしていない場合の救済手段についても規定する．すなわち，この場合，Buyer には製品の受領を拒否する[209]，対象契約を解除する[210]，または Warranty 違反によって被った損害の賠償を請求する[211]といった選択肢が生じうる[212]。

---

[209] U.C.C. § 2-601 (Am. Law Inst. & Unif. Law Comm'n 2002).
[210] *Id.* § 2-711.
[211] *Id.* § 2-714.
[212] *See generally* Davis, *supra* note 197, at 794-95 (quoting E. River S.S. Corp. v. Transamerica Delaval, 476 U.S. 858, 872 (U.S. 1986) ("[A] claim of a nonworking product can be brought as a breach-of-warranty action. Or, if the customer prefers, it can reject the product or revoke its acceptance and sue for breach of contract.") (U.C.C. § 2-711 に基づく請求については契約違反に関するものであり，U.C.C. § 2-714 に基づく請求については Warranty 違反に関するものであるとして，両者は区分できるとする理解を紹介する)。契約上，Warranty 違反に関する時効期間が特別に規定されている場合にはこのような区分が重要な意味を持ちうる。*See generally* Highway Sales, Inc. v. Blue Bird Corp., 504 F. Supp. 2d 630 (D.Minn. 2007) (契約上，Warranty 違反に関する請求の時効期間は1年である旨規定されている一方，契約違反に関する請求の時効期間は4年であった場合において，契約違反に関する請求に基づく権利主張が行われた事案); *but see* Davis, *supra* note 197, at 797 (契約違反に基づく請求と Warranty 違反に関する請求とは明確に区分できるとまではいえない旨を指摘する)。例えば，10.2 条のように Warranty Clause に基づいた請求が Seller に対して行われる場合，その請求は (10.1 条に関する) 契約違反に基づく請求であるとも評価で

66

10.2 条においてはそれら救済手段のほか，欠陥品の提供のために Buyer が被った費用の精算および欠陥品の返還手続きについても規定することで円滑な処理を確保しようとしている．

Section 10.3 Recalls.

If Buyer, any of Buyer's customers, Seller or any Governmental Authority determines that any Products sold to Buyer are Defective and a recall campaign or a service campaign is necessary, either Party may implement such recall or service campaign. Buyer must return Defective Products to Seller or destroy such Products, as determined by Buyer, at Seller's sole cost and risk. Without prejudice to Buyer's rights under Section 10.1 and Section 10.2, if a recall campaign is implemented, at Buyer's option and Seller's sole cost, Seller shall promptly either repair or replace, or credit or refund Prices for, all such returned Products under the terms of Section 10.1 and Section 10.2. The foregoing will apply even if the product warranties under Section 10.1 or any other product warranty applicable to the Products have expired. Seller is liable for all of Buyer's costs associated with any recall campaign if such recall campaign is based on a reasonable determination that either:

(a) the Products fail to conform to either the warranties under this Agreement or applicable Law; or

(b) the basis for the recall arose from Seller's negligence or willful misconduct.

3.27 Product Recall Clause

10.3 条は Seller による Warranty Clause 違反の結果，Buyer が Recall または Service Campaign など(以下，Recall などという)を実施する必要が生じた場合における，Seller の Buyer に対する責任内容を規定する．例えば米国の自動車業

きるのである．*See generally* Med. City Dallas, Ltd. v. Carlisle Corp., 251 S.W.3d 55 (Sup. Ct. Tex. 2007) (Texas 州法 (Tex. Civ. Prac. & Rem. § 38.001(8)) は契約違反に関する請求について，敗訴者から勝訴者に対する弁護士費用の填補を認めているところ，Warranty 違反に関する請求は契約上の救済の性質を有するとして，この Texas 州法の適用を認めた事案).

界における Recall とは，車両製造業者または Department of Transportation's National Highway Traffic Safety Administration (NHTSA という)[213]が車両，車両装備，車両シート，もしくはタイヤなどについて，安全性に関する不適切なリスクを抱えていると判断した場合，または，Federal Motor Vehicle Safety Standards[214]を満たしていないと判断した場合において実施される対象車両の回収措置をいう[215]。この場合，車両製造業者は不適切なリスクが存在する製品の交換を無償で行うことになる[216]。

そこで，契約当事者としては，いかなる場合に自己が Recall などに関する費用を負担することになるかについて注意を払わなければならない。したがって，Product Recall Clause との関係において，(1) Recall などの定義[217]，(2) Recall などの実施の前提としての欠陥原因の究明活動の進め方[218]，および(3) Recall などに関する公的機関との協議の進め方などについて確認すべきであろう[219]。

ARTICLE 11
INDEMNIFICATION

3.28 Indemnification

例えば，Seller が携帯電話の製造業者，そして Buyer が携帯電話の小売業者であり，Seller に起因する理由によって携帯電話が発火した結果，消費者が怪我を負ったとする。消費者としては，病院での治療費などの損害額を携帯電話の直接の売主である Buyer に請求したいところである。そしてこの請求を受け

---

[213] 49 U.S.C. § 30101-30183.
[214] 49 C.F.R. § 571.101-571.500 (1971).
[215] U.S. Dept. of Transp., *Motor Vehicle Defects and Safety Recalls: What Every Vehicle Owner Should Know*, https://www-odi.nhtsa.dot.gov/recalls/recallprocess.cfm (last visited May 11, 2018).
[216] これに対して，Service Campaign とは，安全性に直結はしない不適切なリスクが存在する場合において実施される回収措置をいう。*See* Volkswagen of Am., Inc., *Recall/Service Campaign Lookup*, http://www.vw.com/owners-recalls/ (last visited May 11, 2018).
[217] *See generally id.* ("Recalls address defects relating to motor vehicle safety and non-compliances with Federal Motor Vehicle Safety Standards." "Service campaigns address product technical issues not directly related to safety or compliance and also can be emissions-related in scope.")
[218] 例えば，「[i]f any Products are reasonably determined by the Parties (including by use of statistical analysis or other sampling methodology) to fail to conform to the warranties set forth in this Agreement . . . .」というように，近年では Seller の提供した製品が Warranty 違反を構成するかの検証方法について具体的な例を挙げようと試みる契約も少なくない。
[219] Daniel J. Herling, *The Weakest Link – Why Those Boilerplate Contract Clauses Matter*, Mintz, Levin, Cohn, Ferris, Glovsky and Popeo, P.C. (Aug. 2, 2013), https://www.consumerproductmatters.com/2013/08/the-weakest-link/. (last visited May 11, 2018).

たBuyerとしては，携帯電話の発火についての責任はSellerにあるのだから，自己が消費者に支払った損害額の請求をSellerに対して行うこととなる．この場合においてSellerがBuyerに向けて行うBuyerの損害額の填補を「Indemnification」という．

a. Common Lawにおける取り扱い
「Indemnification」の概念は，Common Lawにおいて認めることができる[220]．しかし，Common LawのもとでIndemnitee（先の例におけるBuyer）がIndemnitor（先の例におけるSeller）に対して「Indemnification」を求めるためには，①Indemniteeが第三者に対して責任を負っていること[221]，および，②Indemnitee自身は第三者に対する責任を発生させた原因について過失がないこと[222]の証明が原則的な要件であるとされる．

b. U.C.C.における取り扱い
U.C.C.においても，SellerからBuyerに向けた「Indemnification」に関する規定が設けられている[223]．

i. 人身損害に関するIndemnification
対象製品の欠陥などによって人身損害を生じさせた場合，その損害は「Indemnification」の対象としてではなく，Implied Warranty of Merchantability

---

[220] *But see* Joseph Peterson & Ashford Tucker, *The Buck Stops Where? Avenues to Indemnification in the Copyright Context*, Intell. Prop. Litig. 21, 4 (first citing Elektra Entm't Group Inc. v. Santangelo, 2008 U.S. Dist. LEXIS 11845, at 6 (S.D.N.Y. 2008); and then citing Lehman Bros., Inc. v. Wu, 294 F. Supp. 2d 504, 505 (S.D.N.Y. 2003)) ("Courts have held that no such rights [to indemnity or contribution] exist under either the Copyright Act or federal common law.") (著作権については，著作権法またはCommon Lawを根拠としたIndemnificationは認められないと推察する)．
[221] *See, e.g.*, McNally & Nimergood v. Neumann-Kiewit Constructors, Inc., 648 N.W.2d 564, 574 (Sup. Ct. Iowa 2002) ("The first principle is that a party who seeks to establish a right to indemnity in an independent action must normally plead and prove it was liable to the injured party.").
[222] *McNally & Nimergood*, 648 N.W.2d, 571 (first citing Evans v. McComas-Lacina Constr. Co., 641 N.W.2d 841, 845 (Sup. Ct. Iowa 2002); then citing Sears, Roebuck & Co. v. Poling, 248 Iowa 582, 588 (Sup. Ct. Iowa 1957); and then citing United States v. Seckinger, 397 U.S. 203 (U.S. 1970)) ("This rule provides that indemnification contracts will not be construed to permit an indemnitee to recover for its own negligence unless the intention of the parties is clearly and unambiguously expressed.").
[223] U.C.C. § 2-312(3) (Am. Law Inst. & Unif. Law Comm'n 2002) ("Unless otherwise agreed a seller who is a merchant regularly dealing in Products of the kind warrants that the Products shall be delivered free of the rightful claim of any third person by way of infringement or the like but a buyer who furnishes specifications to the seller must hold the seller harmless against any such claim which arises out of compliance with the specifications.").

または Implied Warranty of Fitness for a Particular Purpose[224]の違反に関する問題として取り扱われるようである[225]。

なお，人身損害は多額にのぼる可能性があるため，Seller が損害の十分な填補を Buyer に行えないおそれもある．そこで，Buyer は，Seller に人身損害に関する保険の付保をあわせて要求することが少なくない[226]。

ii. 知的財産権などの侵害に関する Indemnification

Seller が「Merchant」[227]である場合，Seller は Buyer に向けて，「対象製品が，第三者からその『権利を侵害しているなど』といった『正当な根拠に基づいた請求』を受けるものではない」ことを保証している．この保証は Seller が Buyer に対象製品を提供した時点で[228]，Buyer が保証違反の存在を知っているかどうかにかかわらず生じる[229]。

(a)「権利を侵害しているなど」(by way of infringement or the like)

U.C.C.の規定自体からは明確ではないものの，第三者の「権利を侵害しているなど」といった主張には，特許権，商標権，または著作権に関するものなどを広く含む[230]．もっとも，この保証はあくまでも対象製品自体に関するものであって，例えば製品受領後に Buyer が対象製品に加えた変更などが第三者の主張の原因である場合には Seller の保証の対象と

---

[224] U.C.C. § 2-314 (Am. Law Inst. & Unif. Law Comm'n 2002).
[225] Tori Levine, *When Product Liability Meets the Uniform Commercial Code*, Wilson Elser (Jan. 19, 2016), https://www.productliabilityadvocate.com/2016/01/when-product-liability-meets-the-uniform-commercial-code/. (last visited May 14, 2018); Cline v. Prowler Industries of Maryland, Inc. A.2d 968, 975 (Sup. Ct. Del. 1980) (quoting Ciociola v. Delaware Coca-Cola Bottling Co., A.2d 252, 256 (Sup. Ct. Del. 1961)). "Liability by a seller or manufacturer of goods for breach of warranty originally was based on tort concepts. Originally the action was always brought as an action on the case for the breach. Gradually, the concept of the nature of the action changed and an action was permitted finally to be brought on the contract itself. Thereafter, rightly or wrongly, actions for breach of an implied warranty were regarded as ex contract." (相手方契約当事者に対して人身損害に関する責任を追及するにあたって，U.C.C. § 2-314 が不法行為責任を追及するための根拠としての機能を有する旨を示した).
[226] 保険に関しては 5.7 (Insurance Clause) において紹介する．
[227] U.C.C. § 2-104 (Am. Law Inst. & Unif. Law Comm'n 2002). *See supra* note 79.
[228] Paul E. McGowan, *Strategies for Indemnification under the UCC Against Claims of Patent Infringement*, 21 Intell. Prop. Litig. 6, 6, https://www.troutman.com/files/Uploads/Documents/IP%20Lit%20Newsletter%20Winter%202010.pdf (last visited Feb. 15, 2018).
[229] *Id.*
[230] McGowan, *supra* note 228, at 9 (citing Pure Country Weavers, Inc. v. Bristar, Inc., 410 F. Supp. 2d 439, 447 (W.D.N.C. 2006)) ("UCC's warranty against infringement applies to copyrights as well as patent and trademark infringement.").

はならない[231].

(b)「正当な根拠に基づいた請求」(rightful claim)
「正当な根拠」に関しても緩やかな解釈がされている．すなわち，第三者の Buyer に対する請求は訴訟にまで発展したものである必要はないし[232]，ましてや，実際に対象製品が第三者の知的財産権を侵害した旨判断される必要もない[233]．第三者の Buyer に対する請求が「根拠のない」[234]ものでない限り足りるとされる[235]．

Seller から「対象製品がある第三者の知的財産権を侵害しているなどといった正当な根拠に基づいた請求を受けるものではない」旨の保証が提供されていたにもかかわらず，Buyer が第三者からそのような請求を受けた場合，Buyer は合理的期間内に Seller に対して通知を行う義務を負う[236]．Buyer からの通知を受けた Seller は Buyer に向けて「Indemnification」に関する義務を負うことになるが[237]，その一環として，自己が第三者との間に

---

[231] *See, e.g.*, Motorola, Inc. v. Varo, Inc., 656 F. Supp. 716, 718–19 (N.D.Tex. 1986) ("The delivery of a good is warranted to be free of all claims of infringement. There is no warranty that a buyer's use of the good will be free of all infringement."); *see also e.g.*, Chemtron, Inc. v. Aqua Prods., Inc., 830 F. Supp. 314, 315 (E.D.Va. 1993) ("[A] buyer, such as Aqua, should not be entitled to purchase goods from a seller, such as Viking, which are not subject to any infringement action, use the non-infringing component goods in an infringing device and incur liability to a third party patentee, Chemtron, and then turn around and attempt to impose liability on the original seller of the component parts.").

[232] Pacific Sunwear of California, Inc. v. Olaes Enterprises, Inc., 167 Cal. App. 4th 466, 482 (Ct. App. Cal. 2008) ("[T]he existence of litigation is neither necessary nor, in itself, sufficient to establish that a claim is 'rightful'. A claim of infringement may be rightful under section 2312(3) whether or not it is ultimately pursued in litigation.").

[233] McGowan, *supra* note 228, at 7 (citing Cover v. Hydramatic Packing Co., 83 F.3d 1390, 1394 (Fed. Cir. 1996)).

[234]「根拠のない」請求であるかどうかについては最終的にその特許権の内容の判断に関わってくることもあるところ，その判断は連邦裁判所で実施されることとなりうる．28 U.S.C. § 1400(b) (1999); *see generally Pacific Sunwear of California, Inc.*, 167 Cal. App. 4th (「根拠のない請求」を排除した趣旨については，訴訟が提起されたことのみをもってなんらの実体的な根拠の検証なしに保証を認めるような事態を制限したものであると評価した).

[235] *See, e.g.*, 84 Lumber Co. v. MRK Techs., Ltd., 145 F. Supp. 2d 675, 680 (W.D. Pa. 2001) ("If claims of patent infringement are seen as marks on a continuum, whatever a 'rightful claim' is would fall somewhere between purely frivolous claims at one end, and claims where liability has been proven, at the other."); *id.* at 680 (quoting Cover v. Hydramatic Packing Co., 1997 U.S. Dist. LEXIS 6275 (E.D.Pa. 1997)) ("[T]he Federal Circuit suggests that a rightful claim does not require a finding of absolute patent liability, a construction with which we do not disagree.").

[236] U.C.C. § 2-607(5)(a) (Am. Law Inst. & Unif. Law Comm'n 2002).

[237] *Id.* § 2-312(3).

おける訴訟をコントロールする旨の申し出を行うことが許容されている[238]。

なお，これらに対して，第三者の請求が Buyer から Seller に対して提示された仕様書などに起因する場合，Buyer が Seller に Indemnification に関する義務を負うことになる[239]。

c. Indemnification と民事訴訟との関係

Indemnitee が対象製品に関して第三者から訴訟を提起された場合，Indemnitee は Indemnitor を訴訟に参加させ，Indemnitor による Indemnification の履行（例えば Indemnitor から第三者に対する直接の金銭賠償）を求めることができる[240]。

Section 11.1 Seller's Indemnification.

Subject to the terms and conditions of this Agreement, including those set forth in Section 11.2, Seller (as "Indemnitor") shall indemnify, defend, and hold harmless Buyer and its representatives, officers, directors, employees, agents, Affiliates, successors, and permitted assigns (collectively, "Indemnitee") against any and all losses, damages, liabilities, deficiencies, claims, actions, judgments, settlements, interest, awards, penalties, fines, costs, or expenses of whatever kind, including reasonable attorneys' fees, fees, and the costs of enforcing any right to indemnification under this Agreement and the cost of pursuing any insurance providers, incurred by Indemnitee (collectively, "Losses"), relating to or resulting from any claim of a third party or Indemnitee alleging:

(a) breach or non-fulfillment of any representation, warranty, or covenant

---

[238] *Id.* § 2-607(5)(b).

[239] *Id.* § 2-312(3); *see id.* § 2-607(6).

[240] Fed. R. Civ. P. 14(a). なお，Indemnitee が Imdemnitor を訴訟に関与させるためには（これを Impleader という）Imdemnitee が Indemnitor に対して有する請求権が Indemnitee と第三者との間の訴訟の根拠となる請求権から派生するものであることが要件となるが，これには「Indemnification」を含む。*See, e.g.,* Index Fund, Inc. v. Hagopian, 417 F. Supp. 738, 744 (S.D.N.Y. 1976) ("The procedural device of impleader may be utilized only when the third-party complaint necessarily depends upon the outcome of the main claim against the defendant."); *see also e.g.,* Eagle Star Ins. Co. of America v. Metromedia, Inc., 578 F.Supp. 184, 2 (D.Vt.) (quoting 6 C. Wright and A. Miller § 1446 at 246-50 (1971)) ("The secondary or derivative liability notion is central and it is irrelevant whether the basis of the third-party claim is indemnity, subrogation, contribution, express or implied warranty, or some other theory.").

72

  under this Agreement by Indemnifying Party or Indemnifying Party's Personnel;

 (b) any grossly negligent or more culpable act or omission of Indemnifying Party or its Personnel (including any recklessness or willful misconduct) in connection with the performance of its obligations under this Agreement; or

 (c) any bodily injury, death of any Person, or damage to real or tangible personal property caused by the willful or grossly negligent acts or omissions of Indemnitor or its Personnel; or

 (d) any failure by Indemnitor or its Personnel to materially comply with any applicable Laws.

3.29 Indemnification Clause

　先に紹介したとおり，「Indemnification」については特定の範囲においてCommon Law および U.C.C.においても認められている．しかし，それにもかかわらずほとんどの契約においては Indemnification Clause が用意されている．これは Common Law との関係においては，Indemnitee から Indemnitor に対する Indemnification の請求に関する要件を不要なものとできること[241]などが理由であると思われる．また，U.C.C.との関係においては，Seller が Buyer に対して Indemnification を要求する場合の具体的な手続きについては必ずしも明確とはいえないことなどが理由であると思われる．

　Indemnification Clause は，Indemnitee が負うことになった特定または不特定の責任および損害について Indemnitor が責任を負う旨の規定であると理解されるが[242]，より詳細にみると，Indemnification Clause は (1) Duty of Indemnification[243]，(2) Duty of Hold Harmless[244]，および (3) Duty to Defend[245]のすべてを含むことが

---

[241] Roger W. Stone & Jeffrey A. Stone, *Indemnity in Iowa Construction Law*, Simmons Perrine Moyer Bergman PLC, 6-7, https://www.spmblaw.com/1CF0B9/assets/Indemnity-in-Iowa-Construction-Law.pdf (last visited May 15, 2018).
[242] *Black's Law Dictionary: Pocket Edition* 376 (4th ed. 2011).
[243] 「Indemnification」とは，ある損害に二次的責任者として対応した者に対して，本来的責任者がその対応に要した費用および損害を填補することをいう．*Black's Law Dictionary: Pocket Edition* 375 (4th ed. 2011); *see, e.g.*, Woodruff Constr. Co. v. Barrick Roofers, Inc., 406 N.W.2d 783, 785 (Sup.Ct. Iowa 1987) (quoting A. Larson, *Workmen's Compensation: Third Party's Action over Against Employer*, 65 NW. U. L. REV. 351, 368–69 ("[A] third party's action for indemnity is not exactly for "damages" but for reimbursement"")).
[244] 「Hold Harmless」とは，他方契約当事者を取引から生じる損害などに関する責任から解放することを

多い.

　Indemnification Clause は，Buyer と Seller との間でどのように製品に関わるリスクを分担するかという問題の解決を図るものである．したがって，Seller としては，以下の事項についての検討を必要とする．また，Buyer としては，Indemnification Clause は Indemnitee に対して厳しい方向で解釈される傾向にあるという事実をふまえ[246]，どのような条件のもとでどのような内容の Indemnification を受けることができるのかについて明確な規定を試みる必要がある[247]．

　　a. Indemnitee の範囲
　Indemnification Clause のもと Seller から補償を受けるべき者としてまず挙げられるのは Buyer である．しかし，Buyer としては 11.1 条のように，Indemnitee にその他の関係者（例えば，「its representatives, officers, directors, employees, agents, Affiliates, successors, and permitted assigns parents, subsidiaries, affiliates, officers, directors, employees, agents, successors, heirs, and assigns」）を Indemnitee に包含し，万全を期したいところである．さらに Buyer としては自己が責任を問われる可能性を可能な限り排除したいとの意図のもと，Indemnitee に「Buyer's customer」を含めることを要求する場合もある．

　　b. Duty to Indemnification
　　　i. Duty to Indemnification の対象
　Common Law のもとで Indemnitee が Indemnitor に対して Indemnification を求めるためには，Indemnitee 自身は第三者に対する責任を発生させた原因について過失がないことが原則的に要求される旨を紹介した．しかし

いう．*Black's Law Dictionary: Pocket Edition* 357 (4th ed. 2011).

[245] 「Duty to Defend」とは，製品に関して紛争が発生した場合において，一方契約当事者が他方契約当事者を防御する義務をいう．*See* Jeffrey W. Cavignac, *Construction Industry Update – The Liability Implications of the Duty to Defend*, Cavignac & Associates (May 2010), http://www.cavignac.com/publications/publicationsconstruction-industry-update/construction-industry-update/ (last visited May 15, 2018); *see also* Troy Hunter, *When Does Contractual Duty to Defend, Indemnify and Hold Harmless Really Kick In?*, Issaquah Law Group, PLLC. (Oct. 12, 2015), http://www.issaquahlaw.com/theamateurlawprofessor/2015/10/12/when-does-contractualduty-to-defend-indemnify-and-hold-harmless-really-kick-in (last visited Feb. 16, 2018).

[246] Angelo Iafrate Const., LLC v. Potashnick Const., Inc., 370 F.3d 715, 721 (8th Cir. 2004) (quoting Chevron U.S.A. Inc. v. Murphy Exploration & Prod. Co., 356 Ark. 324, 330 (Sup. Ct. Ark. 2004)) ("'Indemnity agreements are construed strictly against the party seeking indemnification.'").

[247] *Angelo Iafrate Const., LLC*, 370 F.3d, 721 (quoting *Chevron U.S.A. Inc.*, 356 Ark., 330) ("'[T]he intent of the indemnitor's obligation to indemnify against [the losses] must be expressed in clear and unequivocal terms and to such an extent that no other meaning can be ascribed.'").

Indemnification Clause においては，たとえ第三者に対する責任に関して Indemnitee に過失の認められる場合であったとしても Indemnitor による Indemnification が行われる旨を規定することも可能である．ただし，その場合，Indemnification の対象には Indemnitee の過失に起因するものも含むことを明確に規定することが要求される[248]．

ii. Duty to Indemnification の範囲

Duty to Indemnification は，Indemnitor に対して Indemnitee の「Damages」を賠償する義務を課すことが多い．一般に「Damage」とは，人身損害または物の価値の減少[249]を意味する．ここで問題となるのは，Indemnitor がどのような範囲で Indemnitee に「Damage」を賠償する義務を負うかということである．以下においては，「Damage」の賠償に関する一般的な理解を紹介する．

(a)「Damage」の範囲について契約上規定のない場合

一方契約当事者による契約違反の結果として損害を被った他方契約当事者は，契約締結時，契約違反当事者が契約違反によって生じるであろうと予見しえた範囲において，その責任を問うことができる[250]．ここに「契約違反によって生じるであろうと予見しえた範囲」には，(i) 契約違反の結果として通常生じる事象に基づく損害，および，(ii) (契約違反の結果として通常生じる事象とはいえないが) 契約違反当事者が予見しえた事象に基づく損害が含まれる[251]．

---

[248] Snohomish County Pub. Transp. Benefit Area Corp. v. FirstGroup Am., Inc., 173 Wn.2d 829, 836 (Sup. Ct. Wash. 2012) (quoting Northwest Airlines v. Hughes Air Corp., 104 Wn.2d 152, 154-55 (Sup. Ct. Wash. 1985)) ("'[A] contract of indemnity will not be construed to indemnify the indemnitee against losses resulting from his own negligence unless this intention is expressed in clear and unequivocal terms.'"). そこで次のような規定を設けることになる．「[Indemnitor] shall indemnify the [indemnitee] from and against any and all claims, demands, causes of action, suits or judgments (including costs and expenses incurred in connection therewith) for deaths or injuries to persons or for loss of or damage to property arising out of or in connection with the use and occupancy of the premises by [indemnitor], its agents, servants, employees or invitees whether or not caused by [indemnitee's] negligence.」. See Hunter, supra note 245.

[249] Black's Law Dictionary: Pocket Edition 196 (4th ed. 2011); id. at 466.

[250] See e.g., Western Union Tel. Co. v. Hall, 124 U.S. 444, 455 (U.S. 1887) (quoting Booth v. Spuyten Duyvil Rolling Mills Co., 60 N.Y. 487, 492 (Ct. App. N.Y. 1875)). "[T]he damages for which a party may recover for a breach of a contract are such as ordinarily and naturally flow from the non-performance. They must be proximate and certain, or capable of certain ascertainment, and not remote, speculative or contingent."

[251] See, e.g., Shurtleff v. Occidental Bldg. & Loan Ass'n, 105 Neb. 557, 561 (Sup. Ct. Neb. 1921) (citing Hadley v. Baxendale, 9 Exch. (Eng.) 341, 354) ("[T]he damages recoverable are such as may fairly and reasonably be supposed to have been in the contemplation of the parties at the time of making the contract, as the probable result of a breach of it."); see, also, e.g., Western Union Tel. Co. v. Hall, 124 U.S., 454-55 ("[A] plaintiff may rightfully recover a loss of profits as a part of the damages for breach of a special contract, but in such a case the

(b)「Damage」の範囲について契約上規定のある場合

各契約当事者の「Damage」に関する責任の範囲は，契約上最も重要な事項のひとつとして，できる限り明確なものとなるよう努めるべきである．例えば，Seller による契約違反があった場合において Buyer に生じると想定される事象を具体的に列挙することは，Seller がそれら事象を予見しえたことを裏付けるものとして有用である[252]．

契約上規定される「Damage」としては次のようなものが挙げられる[253]．Seller としてはこれらの Damage のうち，どの範囲までであれば責任を負うことも許容できるのかを検討しつつ，責任対象となる Damage の種類，範囲，および金額の制限を試みることになる[254]．

(i) Direct Damages

一方契約当事者による契約違反から通常生じる事象に基づく他方契約当事者の損害のうち，契約上の義務が履行された場合と同等の効果を得るために要した損害をいう[255]．例えば Seller A が製品を納入できなかったため Buyer が他の Seller B から同種の製品を調達した結果生じた損害（Seller A の販売価格よりも Seller B の販売価格のほうが高額であった場合のその差額）は Direct Damages である．なお，Buyer の逸失利益についても Direct Damages に該当すると判断されうる[256]．

---

profits to be recovered must be such as would have accrued and grown out of the contract itself as the direct and immediate result of its fulfilment."); *see, also, e.g.*, Restatement (Second) of Contracts § 351(1)(2) (Am. Law Inst. 1981).

[252] *Id.* § 351 illust. b.

[253] Glenn D. West et al, *Consequential, Incidental, Direct, Actual and Compensatory Damages: What are they and who gets them? Measures of Damages in Domestic and International Transactions*, 2012 A.B.A. Bus. Sec., https://apps.americanbar.org/buslaw/committees/CL560016pub/materials/Presentation_by_Glenn_West_&_Hermann_Knott_on_Damages_given_at_the_Spring_Meeting_in_Las_Vegas_-_March_2012.pdf (last visited Feb. 16, 2018).

[254] これら Seller の責任範囲の制限との関係については，5.6 (Limitation of Liability Clause) において紹介する．

[255] *See* Brian A. Blum, Contracts Examples & Explanations, 681-82 (6th ed. 2013); *e.g.*, Penncro Assocs., Inc. v. Sprint Spectrum, L.P., 499 F.3d 1151, 1156 (10th Cir. 2007) ("Direct damages refer to those which the party lost from the contract itself—in other words, the benefit of the bargain—while consequential damages refer to economic harm beyond the immediate scope of the contract.").

[256] *Id.* (first citing Source Direct, Inc. v. Mantell, 19 Kan.App.2d 399, 870 P.2d 686, 693 (Ct. App. Kan. 1994); then citing Restatement (Second) of Contracts § 347 (Am. Law Inst. 1981)) ("Lost profits, under appropriate circumstances, can be recoverable as a component of either (and both) direct and consequential damages"); *see* West, *supra* note 253. ただし，逸失利益の請求を行うにあたっては，①その逸失利益は，契約違反がなかったならば，合理的かつ直接的に生じたものであること，ならびに，②その逸失利益の額について合理的な確度をもって示すことが必要とされうる．*See, e.g.*, Rev. Ariz. Jury Instr. (Civil) Contract 19 (5th

(ii) Incidental Damages

一方契約当事者による契約違反の結果として他方契約当事者が要した費用をいう[257]．例えば Seller が Buyer に納入した製品に欠陥があったため，Buyer が返品するまでの間，倉庫を借りてその製品を保管した場合，その倉庫保管に要した費用は Incidental Damages である．

(iii) Consequential Damages

General Consequential Damages と Special Consequential Damages とに分類できる[258]．General Consequential Damages は，一方契約当事者による契約違反から通常生じる事象に基づく他方契約当事者の損害のうち，契約上の義務が履行された場合と同等の効果を得るために要したもの以外の損害をいう（Direct Damages と General Consequential Damages とを併せて General Damages という[259]）．これに対して，Special Consequential Damages は，一方契約当事者による契約違反から通常生じうる事象に基づかない他方契約当事者の損害をいう．したがって，契約違反当事者は，そのような特別の事象を予見しえた場合に限り，Special Consequential Damages を賠償する責任を負う[260]．

例えば，Seller が Buyer に販売した自動車向けサンルーフに欠陥があり，閉じなくなってしまった場合において，Buyer が土砂降りの雨に遭遇し，自動車内のレザーシートが水浸しになってしまったとする．この場合において Buyer のレザーシートに関する損害は Direct Consequential Damages であり，Seller はそれを賠償する責任を負う．レザーシートが水浸しになってしまうことは，欠陥のある自動車向けサンルーフを提供した結果として通常生じる事象といえるためである．

これに対して，上記の例において，Buyer が自動車内に有名選手の直筆サインが付いたフットボールを置いていたところ，土砂降りの雨によって，そのサインが消えてしまった場合はどうであろうか．自動車内にサイン付きのフットボールが置いてあること（またはそのサインが消えてしまうこと）については，欠陥のある自動車向けサンルー

---

ed. 2013).
[257] U.C.C. § 2-715 cmt. 1 (Am. Law Inst. & Unif. Law Comm'n 2002).
[258] Blum, *supra* note 255, at 681-82.
[259] *Id.* at 681.
[260] *See* Restatement (Second) of Contracts § 351 cmt. b. (Am. Law Inst. 1981); *see also* U.C.C. § 2-715 cmt. 3 (Am. Law Inst. & Unif. Law Comm'n 2002); *see generally* Hadley v. Baxendale 9 Exch. (Eng.) 341, 354.

フを提供した結果として通常生じうる事象とはいえないであろう．したがって，Buyer のフットボールに関する損害は Special Consequential Damages であり，Seller は，そのような事象を予見しえた場合でない限り，それを賠償する責任を負わない．

(iv) Actual Damages (Compensatory Damages ともいう)
被契約違反者を，他方契約当事者による契約違反がなかった場合と同じ状況におくことを意図した概念であり，Direct Damages のみならず Consequential Damages をも包含する[261]．

(v) Remote Damages
一方契約当事者に発生した損害ではあるが，他方契約当事者による契約違反の結果発生したとはいえない損害をいう．契約違反者は Remote Damages を賠償する責任を負わない[262]．

(vi) Speculative Damages
一方契約当事者に発生したとはいえない損害をいう．契約違反者は Speculative Damages を賠償する責任を負わない[263]．

(vii) Punitive Damages
不当な行為を行った者に対する制裁的な意味合いで認められる損害である．したがって，Punitive Damages は不法行為法上の請求とされることが主であって，契約法上の請求として認められることはほとんどない[264]．

c. Duty to Hold Harmless
Duty to Hold Harmless は，実質的に Duty to Indemnifiation と同義であると理解されることが多いようである[265]．

---

[261] West, *supra* note 253.
[262] *See, e.g.*, Cardinal Consulting Co. v. Circo Resorts, Inc. 297 N.W.2d 260, 267 (Sup. Ct. Minn. 1980) (first citing Leoni v. Bemis Co., 255 N.W.2d 824 (Sup. Ct. Minn. 1977); then citing Hornblower & Weeks-Hemphill Noyes v. Lazere, 301 Minn. 462, 222 N.W.2d 799 (Sup. Ct. Minn. 1974); then citing Restatement (First) of Contracts § 331(1) (Am. Law. Inst. 1932); and then citing C. McCormick, Handbook on the Law of Damages § 26 (1935)) ("The controlling principle is that speculative, remote, or conjectural damages are not recoverable.").
[263] *See, e.g.*, id.
[264] *See, e.g.*, Restatement (Second) of Contracts § 355 (Am. Law Inst. 1981).
[265] *See* Joann M. Lytle, *Contractual Indemnity and Additional Insured Coverage*, McCarter & English (Dec. 10, 2014), http://www.ctrims.org/CONTRACTUAL_INDEMNITY_AND_ADDITIONAL_INSURED_

d. Duty to Defend

Duty to Defend は，Indemnitee が対象製品に関して訴訟などの紛争に巻き込まれた場合において，Indemnitor が訴訟上または金銭上の防御手段を Indemnitee に向けて提供する義務をいう[266]。Duty to Defend は Indemnitee が紛争に巻き込まれた瞬間に Indemnitor が負担することになる義務であり，ある紛争に関して Indemnitee が確定的に負うこととなった責任について Indemnitor が負担する Duty to Indemnification とは区分して理解される[267]。

なお，Duty to Defend に基づく Indemnitor の負担額については，Indemnitee が付保する Commercial General Liability Insurance の対象とならない場合もあるため，確認が必要となる[268]。

i. Duty to Defend の対象

特にいわゆるパテント・トロールの活動が顕著な事業分野に関する契約においては，Indemnitor による Duty to Defend がいつの時点で発生するのかは重要な交渉事項となる。Indemnitor の Duty to Defend の発生時期の選択肢としては，Indemnitee が第三者から，(1) ライセンスのオファーを受領した

COVERAGE__Connecticut_Valley_RIMS__REVISED_c.pdf (last visited May 15, 2018) (first citing Medcom Holding Co. v. Baxter Travelnol Lab., Inc., 200 F.3d 518 (7th Cir. 1999); and then citing Praetorian Ins. Co v. Site Inspection, LLC, 604 F.3d 509 (8th Cir. 2010)) ("Most courts hold that 'indemnity' and 'hold harmless' are synonymous"); *see also* Kenneth A. Adams, *"Hold Harmless" and "Indemnify"*, Adams on Contract Drafting (Oct. 21, 2006), http://www.adamsdrafting.com/hold-harmless-and-indemnify/ (last visited Feb. 16, 2018); *but see* Fernandez v. K-M Indus. Holding Co., 646 F. Supp. 2d 1150, 1159 (N.D.Cal. 2009) (Duty to Indemnification は Indemnitee が Indemnitor に対して Indemnification を請求できるという積極的権利を付与するものである一方，Duty to Hold Harmless は Indemnitee が Indemnitor から Indemnification の請求を受けることがないという消極的権利を付与したものである旨を示した) ("This interpretation finds support in *Queen Villas*, which addresses the meaning of the term 'hold harmless': Are the words 'indemnify' and 'hold harmless' synonymous? No. One is offensive and the other is defensive -- even though both contemplate third-party liability situations. 'Indemnify' is an offensive right -- a sword -- allowing an indemnitee to seek indemnification. 'Hold harmless' is defensive: The right not to be bothered by the other party itself seeking indemnification.").

[266] *See, e.g.*, Crawford v. Weather Shield Mfg., Inc., 44 Cal. 4th 541, 553 ("The duty promised is to render, or fund, the service of providing a defense on the promise's behalf").

[267] *See, e.g.*, *Crawford*, 44 Cal. 4th, 559 ("[A] clause requiring a party to indemnify another party against defined claims clearly indicates that the indemnity obligation applies only if the indemnitee ultimately incurs such a legal consequence as a result of covered claims. By contrast, under language requiring the indemnitor to defend the indemnitee against any suit or action founded upon a covered claim, the duty to defend arises, as it logically must, as soon as a suit or action is brought against the indemnitee that is founded upon a covered claim, i.e., that asserts a claim within the coverage of both clauses. Necessarily, a duty expressed in this manner does not require a final determination of the issues before the indemnitor is required to mount and finance a defense on the indemnitee's behalf.").

[268] *See* Cavignac, *supra* note 245.

とき，(2) その第三者の権利を侵害している旨の連絡を受領したとき，または (3) 訴訟を提起されたときなどが挙げられる[269]．

ii. Indemnitee の義務の設定

Indemnitor としては，Duty to Defend を適切に実行できるよう Indemnitee からの協力などを得る必要がある場合もある．特に，(1) Indemnitee が対象製品について第三者からある要求を受けた場合，直ちに Indemnitor に通知する義務，(2) Indemnitor が Duty to Defend を遂行するうえで Indemnitee が必要な情報を有する場合にはその情報を Indemnitor に提供する義務，および (3) Indemnitor がその第三者との訴訟または和解を進めるうえで Intemnitee から Indemnitor に向けた権限の付与が必要となる場合はその提供義務[270]などが検討対象となる[271]．

3.30 First Party Indemnification

Indemnification Clause は，Indemnitee が対象製品に関して第三者から訴訟提起されるなどした場合の結果として被った損害の填補を対象として設けられることが多い．では，Indemnitee 自身が Indemnitor に対して，自己が直接被った一次的損害に関する請求を行う場合の根拠とすることはできるのであろうか．例えば，Seller から購入した製品に不具合があったため，その製品と組み合わせた Buyer の製品が破損してしまった場合において，Buyer が Seller に対して製品の瑕疵に関する自己の損害の填補を Indemnification Clause に基づいて請求すること (First Party Indemnification という) は認められるのであろうか．

---

[269] Robert E. Rudnick & Andrew M. Grodin, *Drafting and Negotiating Defense and Indemnification Provisions*, 21 Intell. Prop. Litig. 1, 9 (2010), https://www.gibbonslaw.com/Files/Publication/19c9e523-352d-4328-b044-057b4e02f43c/Presentation/PublicationAttachment/f91b58b8-1c69-4094-9ab2-0af249de9099/draft.pdf (last visited May 18, 2018).

[270] なお，Indemnitee は，第三者との紛争解決内容が自己の Indemnitor に対する Indemnification の請求に影響を及ぼさないよう注意しなければならない．*See, e.g.*, Peregrine Fin. Group, Inc. v. TradeMaven, L.L.C., 909 N.E. 2d 837 (App. Ct. Ill. 2009) (Indemnitor，Indemnitee，および第三者 (Indemnitor が Indemnitee に提供するソフトウェアが自己の保有する特許権を侵害する旨を主張した者) の間で Consent Judgment (当事者間の和解内容に基づいて裁判所の判決を得ることで執行力を付与されるものをいう) (その Consent Judgment には，「訴訟などに要した費用は各当事者の負担とする」旨が含まれていた) を得た後の Indemnitee から Indemnitor に対する Indemnification Clause に基づく請求を否定した事案．そのような Indemnification の請求は Res judicata (すでに前訴で争われた事項または前訴で争うことのできた事項については別訴で争うことを禁止するという原則) によって認められないとしたのである); *see also, e.g.*, Kenneth L. Dorsney, *Res Judicata: Patent Indemnitee Beware!*, 21 Intell. Prop. Litig. 1, 17-18 (2010), https://www.gibbonslaw.com/Files/Publication/19c9e523-352d-4328-b044-057b4e02f43c/Presentation/PublicationAttachment/f91b58b8-1c69-4094-9ab2-0af249de9099/draft.pdf (last visited May 18, 2018).

[271] Rudnick, *supra* note 269, at 10.

この点，First Party Indemnification が認められるためには Indemnification Clause においてその旨が明らかにされていなければならない[272]。そのほか，Indemnification の手続きに関する規定[273]についても注意を払わなければならない。

11.1 条においては，Seller の Buyer に対する Indemnification は「relating to or resulting from any claim of a third party or <u>Indemnified Party</u>」に対して実施される旨明記されているため，First Party Indemnification を認める趣旨であると理解されるものである。Indemnification Clause に基づく補償には Indemnitee が要した弁護士費用も含まれることが多いこともふまえると[274]，Seller としては可能な限

---

[272] See, e.g., Ingwersen v. Planet Group, Inc., 2011 U.S. Dist. LEXIS 43490, 18 (D.Neb. 2011) (quoting Angelo Iafrate Const., LLC v. Potashnick Const., Inc., 370 F.3d 715, 721 (8th Cir. 2004)) ("[T]he intent of the indemnitor's obligation to indemnify against [the losses] must be expressed in clear and unequivocal terms and to such an extent that no other meaning can be ascribed."). なお，Ingwersen 2011 U.S. Dist. LEXIS 43490 においては，次の Indemnification Clause について，First Party Indemnification を認める趣旨のものであるかは明らかでないとして First Party Indemnification に関する請求を認めなかった。「Indemnification Obligations of the Seller. Except to the extent otherwise provided in this Section 9, [Ingwersen] shall indemnify, defend, and hold harmless [Planet] and its officers, directors, employees, and Affiliates, and each of the heirs, executors, successors, and assigns of any of the foregoing (collectively, the "Buyer Indemnified Parties") <u>from, against, and in respect of any and all Losses arising out of or relating to</u>: (a) any breach or inaccuracy of any representation or warranty made by [Ingwersen] in this [SPA] or any certificate or document delivered pursuant to this [SPA]; or (b) any breach of any covenant, agreement, or undertaking made by [Ingwersen] in this [SPA].」; cf. Sequa Coatings Corp. v. N. Ind. Commuter Transp. Dist., 796 N.E.2d 1216, 1229 (「Loss or Damages」に関する規定の内容などをふまえて，First Party Indemnification に関する請求を認めた) ("The plain language of the parties' agreement, however, not only shifted the risk of harm to third parties to Sequa, but also shifted NICTD's loss arising out of an accident at Midwest Crossing to Sequa. For example, the agreement provides: The phrase "Loss or Damage" as used within this Agreement shall be interpreted by the parties to include any and all loss of, damage to, or destruction of any real property, personal property, or environment, including without limitation, damage to or destruction of land, air, water, wildlife, or vegetation, and <u>irrespective of whether the damaged or destroyed property is owned or otherwise possessed by [NICTD], Sequa, or a third party</u>".).

[273] Ingwersen, 2011 U.S. Dist. LEXIS 43490 においては，第三者から Indemnitee が請求を受けた場合に関しては Indemnitor に通知することが規定されていたのに対し，Indemnitee が直接損害を被った場合については Indemnitor への通知に関する規定が存在していないことも，First Party Indemnification を否定する理由の一つとして考慮された。

[274] First Party Indemnification は契約当事者が被った損害に関するものであるから，Indemnitee は 通常，契約違反としての請求もできるはずである (例えば製品に不具合があった場合においては，Buyer が Seller に対して Warranty Clause 違反に基づく損害の填補を主張することができる はずである)。それにもかかわらず First Party Indemnification を主張する最大の意義は，弁護士費用 の請求にあると考える。例えば Buyer が欠陥のあった Seller の製品と組み合わせた Buyer の製品に関する直接の損害を Seller に請求したところ，交渉が難航したため弁護士を雇用したとする。Seller に対する補償請求の根拠を Indemnification Clause とした場合，Indemnification Clause においては Indemnitee が填補を受けうる損害には関連する弁護士費用も含まれていることが通常であるから (例えば 11.1 条においても，「including reasonable attorneys' fees」と規定されている)，Buyer は交渉に要した弁護士費用も Seller に請求しうる可能性が高い。これに対して Seller に対する補償請求の根拠を契約違反とした場合，Buyer が交渉に要

り排除したい規定といえる．

・Attorneys' Fees Clause
　ある契約に関する紛争を解決するために要する社外弁護士の費用は，契約当事者にとって最も大きな「Damage」のひとつである．米国においては，ある紛争の結果訴訟に至ったとしても，勝訴または敗訴にかかわらず一方当事者が他方当事者にその訴訟に要した弁護士費用の請求を行うことはできないのが原則である（American Rule という）[275]．American Rule は，当事者が敗訴時の弁護士費用の負担を恐れるあまり，訴訟提起に踏み切ることを躊躇するといった事態を予防する趣旨を持つ．もっとも American Rule にも例外があり，それは，(1) 契約上格別に弁護士費用を他方契約当事者に請求できる旨の規定（Attorneys' Fees Clause という）がある場合[276]，または，(2) 制定法上，弁護士費用の請求が認められている場合[277]である．

・One-Way Attorneys' Fees Clause
　One-Way Attorneys' Fees Clause は，一方契約当事者にのみ，契約に関する紛争解決に要した弁護士費用の填補を受ける権利を確保する規定であり，契約当事者間で取引上の力関係に大きな差がある場合などに見受けられる[278]．
　しかし One-Way Attorneys' Fees Clause のもと，弁護士費用の填補を義務付けられている契約当事者としては，（相手方契約当事者の要した弁護士費

した弁護士費用の Seller に対する請求は認められない場合がある (この点と関連する American Rule については後述する)．

[275] Baker Botts L.L.P. v. ASARCO LLC, 135 S. Ct. 2158, 2161 (U.S. 2015) (quoting Hardt v. Reliance Standard Life Ins. Co., 560 U.S. 242, 252-53) (U.S. 2010) ("The American Rule provides the 'basic point of reference' for awards of attorney's fees: 'Each litigant pays his own attorney's fees, win or lose, unless a statute or contract provides otherwise.'").

[276] 例えば，次のような規定を設けることになる．「The prevailing party shall have the right to collect from the other party its reasonable costs and necessary disbursements and attorneys' fees incurred in enforcing this Agreement.」; but see Richard Smith, *Attorneys' Fees Provisions in Contracts Parties to a contract can agree on payment of attorneys' fees and costs if a legal dispute arises*, Nolo, https://www.nolo.com/legal-encyclopedia/attorneys-fees-provisions-contracts-32645.html (last visited Feb. 15, 2018) (たとえ契約上 Attorneys' Fees Clause が規定されている場合であっても，必ずしもそれを裁判所が認めるとは限らず，裁判所がより衡平に適うと認めた場合などにおいては填補義務の対象となる弁護士費用の減額または弁護士費用の填補義務自体の免責といった判断を下す場合もある旨を指摘する)．

[277] *E.g.*, Cal. Civ. Proc. § 1021.5; *see, e.g., Baker Botts L.L.P.*, 135 S. Ct., 2161 ("Because the rule is deeply rooted in the common law, this Court will not deviate from it 'absent explicit statutory authority").

[278] One-Way Attorney's Fees Clause にその規定のとおりの効果を認める州は 2012 年時点で 31 州にのぼる．Jeffrey C. Bright, *Unilateral Attorney's Fees Clauses: A Proposal to Shift to the Golden Rule*, 61, Drake L. Rev. 85, 119 (2012), https://lawreviewdrake.files.wordpress.com/2015/06/lrvol61-1-bright.pdf (last visited Feb. 2, 2018)．

用の填補義務を避けるべく）そもそも相手方契約当事者との紛争自体を回避したいとの心理が働きかねない．そして，その結果として，他方契約当事者からの契約に関する各種請求に対する交渉力が損なわれることも十分に想定できる．そこで一部の州[279]においては，One-Way Attorneys' Fees Clause はその内容にもかかわらず，両契約当事者に等しく適用されるものとして解釈する．つまり，両契約当事者は，ある紛争に関する勝訴者である限り，相手方契約当事者に対してその弁護士費用の填補を請求できるものとするのである．

Section 11.2 Exceptions and Limitations on Indemnification.

Notwithstanding anything to the contrary in this Agreement, Indemnitor is not obligated to indemnify, hold harmless, and defend the Indemnitee from and against any claim (whether direct or indirect), under Section 11.1 if such claim or corresponding Losses arise out of or result from, in whole or in part, Indemnitee's or its Personnel's:

(a) gross negligence or more culpable act or omission (including recklessness or willful misconduct); or

(b) bad faith failure to materially comply with any of its obligations under this Agreement.

3.31 Indemnification Clause に基づく義務からの免責

11.2 条においては，Seller が Buyer に対して Indemnification Clause に基づく義務を負わない場合を明示する．

どのような場合を 11.2 条の対象とすべきかについては契約当事者間の交渉事項となるが，例えば Buyer の Damage が Buyer の重過失（gross negligence[280]）に

---

[279] California 州，Florida 州，Hawaii 州，Montana 州，Oregon 州，Utah 州および Washington 州である (Cal. Civ. Code § 1717 (1987); Fla. Stat. Ann. § 57.105(7) (2010); Haw. Rev. Stat. § 607-14 (1997); Mont. Code Ann. § 28-3-704 (2009); Or. Rev. Stat. Ann. § 20.096 (2009); Utah Code Ann. § 78B-5-826 (2008); Wash. Rev. Code. Ann. § 4.84.330 (2011). *Id.* at 115.

[280] Gross negligence については，「reckless indifference to the rights of others」と定義した裁判例をふまえ，「negligence」というよりも「willful misconduct」に近い性質をもったものであると指摘される．David Shine, *Contractual Applications of Negligence/ Gross Negligence Standards: Considerations Under New York Law*, 8, The M&A Law., 10-12 (2005) (citing Sommer v. Federal Signal Corp., 79 N.Y.2d 540, 593 (Ct. App. N.Y.

よる場合についてまで Seller が Indemnification Clause に基づく義務を負うことは衡平に適わないと思われる[281].

> Section 11.3 Seller's Intellectual Property Indemnification.
>
> Subject to the terms and conditions of Section 11.4, Seller shall indemnify, hold harmless, and defend Buyer and its Representatives (collectively, the "Buyer Indemnitee") from and against all Losses arising out of any third-party Claim alleging that any of the Products infringes any Intellectual Property Right.
>
> In addition, if such a Claim is or is likely to be made, Seller may, with Buyer's prior consent and at Seller's expense, exercise the first of the following that is practicable:
>
> (a) obtain for Buyer the right to continue to use and sell the Products consistent with this Agreement;
>
> (b) modify the Products so they are non-infringing and in compliance with this Agreement; or
>
> (c) replace the Products with non-infringing ones that comply with this Agreement;
>
> If the Products, or any part of the Products, become, or in Seller's

---

1992)), http://www.friedfrank.com/siteFiles/Publications/056EFA672B52519D1926370EFAF84809.pdf (last visited Feb. 19, 2018).

[281] *See, e.g.*, Austro v. Niagara Mohawk Power Corp., 66 N.Y. 2d 674 (Ct. App. N.Y. 1985) (Indemnitee の故意的な行為から生じた Indemnitee の損害についてまで補償を要求する Indemnification Clause については執行力を認めなかった); *see also e.g.*, Idone v. Pioneer Sav. and Loan Ass'n, 159 A.D.2d 560 (Sup. Ct. N.Y. 1990) (Indemnitee の (故意的な行為ではないものの)、gross negligence から生じた Indemnitee の損害について補償を要求する Indemnification Clause については無効であるとした); *see generally* 多くの州においては、Indemnitee の過失に関する損害などについてまでも Indemnitee に対する Indemnification を認めるような Indemnification Clause については制約を課する州法 (Anti-indemnification statute という) が設けられており、これは、Construction Contract を中心に、一方契約当事者が他方契約当事者よりも取引上の力関係に大きな差があるといえる場合を対象とする。Matthiesen, *Anti-Indemnity Statutes in All 50 States*, Wickert & Lehrer, S.C., https://www.mwl-law.com/wp-content/uploads/2013/03/Anti-Indemnity-Statutes-In-All-50-States-00131938.pdf (last visited Feb. 27, 2018).

> opinion are likely to become, subject to a Claim that qualifies for intellectual property indemnification coverage under this Section 11.3, Seller shall, at its sole option and expense, notify Buyer to cease using such Products. Seller shall, Buyer 's request, accept the cancellation and return (at Seller's expense) of infringing Products without Buyer having any cancellation liability and refund to Buyer any amount paid for such infringing Products.
>
> Buyer shall notify Seller of third-party Claims against Buyer, and reasonably cooperate in the investigation, settlement, and defense of such Claims at Seller's expense.

3.32 Intellectual Property Indemnification Clause

ある製品がある特許権を侵害するなどとして訴訟となった場合，その対応に関する費用は非常に高額となりうる[282]．Intellectual Property Indemnification Clause は，対象製品によって知的財産権の侵害が発生した場合においてIndemnitor から Indemnitee に向けて行われる Indemnification について規定する．U.C.C.は対象製品について第三者の知的財産権などを侵害しないことの保証に関する規定を有するが，Buyer は Seller に対してそれ以上に広汎なIndemnification を要求する場合も多い．

Indemnification Clause について留意すべき事項についてはすでに紹介したとおりであるが，知的財産権の特質との関係から固有に問題となる事項もある．例えば特許権についてみた場合，特許権侵害に関する第三者の請求としては，(1) Direct Infringement[283]，(2) Inducing Infringement[284]，および (3) Contributory

---

[282] 2015 年において，訴額が$10,000,000 以下の特許訴訟に対して費やされた防御費用の平均額は$2,000,000 であった。Austin Champion, *3 Keys to Effective IP Indemnity Clauses A well-drafted intellectual property indemnity provision helps allocate the litigation risk of alleged infringement of IP rights*, Informa USA, Inc. (September 19, 2016), http://www.industryweek.com/intellectual-property/3-keys-effective-ip-indemnity-clauses (last visited Feb. 15, 2018).

[283] Direct Infringement の成立に関しては特許権侵害者の侵害に関する意識の有無は要件とならない。*E.g.*, Commil USA, LLC v. Cisco Sys., Inc., 135 S.Ct. 1920, 1926 (U.S. 2015) ("[A] defendant's mental state is irrelevant. Direct infringement is a strict-liability offense.").

[284] Inducing Infringement の成立に関しては，①特許侵害者が被侵害特許の存在を知っていたこと，および，②特許権侵害を誘引する自己の行為が特許権侵害を構成することを知っていたことが要件となる。35 U.S.C. § 271(b) (2010); *see, e.g., Commil USA, LLC., Inc.*, 135 S.Ct., 1926 ("In contrast to direct infringement, liability for inducing infringement attaches only if the defendant knew of the patent and that 'the induced acts constitute patent infringement.'").

Infringement[285]が挙げられるところ，Buyer のこれらすべてに関する特許権侵害行為を Seller による Indemnification の対象とするべきかという問題がある．特に Inducing Infringement および Contributory Infringement に関する Indemnification は，Indemnitee の故意的な行為から生じた Indemnitee の損害についてまでの補償を要求する Indemnification Clause の有効性について懐疑的な Common Law の傾向とは相反するものともいえるためである[286]．

Section 11.4 Exceptions to Seller's Indemnification.

Notwithstanding anything to the contrary in this Agreement, Seller is not obligated to, indemnify, hold harmless, or defend any Buyer Indemnitee from and against any claim, whether direct or indirect, under Section 11.3 if such claim or corresponding Losses arise out of or result from, in whole or in part:

(a) use of the Products in combination with any products, materials or equipment supplied to Buyer by a Person other than Seller or its authorized Representatives, if the infringement would have been avoided by the use of the Products without such combination; or

(b) any modifications or changes made to the Products by or on behalf of any Person other than Seller or its Representatives, if the infringement would have been avoided without such modification or change.

3.33 Intellectual Property Indemnification Clause に基づく義務からの免責

11.4 条においては，Seller が Buyer に対して Indemnification Clause に基づく義務を負わない場合を明示する．

どのような場合を 11.4 条の対象とすべきかは，ある場合を Seller の責任に帰することが衡平であるかといった観点をふまえたうえでの契約当事者間の交渉事項となるが，例えば 第三者からの対象製品が第三者の特許を侵害しているな

---

[285] Contributory Infringement の成立については，①特許侵害者が被侵害特許の存在を知っていたこと，および，②自己の行為が特許権侵害を構成することを知っていたことが要件となる．35 U.S.C. § 271(c) (2010); see, e.g., Commil USA, LLC., 135 S.Ct., 1926 ("Like induced infringement, contributory infringement requires knowledge of the patent in suit and knowledge of patent infringement.").

[286] Champion, supra note 282.

どの主張が，(1) Seller の製品と Seller 以外の製品との組み合わせの結果に起因する場合，(2) Seller の製品について Seller 以外の者が加えた改変に起因する場合[287]，または (3) Seller の製品について Seller が Buyer からの指図の結果加えた改変に起因する場合など[288]が挙げられる[289]．

> Section 11.5 Exclusive Remedy.
>
> ARTICLE 11 SETS FORTH THE ENTIRE LIABILITY AND OBLIGATION OF EACH INDEMNITOR AND THE SOLE AND EXCLUSIVE REMEDY FOR EACH INDEMNITEE AND BUYER INDEMNITEE FOR ANY LOSSES COVERED BY ARTICLE 11. NEITHER PARTY SHALL BE LIABLE TO THE OTHER FOR ANY SPECIAL, CONSEQUENTIAL NOR PUNITIVE DAMAGES WHATSOEVER, WHETHER IN CONTRACT, TORT INCLUDING NEGLIGENCE AND STRICT LIABILITY, OR ANY OTHER LEGAL OR EQUITABLE PRINCIPLE.

3.34 Exclusive Remedy Clause

Seller としては自己の責任対象および範囲についてある程度予見することができるよう，以下のように，対象製品に関する Buyer からの損害の請求根拠および自己の責任範囲などを可能な限り明示したいところである．

a. 責任追及に関する根拠の制限

Exclusive Remedy Clause は，責任追求に関する根拠を特定のものに限定する（Exclusive Remedy という）ものである．対象契約に関して行われる一方契約当事者から他方契約当事者に対する請求は，契約上明示された手段がすべてであり，他の救済方法（例えば不法行為法に基づく請求）は認められない旨を規定する[290]．

Exclusive Remedy の典型例としては Liquidated Damages が挙げられる[291]．ただし，Liquidated Damages

---

[287] Cynthia Cannady, Technology Licensing and Development Agreements 174 (2013 ed.).
[288] Rudnick, *supra* note 269, at 10.
[289] さらに，これらの事項に該当する場合においては，Seller が Buyer から Indemnification および Defense を受けること (Reverse Duty to Indemnification and Duty to Defend という) も検討に値する．*See id.*
[290] U.C.C. § 2-719 (1) (Am. Law Inst. & Unif. Law Comm'n 2002).
[291] Lawrence Hsieh, *Sandbagging Provisions; Cumulative vs. Exclusive Remedies* (Aug. 11, 2011), http://gcnewyork.com/columns11/081111hsieh.html (last visited Oct. 24, 2017).

契約法は本来的に Cumulative Remedies[292]の立場を基礎としているから，ある契約において Exclusive Remedy の立場をとる場合においてはその旨を明確に規定する必要がある[293]．

b. 責任範囲の種類による制限

他方契約当事者の損害および請求のうち特定のものに限り責任を負うものとするものである[294]．特に逸失利益などのように金額が多額となりうるもの，または，予見可能性が高くないものについてあらかじめ責任外としておくことで責任の拡大を防止することができる．

c. 責任範囲の金額による制限

他方契約当事者に対して補償する金額をあらかじめ決定し（Liquidated Damages という），それを契約上規定する場合がある[295]（Liquidated Damages Clause という）[296]．Liquidated Damages Clause は，①想定される損害と比べてその Liquidated Damages が合理的であること（ペナルティであると判断されないこと），および，②実際の損害の証明が困難であることを満たす必要があ

の設定があることをもって，自動的にそれが Exclusive Remedy であると認定されるわけではないことに留意する必要がある．Liquidated Damages については後述する．

[292] Cumulative Remedies とは，一方契約当事者から他方契約当事者に向けて行われる法律上の責任追及のうち，そのほかの根拠に基づく責任追及が別途行われることを否定することなしに行われるものをいう．詳細については，6.2 (Cumulative Remedies Clause) において紹介する．

[293] Creighton Univ. v. Gen. Elec. Co., 2009 U.S. Dist. LEXIS 22166, at 27 (D. Neb. 2009) (first citing Neb.Rev.Stat. U.C.C. § 2–719(1)(b) cmt. 2; and then citing Reichert v. Rubloff Hammond, L.L.C., 645 N.W.2d 519, 526 (Neb. Sup. Ct. 2002)) ("'If the parties intend the term to describe the sole remedy under the contract, this must be clearly expressed." It is likewise a principle of Nebraska common law that '[a] contract will not be construed to limit the remedial rights of the parties unless that intention is clearly expressed.'"); *see generally* Consolidation Coal Co. v. Marion Docks, Inc., 2010 U.S. Dist. LEXIS 31365 (W.D. Pa. 2010) (取引対象である石炭の納入遅延に関する Seller の責任について，「the seller "shall" pay the buyer the difference between the total base price under the contract and the price at which the buyer purchases substitute coal」とした契約上の規定は Exclusive Remedy Clause であると判断するには不十分である旨を示した)．

[294] これは Limitation of Liability Clause として規定されることが多い．5.6 (Limitation of Liability Clause) において紹介する．

[295] 例えば，次のような条項を設けることになる．「If Seller breaches its obligations under Section 11 ("Seller's Breach"), Seller shall pay to Buyer an amount equal to [three million United States dollars (3,000,000)/ten percent (10%) of the purchase price of the Products] (the "Liquidated Damages"). The Parties intend that the Liquidated Damages constitute compensation, and not a penalty. The Parties acknowledge and agree that "Buyer's" harm caused by a Seller Breach would be impossible or very difficult to accurately estimate as of the Effective Date, and that the Liquidated Damages are a reasonable estimate of the anticipated or actual harm that might arise from Seller's Breach. Seller's payment of the Liquidated Damages is the Seller's sole liability and entire obligation and Buyer's exclusive remedy for any Seller's Breach.」．

[296] *See, e.g.*, U.C.C. § 2-718 (Am. Law Inst. & Unif. Law Comm'n 2002).

り[297]，これらを満たさない場合，その Liquidated Damages Clause は無効とされる[298]。

なお，Liquidated Damages Clause を規定する場合，Exclusive Remedy Clause もあわせて規定しておかなければ 実質的な意味が損なわれてしまう。契約を根拠としない請求が Liquidated Damages Clause 所定の金額を上回って行われるといった事態を防ぐ必要があるためである。また，万が一 Liquidated Damages Clause が無効であると判断された場合に備える意味では Severability Clause [299]も規定しておくことが望ましい。

ARTICLE 12
REPRESENTATIONS AND WARRANTIES

Section 12.1 Seller's Representations and Warranties.

As of the Effective Date, Seller represents and warrants to Buyer that:

(a) it is a limited liability company duly organized, validly existing, and in good standing in the jurisdiction of its organization;

(b) it is duly qualified to do business and is in good standing in every jurisdiction in which such qualification is required for purposes of this Agreement;

(c) it has the full right, company power, and authority to enter into this

---

[297] Phillips v. Phillips, 820 S.W.2d 785, 788 (Sup. Ct. Tex. 1991) ("In order to enforce a liquidated damages clause, the court must find: (1) that the harm caused by the breach is incapable or difficult of estimation, and (2) that the amount of liquidated damages called for is a reasonable forecast of just compensation.").

[298] *Phillips*, 820 S.W.2d, 789 (原告の被った損失の 10 倍を Liquidated Damages として設定した規定（「If the general partner breaches his trust hereunder, he shall pay to the limited partner as liquidated damages ten times the amount she loses as a result of such breaches of trust. Errors of judgment shall not be considered breaches of trusts.」) は無効であると判断した) ("A contractual provision like the one here by which one party agrees to pay the other some multiple of actual damages for breach of the agreement does not meet either part of the legal test for an enforceable liquidated damages provision. It cannot meet the first prong of the test because the harm caused by the breach of the contract is not incapable or difficult of estimation. The provision assumes actual damages can and will be determined, indeed must be determined, before the prescribed multiplier can be applied. The provision cannot meet the second prong of the test because, instead of attempting to forecast actual damages, it calls for them to be determined and then multiplied.").

[299] Severability Clause については 6.9 (Severability Clause) において紹介する。

Agreement, to grant the rights and licenses granted under this Agreement, and to perform its obligations under this Agreement;

(d) the execution of this Agreement by its Representative whose signature is set forth at the end of this Agreement has been duly authorized by all necessary corporate action of Seller;

(e) when executed and delivered by each of Buyer and Seller, this Agreement will constitute the legal, valid, and binding obligation of Seller, enforceable against Seller in accordance with its terms, except as may be limited by any applicable bankruptcy, insolvency, reorganization, moratorium, or similar laws and equitable principles related to or affecting creditors' rights generally or the effect of general principles of equity; and

(f) it is in compliance with all Laws and Seller's contracts applicable to this Agreement, the Products, and the operation of its business.

(g) to the best of its knowledge it is in compliance with all Laws and Seller's contracts applicable to this Agreement, the Products, and the operation of its business.

3.35 Representation and Warranty Clause

Representation and Warranty Clause は，一方契約当事者の表明した事項に関する他方契約当事者の信頼を保護するものである．

a. Representation の意義

「Representation」とは，ある時点において相手方の信頼を得るべく行われた現在または過去の事実に関する表明をいう[300]．例えば，Seller が Buyer に向けて対象製品は本日現在において最高品質である旨表明した場合，それは Representation に該当するといえる．これに対して将来の事実に関するコメントは単なる意見であり，Representation とは認められないのが原則である[301]．Representation 違反は不法行為としての Misrepresentation を構成しうる．その場

---

[300] Stark, *supra* note 1, at 12.
[301] Stark, *supra* note 1, at 13, 140-41 (将来の事実に関する表明保証は実質的には Covenant であると指摘する).

合の被表明者がとりうる救済方法は契約の撤回または損害の賠償請求である[302]。

b. Warranty の意義

「Warranty」とは，保証者による保証内容が正確であること[303]の保証である。したがって Warranty も現在または過去の事実に対して行われるものである。Warranty 違反は，被保証者から保証者に対する損害の賠償請求などを可能とする[304]。

このように「Representation」と「Warranty」とは異なる意義を持つため[305]，相手方契約当事者に Representation と Warranty の双方を要求することにも理由が認められる[306]。なお，U.C.C.の適用がある「Goods」の売買契約の場合，格別の規定がない限り，売主が製品に関する所有権を有していること，および，製品にはなんらの担保権も付されていないことが保証されている[307]。

c. Representation and Warranty の対象の特定

契約当事者の責任範囲を画するためには，Representation and Warranty（以下，表明保証という）の対象を明確にする必要がある。

---

[302] Glenn D. West & W. Benton Lewis, Jr., *Contracting to Avoid Extra-Contractual Liability—Can Your Contractual Deal Ever Really Be the "Entire" Deal?*, 65 The Bus. Law. 999, 1008 (2009), https://www.weil.com/~/media/files/pdfs/Extra-Contractual%20Liability%20Article.pdf (last visited Feb. 22, 2018); *see also* Richard A. Lord, 18 Williston on Contracts § 52:45, §69:5 (4th ed.).

[303] これに対して，Representation の一環として提供されるものではない Warranty (Representations of Warranty Clause ではなく Warranty Clause に基づいて行われる Warranty を指す。例えば製品の品質に関する Warranty である）については将来の事実に関する保証（例えば契約締結日から1年間は製品仕様を満たす旨の保証）も可能である。Stark, *supra* note 1, at 142.

[304] Stark, *supra* note 1, at 16-18.

[305] *See also* Thomson Reuters Practical Law, *Representations and Warranties*, https://content.next.westlaw.com/Document/I1559f7a3eef211e28578f7ccc38dcbee/View/FullText.html?contextData=(sc.Default)&transitionType=Default&firstPage=true&bhcp=1 (last visited Jun. 18, 2018) ("A representation is an assertion as to a fact, true on the date the representation is made, that is given to induce another party to enter into a contract or take some other action. A warranty is a promise of indemnity if the assertion is false. The terms 'representation' and 'warranty' are often used together in practice. If a representation is not true it is 'inaccurate.' If a warranty is not true it is 'breached.'").

[306] Stark, *supra* note 1, at 138; *but see* Kenneth A. Adams, *Eliminating The Phrase Represents And Warrants From Contracts*, 16 The Tenn. J. of Bus. L., 203, 218-20 (2015), http://www.adamsdrafting.com/wp/wp-content/uploads/2015/06/Adams-Eliminating-the-Phrase-Represents-and-Warrants-from-Contracts.pdf (last visited Feb. 22, 2018) (Representation と Warranty の併記については，それが被表明保証者の救済方法を拡張することには寄与するわけではなく，いたずらに契約を複雑化させるものであって適当でないと指摘する）。

[307] U.C.C. § 2-312 (Am. Law Inst. & Unif. Law Comm'n 2002).

i. 表明保証の対象

「To the best of knowledge」の一節は，表明保証の対象を表明保証者の認識の範囲に限ることで，表明保証者が不測の表明保証違反[308]を構成してしまうような事態を予防するものである．

なお，単に「to my knowledge」とするよりも「to the best of knowledge」とした方がより手厚いのではないかとの問題意識もあるようであるが，認識の有無に「best」のような表現はあてはまらず，大きな違いはないとする見解がある[309]．

ii. 表明保証の提供時期

表明保証は契約締結時点における事実に関して行うことも，また，過去の特定時点における事実に関して行うことも可能[310]であるため，契約上の表明保証がいつの時点に対するものであるかを明示することは重要である．なお，格別の規定がない場合，その表明保証は契約締結時点における事実に関して行われたものであると理解される[311]．

ARTICLE 13
CERTAIN OBLIGATIONS OF SELLER

3.36 Covenant

「Covenant」とは，契約上で規定された合意事項または約束事項であり[312]，契約当事者に履行義務を負わせるものである．契約上 Covenant を列挙する場合においては，義務を表す単語であると一般に理解されている「shall」を使用するべきであり，「agree」または「(is) responsible」のような単語の使用は避けるべきとされる[313]．

---

[308] 例として，不動産売買契約において「契約締結日現在において家屋は住居に適していること」を表明保証したところ，実際には当日到来した台風によって家屋が破損していたような場合が挙げられる．
[309] Kenneth A. Adams, *Revisiting "To the Best of Its Knowledge" (Plus Thoughts on the Marketplace of Ideas)*, Adams on Contract Drafting (Sep. 20, 2009), http://www.adamsdrafting.com/revisiting-to-the-best-of-its-knowledge/ (last visited Feb. 22, 2018).
[310] Stark, *supra* note 1, at 139 (citing Restatement (Second) of Contracts § 156 cmt. c (Am. Law Inst. 1981)).
[311] *Id*, at 138.
[312] *Black's Law Dictionary: Pocket Edition* 182 (4th ed. 2011).
[313] Stark, *supra* note 1, at 151-57. したがって，例えば，「Buyer agrees to pay (is responsible for paying) $100,000 to Seller before January 1, 2020」と規定するのではなく，「Buyer shall pay $100,000 to Seller before January 1, 2020」と規定するべきである．

a. Covenant に関する違反

　契約当事者が Covenant の履行を怠った場合，相手方当事者はそれに伴う損害の賠償請求または Specific Performance[314]の履行を請求することができる。また，その Covenant の履行の懈怠が契約に重大な影響を及ぼす場合においては契約の解除もできる[315]。

b. Representation and Warranty と Covenant の区分

　Representation and Warranty は現在または過去の事実に関する表明保証であり，将来の事実に対して提供されるものではない。これに対して Covenant は将来特定の義務を履行することの担保として提供することができる。

Section 13.1 General Compliance with Laws Covenant.

Seller shall at all times comply with all Laws applicable to this Agreement and its obligations under this Agreement, including Seller's sale of the Products.

Without limiting the generality of the foregoing, Seller shall:

(a) at its own expense, maintain all certifications, credentials, licenses, and permits necessary to conduct its business relating to the sale of the Products; and

(b) not engage in any activity or transaction involving the Products, by way of shipment, use, or otherwise, that violates any Law.

Section 13.2 Ingredients and Materials Disclosure.

On Buyer's written request, Seller shall promptly provide to Buyer, in such form and detail as Buyer requests, a list of all ingredients and

---

[314] Specific Performance とは，損害賠償による救済が被契約違反者の救済に適当ではないと思われる場合，または，損害額が算定できない場合において，裁判所の裁量のもと決定される救済方法である。*Black's Law Dictionary: Pocket Edition* 703 (4th ed. 2011).

[315] Stark, *supra* note 1, at 25. ただし，これは Common Law における理解であり，U.C.C.の適用のある契約における理解については 4.3（契約の解除）において紹介する。

materials incorporated in the Products, the amount of such ingredients and materials, and information concerning any changes in or additions to such ingredients and materials.

(a) Without limitation of the foregoing, on Buyer's written request, Seller shall provide to Buyer all information (in sufficient detail), with written certifications thereof, to enable Buyer to timely comply with all of Buyer's and Buyer's customers' due diligence, disclosure and audit requirements under Section 1502 of the Dodd-Frank Wall Street Reform and Consumer Protection Act (the "Dodd-Frank Act") and Rule 13p-1 and Form SD under the Securities Exchange Act of 1934, and all similar, applicable statutes and regulations, including due inquiry of Seller's supply chain and certifications by such suppliers identifying conflict minerals (as defined in Section 1502(e)(4) of the Dodd-Frank Act) contained in each Product and the country of origin of such conflict minerals or, following due inquiry, why such country of origin cannot be determined.

(b) For each shipment of Products, Seller shall provide Buyer, in writing, sufficient advance warning and notice (in addition to including appropriate labels on Products, containers, and packing) of any hazardous or restricted material that is an ingredient or a part of the shipment, together with such special handling instructions as may be necessary to advise logistics providers, handlers of the Products, and personnel of how to exercise that measure of care and precaution that will comply with any applicable Laws and prevent bodily injury or property damage in the handling, transportation, processing, use, or disposal of the Products, containers, and packing.

3.37 Dodd-Frank Act

Dodd-Frank Act[316]は，米国証券取引委員会（U.S. Securities and Exchange Commission）における株式発行者に対して，(1)自社製品に関する Conflict Mineral[317] の使用の有無，(2) 使用する Conflict Mineral が特定国[318]に由来するか

---

[316] Conflict Minerals Release No. 34,677,16 (Aug. 22, 2012), https://www.sec.gov/rules/final/2012/34-67716.pdf (last visited Feb. 22, 2018).

[317] Gold, Tantalum, Tin, および Tungsten をいう。Business & Human Rights Resource Centre, *Implementation*

の確認，および (3) Conflict Mineral の購入が特定の団体を利しているかの確認とその結果の報告義務を課する[319]．これらは，Conflict Minerals の採掘過程において労働者に対する人権侵害行為が見受けられること，および，Conflict Minerals の売買による収益が特定国周辺地域における武力紛争の資金源になっていることをふまえたうえでの要請である[320]．

　対象企業が特定国に由来する Conflict Mineral を使用していたとしても，その Conflict Mineral に関する取引自体の停止までをも要求されるわけではない．しかし，対象企業は人権侵害や武装勢力の資金源となるような取引を行わぬよう適切な対処に向けて活動していることを示す必要がある[321]．

　Buyer が Seller の製品を自社の製品の一部として使用する場合，Seller の製品についてまで個別に Dodd-Frank Act 要求事項について確認することは現実的でない場合もある．そこで，13.2 条は，Seller に対して，Buyer が Dodd-Frank Act を遵守するにあたって必要となる協力を提供する義務を課している．

---

of US Dodd-Frank Act rule on conflict minerals: Commentaries, guidance, company actions, https://business-humanrights.org/en/conflict-peace/conflict-minerals/implementation-of-us-dodd-frank-act-rule-on-conflict-minerals-commentaries-guidance-company-actions (last visited Feb. 22, 2018).

[318] Angola, Burundi, Central Africa Republic, Democratic Republic of the Congo (DRC), Rwanda, South Sudan, Tanzania, The Republic of the Congo, Uganda, および Zambia を指す．Ernst & Young Global Limited, *Dodd–Frank Section 1502 and the SECs final rule*, http://www.ey.com/us/en/services/specialty-services/climate-change-and-sustainability-services/conflict_minerals_dodd_frank_section (last visited Feb. 22, 2018).

[319] Business & Human Rights Resource Centre, *supra* note 317.

[320] Ernst & Young Global Limited, *supra* note 318．なお，2015 年においては対象企業のうち 21%の企業が Dodd-Frank Act の基準を満たしていたとの調査結果がある．Global Witness, *US Conflict Minerals Law Section 1502 of U.S. Dodd Frank Act: the landmark US law requiring responsible minerals sourcing* (Nov. 5, 2017), https://www.globalwitness.org/en-gb/campaigns/conflict-minerals/dodd-frank-act-section-1502/ (last visited May 30, 2018).

[321] *Id.*

CHAPTER 4 / ENDGAME PROVISIONS

Endgame Provisions は，契約の終期，契約の解除事由，および契約終了または契約解約の効果について規定する[322]．これらは画一的なものでは足りず，取引の実態をふまえた適切な内容であることが期待される．

ARTICLE 14
TERM AND TERMINATION

Section 14.1 Initial Term.

The term of this Agreement commences on the Effective Date and continues for a period of five (5) years, unless and until earlier terminated as provided under this Agreement or applicable Law (the "Initial Term").

4.1 契約期間

　契約当事者がビジネスに関してある契約関係に入るのは，何らかのビジネス上の利益が見込めるためにほかならない．したがって，そのビジネス上の利益を実現するため，または，そのビジネスに投下した資本を回収するだけに必要と思われる期間については相手方契約当事者を契約の条件に拘束する必要があり，その期間を「Term」として設定することになる．

　なお，「Term」の終期については祝休日などとの兼ね合いからくる不都合を回避する意味で，「Effective Date から 5 年」といった周年を基礎とした規定よりも特定の期日を明示した規定とするべきとの指摘もある[323]．

---

[322] *But see* Stark, *supra* note 1, at 25 (Dispute Resolution Clause を Endgame Provisions に包含する)．本書においては，Dispute Resolution Clause を General Provisions の一部として紹介する．*See generally* Practical Law Corporate & Securities and Practical Law Commercial Transactions, Boilerplate Clauses, Thomson Reuters, https://1.next.westlaw.com/Document/I0f9fe56def0811e28578f7ccc38dcbee/View/FullText.html?contextData=(sc.Default)&transitionType=Default&firstPage=true&bhcp=1&OWSessionId=88fc4d23889b461c8fd8b9bf1401398f&isplcus=true&fromAnonymous=true (last visited Jun. 27, 2018).

[323] Sarah Kahn et al., *When to Call it Quits and How to Survive the Break-Up -- Termination Clause Drafting Tips*, 18, https://www.acc.com/chapters/ncr/upload/Termination-Clause-Drafting-5-19-2015.pdf (last visited Jun. 18, 2018).

Section 14.2 Renewal Term.

Upon expiration of the Initial Term, this Agreement automatically renews for additional successive three (3) years unless and until either Party provides notice of nonrenewal at least thirty (30) days before the end of the then-current term, or unless and until earlier terminated as provided under this Agreement or applicable Law (each a "Renewal Term" and together with the Initial Term, the "Term"). If the Term is renewed for any Renewal Term(s) pursuant to this Section 14.2, the terms and conditions of this Agreement during each such Renewal Term are the same as the terms in effect immediately prior to such renewal, subject to any change in Prices payable for the Products and payment terms during the applicable Renewal Term as set forth in this Section 14.2.

If either Party provides timely notice of its intent not to renew this Agreement, then, subject to Section 14.1, unless earlier terminated in accordance with its terms, this Agreement terminates on the expiration of the then-current Term.

4.2 Evergreen Clause

　契約によっては，その契約条件について再度の交渉が行われる，または，契約期間の終了に関する手続きがとられるといった事態が生じない限り，契約期間が満了した後もなお自動的に契約が更新される旨の規定を設けている場合があり，これを Evergreen Clause という。Evergreen Clause は，格別の必要性が認められない場合においては「Initial Term」満了後の契約の再交渉を不要とすることで，取引関係継続の容易性を確保することを目的とする[324]。

　もっとも Evergreen Clause は契約当事者を当初設定した契約期間を超えてもなお拘束する効果を持つため，その有効性が問題とされる場合もあり[325]，適用

---

[324] Andrew C. Voorhees, *The Enforceability of "Evergreen Clauses"*, Weltman, Weinberg & Reis Co., LPA (Feb. 11, 2016), http://www.weltman.com/?t=40&an=49799&format=xml&p=7735 (last visited Feb. 23, 2018).

[325] N.Y. Gen.Oblig. § 5-903 (2014) (Service Contract などに関する契約に自動更新条項が含まれている場合，Service などの提供者は，相手方契約当事者に対して，相手方契約当事者が契約の更新を行わない旨を通知すべきとされる期限の 15 日前から 30 日前までの間に，その義務の存在を認識させるような通知を行う必要があり，これに反した自動更新は認められないとする); Cal. Bus. & Prof. § 17600-17606

法との関係に留意が必要とされる.

> Section 14.3 Buyer's Right to Terminate the Agreement.
>
> Buyer may terminate this Agreement (including all related Individual Transactions in accordance with Section 5.3), on notice to Seller:
>
> (a) except as otherwise specifically provided under this Section 14.3, if Seller is in material breach of any representation, warranty, or covenant of Seller under this Agreement and either the breach cannot be cured or, if the breach can be cured, it is not cured by Seller within a commercially reasonable period of time under the circumstances, in no case exceeding ten (10) Business Days following Seller's receipt of notice of such breach;
>
> (b) if Seller repudiates, or threatens to repudiate, any of its obligations under this Agreement;
>
> (c) if Seller:
>
> > (i) becomes insolvent or is generally unable to pay, or fails to pay, its debts as they become due;
> >
> > (ii) files or has filed against it, a petition for voluntary or involuntary bankruptcy or otherwise becomes subject, voluntarily or involuntarily, to any proceeding under any domestic or foreign bankruptcy or insolvency Law;
> >
> > (iii) seeks reorganization, arrangement, adjustment, winding-up, liquidation, dissolution, composition, or other relief with respect to it or its debts;
> >
> > (iv) makes or seeks to make a general assignment for the benefit of its creditors; or

---

(2012) (消費者契約における自動更新条項は「clear and conspicuous」であることを要求する); *see* Perrie Michael Weiner & Edward D. Totino, *California's Automatic Renewal Law: three recent decisions, and what they mean for businesses*, DLA Piper (Mar. 16, 2017), https://www.dlapiper.com/en/us/insights/publications/2017/03/california-automatic-renewal-law/ (last visited Feb. 23, 2018).

(v) applies for or has a receiver, trustee, custodian, or similar agent appointed by order of any court of competent jurisdiction to take charge of or sell any material portion of its property or business;

(d) if Seller fails to provide Buyer, within a commercial reasonable time after Buyer's request (but in no case exceeding ten (10) Business Days after such request with adequate and reasonable assurance of Seller's financial and operational capability to timely perform Seller's obligations under this Agreement;

(e) in the event of a Force Majeure Event affecting the Seller's performance of this Agreement for more than twenty (20) consecutive days;

(f) if, without obtaining Buyer's prior written consent, (i) Seller sells, leases, or exchanges a material portion of Seller's assets, (ii) Seller merges or consolidates with or into another Person, or (iii) a change in Control of Seller occurs, unless in the case of a merger or consolidation of Seller with another Person, Seller is the surviving entity and has a net worth greater than or equal to its net worth immediately prior to the merger or consolidation; or

(g) at its option, at any time and for any reason.

Any termination under this Section 14.3 is effective on Seller's receipt of Buyer's notice of termination or any later date set out in the notice.

Section 14.4 Effect of Expiration or Termination.

(a) Unless Buyer directs otherwise, any termination under Section 14.2 or Section 14.3 automatically terminates all related Individual Transactions under Section 5.2.

(b) Upon the expiration or earlier termination of this Agreement, Seller shall promptly:

(i) return to the other Party or destroy all documents and tangible materials and any copies containing, reflecting, incorporating, or based on the other Party's Confidential Information;

(ii) permanently erase all of the other Party's Confidential Information from its computer systems, except for copies that are maintained as archive copies on its disaster recovery and/or information technology backup systems. Each Party shall destroy any such copies upon the normal expiration of its backup files; and

(iii) certify in writing to the other Party that it has complied with the requirements of this Section 14.4.

(c) The Party terminating this Agreement, or in the case of the expiration of this Agreement, each Party, shall not be liable to the other Party for any damage of any kind (whether direct or indirect) incurred by the other Party by reason of the expiration or earlier termination of this Agreement. Termination of this Agreement will not constitute a waiver of any of the terminating Party's rights, remedies, or defenses under this Agreement, at law, in equity, or otherwise.

4.3 契約の解除

14.3 条は Buyer による契約上の解約権を確保するものである．解約権は特定事由が発生した場合（Termination for Default という）に認められていることが多く，例えば，相手方契約当事者に契約違反があった場合，相手方当事者の財務状況が悪化した場合，または災害が発生した結果，一方契約当事者の契約上の義務の履行に支障が生じた場合などが挙げられる．また，解約権は契約当事者の自由な意思に基づいて行使できる旨を認めることも可能である（Termination for Convenience という）[326]．一方契約当事者による解約権が行使された場合，両

---

[326] 契約上の解約権 (Termination for Default および Termination for Convenience) をまとめて Contractual Termination という．これに対して Common Law 上認められる解約権を Common Law Termination という．Common Law Termination は，格別契約で排除されていない限り，Contractual Termination とは別個の根拠として主張可能である．Jeremy Andrews & Talia Taylor, *Termination of commercial contracts*, DLA Piper (Mar. 15, 2016), https://www.dlapiper.com/en/uk/insights/publications/2016/03/termination-of-commercial-contracts/ (last visited Feb. 23, 2018). なお，本契約における Contractual Termination の基礎となる事由には Common Law Termination の基礎となる事由も含まれている．

契約当事者は未履行の契約上の義務から解放されることになるのが原則である[327]。

a. 契約違反に基づく契約の解除
14.3(a)条は，Seller が契約に違反した場合において，Buyer に解約権を認めている。このような場合における Common Law および U.C.C.における取り扱いは以下のとおりである。

i. Common Law における取り扱い
一方契約当事者が Common Law に基づいて契約を解除するためには，相手方契約当事者に「Material Breach」[328]が認められる必要があるのが原則である。一方契約当事者が契約に関する Material Breach を起こした場合，他方契約当事者は自己の契約上の義務の履行から解放されるとともに Material Breach から生じた損害の賠償を請求することができる[329]。これを Doctrine of Material Breach[330]という[331]。

したがって，ある契約違反が「Material Breach」に該当するかどうかは重要な問題であり，契約当事者間で論争の対象となることも少なくない[332]。
そこで，特に重要な契約上の義務については，その不履行が「Material

---

[327] Ann B. Graff & Ryan P. Stewart, *Model Jury Instructions: Construction Litigation, ch. 11 Termination* 182 (2d ed. 2015).
[328] Restatement (Second) of Contracts § 241 (Am. Law Inst. 1981). *See supra* note 91.
[329] なお，一方契約当事者の契約違反が「Material Breach」に該当しないとしても，他方契約当事者は損害の賠償を請求することはできる。*See generally id.* § 347 (Am. Law Inst. 1981).
[330] Doctrine of Substantial Performance (一方契約当事者が契約上の義務を実質的に履行している限り，他方契約当事者は，自己の義務の履行を拒絶することはできない) は Doctrine of Material Breach と表裏一体の関係にある。49 Tex. Prac., Contract Law § 9.3.
[331] Doctrine of Material Breach と関連するものとして The First Material Breach Rule (いったん Material Breach を発生させた契約当事者はそれ以降に相手方契約当事者が発生させた Material Breach から生じた損害の賠償の請求を行うことが認められないという原則) がある。ただし，(1) Material Breach を発生させた契約当事者がすでにその Material Breach を「Cure」した場合，または，(2) 相手方契約当事者が Material Breach を認容した場合においては The First Material Breach Rule は適用されない。J. Ross Pepper, *The First Material Breach Rule in Tennessee*, Pepper Law PLC (Jul. 15, 2014), https://www.nashvillebusinesslitigationlawyersblog.com/2014/07/first-material-breach-rule-tennessee.html (last visited Feb. 23, 2018).
[332] そこで「Material Breach」自体の定義を試みることも有用であり，例えば，次のような規定を設けることになる。「"Material Breach" means, with respect to a given breach, that a reasonable person in the position of the nonbreaching party would wish to terminate this agreement because of that breach.」. Kenneth A. Adams, *"Material Breach"*, Adams on Contract Drafting (Nov. 11, 2007), http://www.adamsdrafting.com/material-breach/ (last visited May 4, 2018).

Breach」を構成する旨明示しておくことが望ましい[333].

ii. U.C.C.における取り扱い

U.C.C.の適用対象となる契約については Doctrine of Material Breach の適用はなく，代わりに Perfect Tender Rule が適用される．Perfect Tender Rule においては，Seller は Buyer と合意した製品に関するすべての仕様を忠実に満たす責任を負うため，相手方契約当事者に契約違反が認められればそれがいかに些細なものであっても契約解除の根拠とできる．

なお，U.C.C.の適用対象となる契約であってもそれが Installment Contract である場合においては Perfect Tender Rule の適用はない[334]．したがって，一方契約当事者に契約上の義務の不履行があったとしても，他方契約当事者はそのことのみをもって Installment Contract 全体について自己の契約上の義務の履行を拒絶することはできない．Installment Contract 全体について他方契約当事者が契約上の義務の履行を拒絶するためには，相手方契約当事者の契約上の義務の不履行が Installment Contract 全体の価値を著しく損なわせているといえる状況が必要なのである[335]．

b. Repudiation に基づく契約の解除

14.3(b)条においては，Seller が契約上の義務の履行を拒絶（repudiation）するなどした場合において Buyer に契約の解除権を認めている．もっとも，本契約の場合，履行期が到来したのちの Seller による repudiation については，14.3(a)条（または Common Law もしくは U.C.C.）の契約違反に基づく契約の解除の問題となることが多いはずであるから，14.3(b)条の意義は，主として履行期が到来していない場合において Seller による repudiation の意思表示があった場合に認められる．

すなわち，この場合において，契約法は，①履行拒絶を示唆する言動が明確[336]かつ任意[337]にとられたこと，ならびに，②履行期到来後に実際にその言

---

[333] Richard Stim, *Breach of Contract: Material Breach How do you know whether your contract is "irreparably broken" in the eyes of the law?*, Nolo, https://www.nolo.com/legal-encyclopedia/breach-of-contract-material-breach-32655.html (last visited May 4, 2018). 例えば，次のような規定を設けることが考えられる.「The Parties agree that, in particular but not limited to, any breaches of [the warranties and representations provided to Buyer under Section 12.1] shall constitute and be considered material breach.」.

[334] U.C.C. § 2-612 (Am. Law Inst. & Unif. Law Comm'n 2002).

[335] *Id.* § 2-612(2).

[336] *See, e.g.*, EastBanc, Inc. v. Georgetown Park Assocs. II, L.P., 940 A.2d 996, 1005 (D.C. Ct. App. 2008) (quoting Order of AHEPA v. Travel Consultants, Inc., 367 A.2d 119, 125 (D.C. Ct. App. 1976) ("For a repudiation of a contract by one party to be sufficient to give the other party the right to recover for breach, the

動が具体化したならばそれは「Repudiation」[338]を構成するであろうこと[339]を要件として（Anticipatory Repudiation という），他方契約当事者による契約の解約権を認める[340]．

しかし，実際にはこれらの要件を満たしているかどうかを正確に判断することは容易でなく，他方契約当事者が契約の解除に踏み切ることを躊躇することも少なくない．したがって，Seller による「threatens to repudiate」があったことのみをもって Buyer に契約の解除権を認める 14.3(b)条は，このような問題の解決を図るものであると評価できる．

なお，一方契約当事者が Repudiation を行った場合，他方契約当事者はそれ以降，自己の損害を軽減する義務を負う[341]．

c. 財務状況の悪化に基づく契約の解除

14.3(c)条は，一方契約当事者が倒産またはそれに類似した状況に陥った場合における他方契約当事者の契約解除権を規定したものである（Ipso Facto Clause という[342]）．しかし，Ipso Facto Clause は倒産手続きとの関係では原則

---

repudiating party must have communicated, by word or conduct, unequivocally and positively its intention not to perform.").

[337] *See generally* Blum, *supra* note 255, at 638.

[338] この場合における「Repudiation」とは，他方契約当事者にとっての対象契約の価値を著しく毀損するような言動をいう．*See* Restatement (Second) of Contracts § 250 (Am. Law Inst. 1981).「Repudiation」の例として，履行拒絶の意思を明確に相手方当事者に伝えた場合，契約上の義務の履行を不可能とする行動がとられた場合（例えば，金銭消費貸借契約のもと借入金の返済義務を負う債務者が，その借入金の返済が不可能となるほど多額の借り入れを第三者から行った場合），および契約上の目的物が第三者に移転した場合（例えば，対象契約が売買契約である場合において Seller がその対象物を第三者に売却した場合）が挙げられる．*See* Richard Stim, *Breach of Contract: Anticipatory Breach (Repudiation) Contracts can be broken as soon as one party indicates that it can't -- or won't -- meet its obligations*, Nolo, https://www.nolo.com/legal-encyclopedia/breach-of-contract-anticipatory-breach-32653.html (last visited Feb. 20, 2018); *see also* Black's Law Dictionary: Pocket Edition 649 (4th ed. 2011)（この意味における Repudiation を Total Repudiation と表現する）．

[339] Blum, *supra* note 255, at 640; *see generally* Coast-To-Coast Fin. Corp. v. United States, 60 Fed. Cl. 707, 711 (Fed. Cl. 2004) ("The concepts of repudiation, total breach, and restitution are thus linked in contract law. If a party repudiates a contract at a time when there is still substantial performance remaining (other than simply payment of the contract price), or if a party commits a breach which the other party can treat as 'total,' then restitution can be an appropriate remedy.").

[340] *See, e.g.*, Dow Chem. Co. v. United States, 226 F.3d 1334, 1344 (Fed. Cir. 2000) ("The injured party can choose between terminating the contract or continuing it."); *see also* U.C.C. § 2-610 (Am. Law Inst. & Unif. Law Comm'n 2002).

[341] 他方契約当事者が損害軽減義務を負う根拠については，相手方契約当事者からの Repudiation に伴い，自己の損害を軽減する機会の提供を受けたとも評価できることを挙げるものがある．Stim, *supra* note 338.

[342] 「Ipso facto」は「by the very nature of the situation」を意味する．Kenneth A. Adams et al., *Termination-on-*

として執行力がないため[343]，Ipso Facto Clause に意義が認められるのは，相手方契約当事者が倒産状態にあるもののいまだ倒産手続きに入っていないような状況との関係であるといえる[344]。

d. Adequate Assurance の提供の懈怠に基づく契約の解除

14.3(d)条においては，Buyer が Seller に対して「Adequate Assurance」を要求する権利，および，Buyer が Seller から「Adequate Assurance」を得られない場合における Buyer の契約の解除権を規定する。ここに「Adequate Assurance」[345]とは，相手方契約当事者の契約履行能力に疑義が生じた場合において要求する，将来の契約義務の履行に関する適切な保証をいう。

Adequate Assurance の要求は，一方契約当事者が他方契約当事者の契約上の義務の履行に合理的な疑問を持つにいたったものの，それが Anticipatory Repudiation に該当するとまでは言い難い場合(例えば，Buyer が資金繰りに窮しており，他の取引先との関係においてはすでに支払い遅延に陥っているとのうわさを聞いたような場合)において特に有用である。

すなわち，その場合，一方契約当事者は他方契約当事者に Adequate Assurance を要求するという手続きを踏むことで，その後に Adequate Assurance を得ることができない場合においては，その契約を撤回したものとみなしたうえで自己の契約上の義務の履行を拒否することが契約法上[346]認められるのである[347]。

Bankruptcy Provisions: Some Proposed Language, Business Law Today (June 2014), https://www.americanbar.org/publications/blt/2014/06/07_adams.html (last visited Feb. 23, 2018).

[343] *See, e.g.*, In re W.R. Grace & Co., 475 B.R. 34, 152 (D. Del. 2012) (first citing In re EBC I, Inc., 356 B.R. 631, 640 (Bankr. D. Del. 2006); then citing In re Lehman Bros. Holdings, Inc., 422 B.R. 407, 414-15 (Bankr. S.D.N.Y. 2010); then citing In re Hutchins, 99 B.R. 56, 57 (Bankr. D. Colo. 1989); and then citing In re Rose, 21 B.R. 272, 276-77 (Bankr. D.N.J. 1982) ("[I]t is well-established that *ipso facto* clauses are unenforceable as a matter of law under the Bankruptcy Code."). Ipso Facto Clause は 11 U.S.C. § 541(c), § 363(l), および § 365(e)(1) のおのおのとの関係で問題があるとされる。例外は，例えばある女優の映画出演契約のように，その契約の義務の履行が相手方契約当事者以外の者によって履行されることが合理的に予期されていないといえる場合 (Personal Service Exception という) である。11 U.S.C. § 365(e)(2) (2005)。

[344] この点に着目した場合，次のような規定を設けることになる。「Buyer may terminate this Agreement (including all related Individual Transactions in accordance with Section 5.2), on notice to Seller if Seller fails generally to pay its debts as they become due unless those debts are subject to a good-faith dispute as to liability or amount or acknowledges in writing that it is unable to do so.」。

[345] *See* U.C.C. § 2-609 (Am. Law Inst. & Unif. Law Comm'n 2002).

[346] 伝統的に Common Law において契約当事者が自己の契約義務の履行を控えることが認められるのは，相手方契約当事者が「Repudiation」に該当する言動をとった場合，すなわち，(1) 相手方契約当事者が(契約上の義務の履行期が到来しているにもかかわらず) その義務の履行を怠った場合，または，(2) 相手方契約当事者が(契約上の義務の履行期の到来前ではあるが) その義務を履行しない旨を明らかにし

e. Force Majeure Event の発生に基づく契約の解除

14.3(e)条は，Force Majeure Event が発生した結果 Seller の契約上の義務の履行に支障が生じたような場合において Buyer に解約権を認めるものである。

本契約の全体を通してみると，14.3(e)条と 18.5 条（Force Majeure Clause）とによって契約当事者間で Force Majeure Event にまつわるリスクの分担を図っていると評価できる。すなわち，Seller は契約上の義務の履行の遅延については 18.5 条のもと Buyer から責任を問われることはない一方，Buyer による解約権の行使の結果に伴う Seller 自身の損害については 14.3(e)条のもと受忍することになるのである。

f. Change of Control に基づく契約の解除

14.3(f)条は，Seller の所有者などについて変更が生じた場合（Change of Control という）において Buyer に契約の解除権を認める。一方契約当事者の新所有者の顔ぶれ次第では，他方契約当事者はもはや契約関係の継続を希望しなくなる場合もありうるということに配慮した規定である。ただし，「Change of Control」については確定的な定義がないため[348]，契約上でその定義を明確にすることが望ましい。

g. 自由意思に基づく契約の解除

14.3(g)条は，Termination for Default に該当する事象が見当たらない場合においても契約当事者の自由意志による解約権の行使を認める Termination for

---

た場合に限られる。Eric Fishman & Sara Stinson, *Protect Expectations with an Adequate Assurances Provision*, Pillsbury Winthrop Shaw Pittman LLP., https://www.pillsburylaw.com/images/content/4/2/v2/4295/ProtectExpectationswithanAdequateAssurancesProvision-CorporateCo.pdf (last visited Feb. 23, 2018). しかし，現代においては Adequate Assurance の概念を認める州も見受けられる (Colorado 州および Maine 州などは Adequate Assurance に関する権利を広く認める可能性を示唆する。*E.g.*, Carfield & Sons, Inc. v. Cowling, 616 P.2d 1008 (Ct. App. Colo. 1980); *e.g.*, Drinkwater v. Patten Realty Corp., 563 A.2d 772 (Sup. Jud. Ct. Me.))。New York 州は U.C.C.の適用対象である契約と類似した特徴を持つと判断した契約に対してのみ Adequate Assurance の概念を認める傾向にある。*E.g.*, Norcon Power Partners, L.P. v. Niagara Mohawk Power Corp., 92 N.Y.2d 458 (Ct. App. N.Y. 1998) (電力の売買契約に対する Adequate Assurance の概念を認めた事案)。これらに対して，West Virginia 州は U.C.C.の適用対象である契約以外には Adequate Assurance の概念を認めないとする。*E.g.*, Mollohan v. Black Rock Contracting, 160 W. Va. 446 (Sup. Ct. W. Va.)。なお，Restatement (Second) of Contracts は Adequate Assurance の概念を認める。Restement (Second) of Contracts § 251 (Am. Law Inst. 1981).

[347] U.C.C. § 2-609 (Am. Law Inst. & Unif. Law Comm'n 2002).

[348] *See* Jennifer Tsai, *What is Change of Control and How Does It Operate?* (Dec. 10, 2015), https://info.kirasystems.com/blog/what-is-change-of-control-and-how-does-it-operate (last visited Feb. 23, 2018).

Convenience を規定したものである[349]．したがって，例えばソフトウェア売買契約に関して，Seller がそのソフトウェアの開発費を負担することになっている場合など，契約の初期段階で一方契約当事者が相当程度の資金を投下する必要がある場合においては，相手方契約当事者に Termination for Convenience を認めることは高いリスクとなるため注意する必要がある．

i. 解約権行使に関する制約

Termination for Convenience Clause に基づく解約権の行使も無制約ではないが，その制約の程度については，対象契約が Federal Contract[350]であるのか，または，Federal Contract 以外の契約であるのかによって異なる[351]．

(a) 対象契約が Federal Contract である場合

例えば，連邦政府との契約においては，連邦政府の Termination for Convenience Clause に基づく解約権行使に関する裁量は非常に広く[352]，被解約者が解約に異議を唱えるためには，少なくともその権利行使が「Bad Faith」[353]に行われたこと，または，明確な裁量の濫用であることを証明する必要がある[354]．

---

[349] 連邦政府が契約した Construction Contract を Termination for Default に基づいて解約したものの実際には Termination for Default を構成する事実が認められなかった場合には，Termination for Convenience に基づく解約権が行使された旨を擬制する 48 CFR 52.249-8(g) (2012) はこの趣旨が顕著な例といえる．
[350] Federal Contract とは，例えば連邦政府と民間事業者との間の商品売買契約のように，連邦政府が直接の利益を受けることとなる契約をいう．*See* Univ. of Pitt., *Basics of Federal Contracting*, http://www.research.pitt.edu/fcs-basics-federal-contracting (last visited Jul. 18, 2018); *see also*, Michael F. Saunders, *Federal Contract Common Law and Article 2 of the Uniform Commercial Code: A Working Relationship*, 20 B.C.L. Rev. 680, 680 n. 3 (1979).
[351] Robert K. Cox, *Termination for Convenience Clauses – Limitless or Limited Authority to Terminate?* (Jul. 12, 2013), http://www.williamsmullen.com/print/43033 (last visited Feb. 23, 2018).
[352] *See, e.g.*, Torncello v. United States, 681 F.2d 756, 770 (Ct. Cl. 1982) (internal citation omitted) (連邦政府が Termination for Convenience に基づく解約権を行使した場合においては，その解約権行使の不当性に関して他方契約当事者に極めて高度の証明責任が課される旨を示した) ("[T]he government, unlike private parties, is assumed always to act in good faith, subject only to an extremely difficult showing by the plaintiff to the contrary. As this court has phrased it, in a case specifically involving convenience termination: it requires 'well-nigh irrefragable proof' to induce the court to abandon the presumption of good faith dealing.").
[353] 「Bad Faith」とは，契約を尊重する意思もまったくないような意図で契約関係に入ったような場合をいう．*See, e.g.*, Continental Collection & Disposal v. United States, 29 Fed. Cl. 644, 652 (Fed. Cl. 1993) ("Since good faith is presumed unless bad faith is demonstrated, the government is prevented only from engaging in actions motivated by a specific intent to harm the plaintiff."); *see also* Ann B. Graff & Ryan P. Stewart, *Model Jury Instructions: Construction Litigation*, ch. 11 Termination 182 (2d ed. 2015); *see generally* Vila & Son Landscaping Corp. v. Posen Constr. Inc., 99 So. 3d 563, 567 (Ct. App. Fla. 2012) (internal citation omitted) (「Bad Faith」は，契約法において一般に契約当事者に要求される Implied Covenant of Good Faith が果たされていないことを示すための Bad Faith (主観的な Bad Faith は要求されない) とは異なり，主観的な

(b) 対象契約が Federal Contract 以外の契約である場合

契約当事者による Termination for Convenience Clause に基づく解約権行使は，それが「Good Faith」[355]および「Fair Dealing」[356]にかなうものであることを条件として許容される[357]。

ii. 解約権行使に伴う被解約者に対する補償

Termination for Convenience に基づく解約は，被解約者に責めに帰すべき事由がない場合であっても認められるものである[358]。したがって，被解約者としては 14.4 条(c)のような規定を容易に受け入れるべきではなく，解約者による解約権行使時によって被った損害について一定範囲で填補が受けられるよう交渉すべきである[359]。

Bad Faith を要求するものである旨を示した) ("[C]ourts placed limits on the government's broad discretion to terminate for convenience so that its contracts would not fail for lack of consideration, and one of those limits is that the government may not exercise its discretion in bad faith; the concept of 'bad faith' as used in these cases refers to subjective bad faith .... In contrast, 'bad faith' in the context of the common law notion of breach of the implied covenant of good faith does not require a showing of subjective bad faith.").

[354] *See, e.g.*, John Reiner & Co. v. United States, 325 F.2d 438, 442 (Ct. Cl. 1963) ("Under an all-inclusive termination for convenience clause, the government has the right to terminate at will, and in the absence of bad faith or clear abuse of discretion the contracting officer's election to terminate is conclusive.").

[355] *See, e.g.*, Ram Eng'g & Constr., Inc. v. Univ. of Louisville, 127 S.W.3d 579, 586 (Sup. Ct. Ky. 2003) (Termination が「Good Faith」であるかどうかについては，Termination を必要とするような事情の変更があったかによって判断する旨を示した) ("The purposes and policies of the Code set forth in KRS 45A.010 are best implemented by requiring a substantial change in circumstances, thus ensuring that Kentucky's procurement system is one of quality and integrity.").

[356] *See, e.g.*, Questar Builders, Inc. v. CB Flooring, LLC, 410 Md. 241, 279 (Ct. App. Md. 2009) ("[W]e hold that termination for convenience rights, like that provided for in Paragraphs 12 and 14 of this Subcontract, may be enforceable, subject to the implied limitation that they be exercised in good faith and in accordance with fair dealing.") (ただし，連邦政府による Termination for Convenience Clause に基づく解約権の行使の妥当性の判断に関する「"well-nigh irrefragable proof" of wrongdoing to establish bad faith」の基準を本事案に用いることは適切ではないとしつつも，この考え方は Maryland 州が契約当事者である場合には適用されない旨を示している)。

[357] *See, e.g.*, Vila & Son Landscaping Corp. v. Posen Constr. Inc., 99 So. 3d 563 (Ct. App. Fla. 2012) (General Contractor が契約済みの Subcontractor よりもさらに良い価格条件を提示してきた新たな Subcontractor と契約するべく，Subcontractor との契約を Termination for Convenience Clause に基づいて解約することは Bad Faith ではない旨を示した事案)。

[358] そのような契約の解除権の行使は Termination for Convenience Clause に従って行われるものであるため，契約違反を構成するものでもなく，被解約者はその損害を請求することができないのが原則となる。*See generally* Cox, *supra* note 351.

[359] 契約解約までの間に被解約者が費やしたコストなどの請求を認める例が多いようである。その場合，次のような規定を設けることになる。「Upon termination of this Agreement in accordance with Section 14.3(g), Buyer shall pay to Seller the following amounts without duplication: (i) the price applicable to the Agreement or the Individual Transaction that have been completed and delivered; and (ii) the actual costs

CHAPTER 4 / ENDGAME PROVISIONS　*107*

> Section 14.5 Survival.
>
> Subject to the limitations and other provisions of this Agreement, the representations and warranties of the Parties contained herein shall survive the expiration or earlier termination of this Agreement.
>
> This Section 14.5 shall not be construed as a description of a contractual statute of limitations that required Buyer to commence litigation within the period of time.
>
> All other provisions of this Agreement will not survive the expiration or earlier termination of this Agreement.

4.4 Survival Clause

　ある契約が終了した場合，その契約に関する契約当事者の履行義務はそれ以降，存在しないものとなるのが原則である[360]．
　しかし，例えば，他方契約当事者から受領した秘密情報を秘密に保持する義務など，契約が終了したとしてもなお契約当事者の履行義務の存続が必要なものもある．Survival Clause はこの点を考慮し，特定の条項については契約終了後も引き続き効力を有する旨を規定するものである．

　・Statute of Limitations との関係
　Survival Clause は一方契約当事者の履行義務を継続させることになるわけであるから，他方契約当事者は Survival Clause が自己の権利の保護にとって有益なものであると理解することになろう．しかし，この理解が必ずしも妥

---

incurred by Seller in accordance with the Agreement or the Individual Transaction for the actual cost of work in process and materials. Payments made under this Section [14.4(d)] shall not exceed the aggregate price applicable to the Agreement or the Individual Transaction.]; *cf.* Mega Constr. Co. v. United States, 29 Fed. Cl. 396, 475 (Fd. Cl. 1993) (quoting Dairy Sales Corp. v. United States, 219 Ct. Cl. 431, 593 (Ct. Cl. 1979)) (建設業者が連邦政府から請け負った郵便局の建設契約が Termination for Convenience に基づき連邦政府によって解約された事案において，建設業者による履行済み部分に関する営業利益の請求については認める一方，末履行部分の営業利益の請求については認められない旨を示した) ("Even under a termination for convenience, the contractor may only recover profit on work it actually performed. Anticipated but unearned profit is never recoverable.").

[360] Hellmuth & Johnson, *Understanding Contract Termination* (Nov. 15, 2011), http://www.hjlawfirm.com/blog/53-understanding-contract-termination (last visited Mar. 26, 2018).

当しない場合もある．つまり，①Survival Clause によって延長されたある契約条項の効力存続期間が本来の法律上の時効期間よりも短い場合で，かつ，②Survival Clause が時効期間自体を短縮する意図で用意されたものであると認められた場合，Buyer は，Survival Clause によって延長された期間内に Survival Clause の対象である権利を Seller に対して主張しなければ，その権利自体を失うことになりかねないとされるのである[361]．

したがって，契約当事者は，14.5 条のように，Survival Clause を上記の要件②との関係に留意した規定を設ける必要がある．

---

[361] *See, e.g.*, State Street Bank and Trust Co. v. Denman Tire Corp. 240 F.3d 83 (1st Cir. 2001) (「[S]eller's representations and warranties shall expire on the second anniversary of closing imposed limitations period on claims」との規定について，対象期間内での訴訟提起を求めた契約上の時効規定である旨示した); *cf.* Hurlbut v. Christiano 405 N.Y.S.2d 871 (Sup. Ct. N.Y.) (Nursing home の売買契約において Buyer から Seller に提供された Buyer による法令の遵守に関する表明保証の違反が問われた事案．「The parties hereto further agree that the representations and warranties set forth in Sections 4.01(d) and 4.03(g) of the Purchase Agreement between them dated February 29, 1972 shall survive the closing for a period of three (3) years.」との規定について，この規定は時効を短縮するために用意されたものではなく，表明保証に関する違反事実があった場合においては Seller から Buyer に対する対象期間内の通知を求めたものである旨を示した)．

CHAPTER 5 / OTHER SUBSTANTIVE PROVISIONS

Other Substantive Provisions は，Action Provisions と同様に，契約当事者の権利および義務を規定するものの，その権利および義務の内容は画一的なものとなる傾向にある．

ARTICLE 15
CONFIDENTIALITY

5.1 Confidentiality Clause

Confidentiality Clause は，対象契約に関して開示される秘密情報の保護に関する規定である．例えば，Buyer にとっては注文数量，Seller にとっては販売価格などが秘密情報に該当しうる．通常の取引においては秘密保持契約を別に締結していることも多いと思われるが，それと明確な適用領域の区分がなされているかにかかわらず，本契約のような製品売買契約においては Confidentiality Clause が設けられていることが多い．

a. 秘密情報と Trade Secrets

Confidentiality Clause との関係で理解しておくべき事項として，秘密情報と Trade Secrets との関係がある．ある秘密情報が Trade Secrets[362]に該当する場合は Trade Secret Law[363]および Common Law による保護を受けることになるためである．ここにある秘密情報が Trade Secrets に該当するといえるための要件は，①情報保持者にとって有価値であること，および，②秘密性があることである[364]．

---

[362] Restatement (Third) of Unfair Competition § 39 (Am. Law. Inst. 1995) において，Trade Secret は次のように定義されている．"A trade secret is any information that can be used in the operation of a business or other enterprise and that is sufficiently valuable and secret to afford an actual or potential economic advantage over others."．

[363] Trade Secret Law は伝統的には州法の領域である．2014 年 11 月時点で New York 州および Massachusetts 州を除く 48 州が Uniform Trade Secrets Act を採用している．Ronald T. Coleman, Jr. et al., *Trade Secrets – The Basic Principles and Issues. ABA Litigation Section "Core Knowledge" Project* (Nov. 2014), 1, https://www.americanbar.org/content/dam/aba/publications/litigation_committees/intellectual/trade-secrets-the-basic-principles-and-issues.authcheckdam.pdf (last visited Feb. 20, 2018). なお，Trade Secrets に関する連邦法としては Defend Trade Secrets Act of 2016 および Economic Espionage Act of 1996 が用意されている．

[364] *Id.* at 3.

b. Confidentiality Clause の意義

　Confidentiality Clause の存在は上記の要件②を裏付けるものであり，対象情報が Trade Secrets に該当することを支える手段として有用である[365]。また，Trade Secret Law は，Trade Secrets の所有者に Trade Secrets の受領者などによる Misappropriation[366]に対する制裁を認めるものにすぎず，例えばリバースエンジニアリングのような行為を抑止することはできない[367]。Confidentiality Clause はそのような行為をも広く包含することで Trade Secrets のさらなる保護を図ることができる。

　また，ある秘密情報が Trade Secrets に該当しない場合においては，Confidentiality Clause は Trade Secret Law などの法律では保護のない情報に対して新たに保護を図るものであるといえる[368]。

Section 15.1 Scope of Confidential Information.

From time to time during the Term, either Party (the "Disclosing Party") may disclose or make available to the other Party (the "Receiving Party") information about its business affairs, Products and services, Forecasts, confidential information, and materials comprising or relating to Intellectual Property Rights, Trade Secrets, third-party confidential information, and other sensitive or proprietary information. Such information, as well as the terms of this Agreement, whether orally or in written, electronic, or other form or media constitutes "Confidential

---

[365] *Id.* at 5 (citing Convolve, Inc. v. Compaq Computer Corp., 527 Fed. Appx. 910 (Fed. Cir. 2013)) ("[I]t helps if the plaintiff has identified the particular information or material as being confidential or proprietary in the normal course of its business or in connection with a specific disclosure under a non-disclosure agreement, rather than trying to make the argument for the first time in litigation."). ただし，Confidentiality Clause の存在が Trade Secret Law に基づく救済を受けるための必要条件というわけではない。*See, e.g.*, Nilssen v. Motorola, Inc., 963 F. Supp. 664, 679-80 (N.D. Ill. 1997) ("While an express confidentiality agreement may certainly suffice to define the duty of confidentiality necessary for action under Act § 2(b)(2)(B)(II), the existence of such an agreement is not a prerequisite to such an action").
[366] Trade Secrets の取得者による行為のうち，自己の利益を図り，かつ，不当に Trade Secrets の所有者の権利を毀損する目的でなされるものをいい，Common Law 上の不法行為に該当する。*Black's Law Dictionary: Pocket Edition* 487 (4th ed. 2011).
[367] Coleman, *supra* note 363, at 7.
[368] さらに，Confidentiality Clause が存在しない場合であっても，当事者間に客観的に Confidentiality に関する合意があるといえる場合においては，黙示の秘密保持に関する合意が認められる (Implied Duty of Nondisclosure という)。Woodrow Hartzog, *Reviving Implied Confidentiality*, 89 Ind. L.J., 763, 775-94 (2014), http://ilj.law.indiana.edu/articles/12-Hartzog.pdf (last visited Feb. 22, 2018).

CHAPTER 5 / OTHER SUBSTANTIVE PROVISIONS *111*

> Information" hereunder; provided, however, Confidential Information must be marked as "confidential", "proprietary", or similar legend. If disclosed in verbal or visual form, Confidential Information must be reduced to writing, marked, and delivered to the Receiving Party within thirty (30) days.

5.2 Confidential Information である旨の表示

　Confidentiality Clause においては、秘密情報に「Confidential である旨の表示」を付する旨要求することが適当である[369]。「Confidential である旨の表示」は、Receiving Party にとっては自己が Confidentiality Clause に基づき負う義務の範囲を明確にするという利益をもたらし、また、Disclosing Party にとっては Trade Secrets の秘密性に関する要件の補強となるという利益をもたらす。

　なお、例えば、Disclosing Party が自己の開示する秘密情報に Confidential Information である旨の表示を怠るなど、実務上 Confidentiality Clause に従った取り扱いがされなかった場合においては、その秘密情報は Confidentiality Clause による救済はもちろん、Common Law による救済も受けられなくなる可能性があるため[370]注意深く対応しなければならない。

> Section 15.2 Exclusions.
>
> Confidential Information excludes information that, at the time of disclosure and as established by documentary evidence:
>
> (a) is or becomes generally available to and known by the public other than as a result of, directly or indirectly, any breach of this Section 15 by the Receiving Party or any of its Representatives;

---

[369] Coleman, *supra* note 363, at 5.
[370] *See, e.g., Nilssen*, 963 F. Supp., 680 (N.D. Ill. 1997) (internal citation omitted) (Confidentiality Agreement において要求される Confidential Information である旨の表示を欠いた秘密情報については Implied Duty of Nondisclosure も認められない旨を示した) ("[B]ecause a confidentiality agreement is a valid contract enforceable according to its terms, Illinois law precludes the finding of 'any implied duty of nondisclosure' that 'would directly contradict the express agreement of the parties'."); *see also e.g., Convolve, Inc.*, 527 Fed. Appx., 925 (Fed. Cir. 2013) ("If the parties have contracted the limits of their confidential relationship regarding a particular subject matter, one party should not be able to circumvent its contractual obligations or impose new ones over the other via some implied duty of confidentiality.").

(b) is or becomes available to the Receiving Party on a non-confidential basis from a third-party source, provided that such third party is not and was not prohibited from disclosing such Confidential Information;

(c) was known by or in the possession of the Receiving Party or its Representatives before being disclosed by or on behalf of the Disclosing Party; or

(d) was or is independently developed by the Receiving Party without reference to or use of, in whole or in part, any of the Disclosing Party's Confidential Information.

Section 15.3 Compelled Disclosure.

This Section 15 will not prevent disclosure of Confidential Information in response to a valid order of a court or other governmental body or to comply with regulatory obligations; provided, however, the Receiving Party shall promptly give prior written notice to the Disclosing Party to the extent permitted by law or such order, so that the Receiving Party, if necessary, may seek a protective order or other appropriate remedy requiring that the Confidential Information or the documents so disclosed be used only for the purpose for which the order was issued.

5.3 秘密保持義務の不発生

例えば Seller が Buyer に対象製品の価格を秘密情報であるとして開示した場合において，実はそれら価格情報はすでに Seller のホームページに掲載されていたとする。この場合，Buyer としてはすでに一般に公開されている情報について Seller から直接開示を受けたことのみをもって Confidentiality Clause のもとで秘密情報として取り扱う義務を負うことは納得がいかないであろう[371]． 15.2

---

[371] 一般に入手できる情報については，Trade Secrets との関係においても「秘密性があること」の要件を満たさないといえる. *See, e.g.* Pope v. Alberto-Culver Co., 296 Ill. App. 3d 512, 515 (App. Ct. Ill. 1998) (internal citation omitted) ("Under the Act, whether the information sought to be protected qualifies as a trade secret focuses fundamentally on the secrecy of such information. Under the first statutory requirement, the information at issue must be substantially secret to impart economic value to both its owner and its competitors because of its relative secrecy. This requirement precludes trade secret protection for information generally

条の規定する Exclusions Clause は，このように Confidentiality Clause のもと Receiving Party に秘密情報としての管理を要求することが相当といえない場合において，Receiving Party を Confidentiality Clause の規定する秘密保持義務から解放するものである．

a. 公的機関の要請に基づいた情報開示

Confidentiality Clause において散見されるのが，Exclusions Clause の対象事由のひとつに，裁判所など公的機関から秘密情報の開示要請を受けた場合を含めているものである[372]．たしかにそれら公的機関からの開示要請については適宜それに従わざるをえないから，その開示行為が Confidentiality Clause 違反を構成しないよう契約上の規定を設ける必要がある．しかし，秘密情報の開示はあくまでその公的機関の要請との関係とでのみ許されるべきであり，その要請を受けたことをもって，以降，対象情報が秘密情報に該当しないものとして取り扱われるべきではない．

したがって，15.3 条のように，公的機関からの開示要請があった場合については Exclusions Clause とは別の条項を設け，公的機関からの要請との関係でのみ，対象情報の開示が Confidentiality Clause 違反を構成しないように手当てすることが適当と思われる[373]．

b. 法律上の要請に基づいた情報開示

15.3 条においては，Receiving Party が法律または規則などを遵守するうえで必要となる場合における秘密情報の開示も許容している．しかし，契約当事者としては自己の開示する秘密情報の重要性も考慮した上で，その対象がいたずらに広汎とならぬよう注意すべき場合がある[374]．

---

known or understood within an industry even if not to the public at large.").

[372] 例えば，次のような規定を設けている場合がある．「The obligations set forth in Sections 15 above shall be inapplicable to any information which … (e) is required to be disclosed by the receiving party pursuant to a subpoena or similar order from a court, agency or other similar authority, provided that the receiving party gives to the disclosing party reasonable notice of such required disclosure to allow the disclosing party to defend against such subpoena or order.」．

[373] *See generally* Richard Harroch, *The Key Elements Of Non-Disclosure Agreements*, Forbes Entrepreneurs (Mar. 10, 2016), https://www.forbes.com/sites/allbusiness/2016/03/10/the-key-elements-of-non-disclosure-agreements/#30661cf7627d (last visited Feb. 22, 2018) (公的機関からの要請があった場合については，Exclusions Clause とは別の検討事項である旨を示唆する)．

[374] Marine Midland Realty Credit Corp. v. LLMD of Mich., Inc., 821 F. Supp. 370 (E.D. Pa 1993) (一方契約当事者が，自ら任意に開始した訴訟手続きにおいて他方契約当事者の秘密情報の開示を Confidentiality Clause の Exclusions Clause (「certain information would be kept confidential unless required by law or judicial or administrative order or regulation」) に基づき行おうとした事案．他方契約当事者は，契約当事者が自己

c. Residual Clause

　Receiving Party は必ずしも Disclosing Party とのみその秘密情報に関するビジネスを行っているとは限らず，むしろ，同種のビジネスを他の顧客向けにも行っていたり，または，同種ビジネスに関する自社単独での開発活動を実施していることも少なくない．

　そのような場合，Receiving Party は，自己の有する情報が果たして Disclosing Party から受領した秘密情報であるのかそうでないのかを区分できない可能性があるし，また，そのような情報を Receiving Party の秘密保持義務の対象とするのでは Receiving Party の活動を大きく制約することになってしまう．そこで，秘密情報のうち Receiving Party が意図せず自己の記憶として有する秘密情報（Residual Information という）についてはその自由な利用を認める[375] Residual Clause[376]を設ける場合がある．

　しかし，Residual Clause の設定は Disclosing Party に不利益をもたらしかねない．例えば，Receiving Party が秘密情報を当初の目的外に利用した場合または第三者に開示した場合において，Disclosing Party がその行為は Confidentiality Clause に違反する旨を指摘したとする．この場合，Receiving Party から，その情報は Residual Information に該当し，Residual Clause においてその利用が認められているとの反論がされたならば，Disclosing Party がそれを否定すること（すなわち，その秘密情報は Receiving Party が意図せず自己の記憶としていた情報ではない旨を証明すること）は非常に困難なのである[377]．

　したがって，Disclosing Party は Residual Clause の利用に関する制約などを設けるべく交渉することが推奨される[378]．

の意思で開始した訴訟手続きにおける情報開示は Exclusions Clause に該当しない旨を主張したが，裁判所は，契約当事者間で格別に Exclusions Clause の適用対象を限定していない限り，そのような縮小解釈はされない旨を示した）．

[375] Rahul Kapoor & Shokoh H. Yaghoubi, *Residuals Clauses in IP Agreements and NDAs*, The Nat'l L. Rev. (Oct. 26, 2017), https://www.natlawreview.com/article/residuals-clauses-ip-agreements-and-ndas (last visited Mar. 2, 2018).

[376] 例えば次のような規定を設けることになる．「Receiving Party shall be free to use the residuals resulting from access or work with the Confidential Information of the Disclosing Party for any purpose; provided, that the Receiving Party shall not disclose the Confidential Information which excludes residuals except as permitted pursuant to the terms of this Article 15.」．

[377] *Id.* Kapoor, *supra* note 375.

[378] *Id.* (Residual Clause に関する制約として，(1) Disclosing Party から Receiving Party に向けた Residual Information に関するライセンス権を供与するものではないこと，(2) Residual Information の活用は Receiving Party の内部でのみ許容されるものであって第三者に開示することまでは認められないこと，

d.「To the extent of permitted by law」

15.3 条のように,「法律によって許容される限り」の意味で,「to the extent permitted by law」との一節が契約文中に挿入される場合がある.「To the extent of permitted by law」は, ある規定が法律上何らかの制約を課されうる場合においてもなお, その法律による制約を受けない範囲において, その規定の有効性を確保することを目的とする[379].

Section 15.4 Protection of Confidential Information.

The Receiving Party shall, for three (3) years from disclosure of such Confidential Information:

(a) protect and safeguard the confidentiality of the Disclosing Party's Confidential Information with at least the same degree of care as the Receiving Party would protect its own Confidential Information, but in no event with less than a commercially reasonable degree of care;

(b) not use the Disclosing Party's Confidential Information, or permit it to be accessed or used, for any purpose other than to exercise its

---

または, (3) 秘密情報のうち, 特に重要なものについては, Residual Information の対象外であることを明示することなどを挙げる).

[379] *See, e.g.*, Brooks v. Judlau Contr., Inc., 11 N.Y.3d 204 (Ct. App. N.Y. 2008) (Contractor が Subcontractor に対して Indemnification Clause に基づく補償を求めた事案. Indemnification Clause の一部は次のとおりであった. "The Subcontractor shall, <u>to the fullest extent permitted by law</u>, hold the Contractor and the Owner, their agents, employees and representatives harmless from any and all liability, costs, damages, attorneys' fee, and expenses from any claims or causes of action of whatever nature arising from the Subcontractor's work, including all claims relating to its subcontractors, suppliers or employees, or by reason of any claim or dispute of any person or entity for damages from any cause directly or indirectly relating to any action or failure to act by the Subcontractor, its representatives, employees, subcontractors, or suppliers.". Subcontractor は「to the fullest extent permitted by law」は, 州法で禁止される Indemnitee の過失に基づく損害に関する Indemnification までをも包含して Indemnification を認める趣旨であり, そのような一節を含む Indemnification Clause は無効である旨を主張した. しかし, 裁判所は,「to the fullest extent permitted by law」は, むしろ Indemnification の適用範囲を州法で許容される範囲内に縮小するものであって, Indemnification Clause を無効とするものではない旨を示した); *but see* Kenneth A. Adams, *"To the Extent Permitted by Law"*, Adams on Contract Drafting (Jan. 21, 2011), http://www.adamsdrafting.com/to-the-extent-permitted-by-law/ (last visited Apr. 11, 2018) (「to the fullest extent permitted by law」には実質的な意義が認められない旨を指摘する).

rights or perform its obligations under this Agreement; and

(c) not disclose any such Confidential Information to any Person, except to the Receiving Party's Representatives who need to know the Confidential Information to assist the Receiving Party, or act on its behalf, to exercise its rights or perform its obligations under this Agreement.

Section 15.5 Term.

The Receiving Party shall be responsible for any breach of this Section 15 caused by any of its Representatives. The provisions of this Section 15 shall survive termination or expiration of this Agreement for any reason for a period of three (3) years after such termination or expiration. On the expiration or earlier termination of this Agreement, or at any time during or after the Term, at the Disclosing Party's written request, the Receiving Party and its Representatives shall, under Section 14.4(b)(i), promptly return or destroy all Confidential Information and copies thereof that it has received under this Agreement.

5.4 秘密保持義務の継続期間

　Disclosing Party としては，Receiving Party にどの程度の期間，秘密保持義務を負わせるべきであろうか．この点については，秘密保持期間の始期とそれ以降の秘密保持期間の設定が検討事項として挙げられる．

　a. 秘密保持期間の始期
　Buyer としては，例えば，本契約終了直前に Buyer が Seller に開示した製品の仕様情報などについては，本契約終了後もなお相当期間，Seller が Buyer の競合企業に開示するといった事態を防止できるように手当てする必要がある．したがって，Disclosing Party にとっては，対象契約の締結日を秘密保持期間の始期とするのではなく，Disclosing Party から Receiving Party に対する秘密情報の開示時点を秘密保持期間の始期とする旨規定する[380]ことが得策と

---

[380] See generally Aileene Koh, *Duration Clauses in Non-Disclosure Agreements*, EveryNDA (Nov. 15, 2017),

思われる。

　b. 秘密保持期間の設定
　秘密保持期間をどの程度のものとすべきかについては，(1) 無制限のものとする，または，(2) 一定期間のものとする，という選択肢があるが，以下のとおり，おのおのについて課題がある。

　　i. 秘密保持期間を無制限とした場合
　Disclosing Party としては，Receiving Party による秘密保持義務の存続期間を無制限とできれば自己の秘密情報を手厚く保護できるとも思える。しかし，Trade Secrets に該当しない秘密情報についてはあくまでその秘密情報を保護するに合理的な範囲での制約が許容されるにすぎない[381]。
　したがって，Trade Secrets に該当しない秘密情報について無制限に秘密保持義務を負わせる内容を有する Confidentiality Clause は不合理であるとしてその執行力が認められない可能性がある[382]。これに対して，Trade Secrets については，その秘密性が確保されている限り保護に値するため[383]，Receiving Party に無制限の秘密保持義務を負わせることも認められうる[384]。

　　ii. 秘密保持期間を一定期間とした場合
　秘密情報が Trade Secrets である場合，Disclosing Party としては，Trade Secret Law における保護を引き続き受けることのできるよう，Receiving Party にも秘密情報を Trade Secrets として取り扱うよう義務付ける必要がある。ところが，Confidentiality Clause において秘密保持期間を一定期間として設定した場合，その秘密保持期間満了日以降，その秘密情報をどのよう

---

https://everynda.com/blog/duration-clauses-non-disclosure/ (Feb. 21, 2018).

[381] 秘密保持義務は性質上，取引に関する制限 (restraint of trade) と関連してくるため，相手方契約当事者に対する秘密保持義務の負荷はその秘密情報を保護するために合理的に必要と認められる限度でのみ許容されるのである。*See generally* Alex Ross, *International report - Protecting trade secrets using non-disclosure agreements*, Global Business Media Group, http://www.iam-media.com/reports/detail.aspx?g=8faaadd8-a19f-418b-85a7-eb9c3a737694 (last visited Feb. 21, 2018).

[382] Mike Tobin, *Time Limits in Confidentiality Agreements: Traps for the Unwary*, Parker Poe Adams & Bernstein LLP (Oct. 30, 2013), http://pcgc.parkerpoe.com/time-limits-in-confidentiality-agreements-traps-for-the-unwary/ (last visited Feb. 21, 2018); *see, e.g.*, Lasership, Inc. v. Watson, 79 Va. Cir. 205 (Cir. Ct. Va. 2009); *see also e.g.*, Augusta Medical Complex, Inc. v. Blue Cross of Kansas, Inc., 227 Kan. 469 (Sup. Ct. Kan. 1980).

[383] *See* Fla. Stat. § 542.335(1)(d)(1) (2011); *see also* Fla. Stat. § 542.335(1)(e) (2011); *see also e.g.*, Zodiac Records, Inc. v. Choice Envtl. Servs., LLC, 112 So. 3d 587, 588-89 (Ct. App. Fla. 2013) (Florida 州法において は Trade Secrets と Trade Secrets に該当しない秘密情報との間において，秘密保持義務を課すことのできる期間に差を設けていることを指摘する)。

[384] Tobin, *supra* note 382.

に取り扱うかは基本的に Receiving Party の裁量に委ねられる．このため，その秘密情報はもはや「秘密であること」の要件を満たさないとして Trade Secrets とは認められない可能性を生じさせる[385]．

これらをふまえると，秘密保持期間の設定は Trade Secrets に該当する秘密情報と Trade Secrets に該当しない秘密情報とで区分することが最適と思われる．多くの Trade Secrets の開示が想定される場合においてはこの点に配慮した規定も十分検討に値するであろう[386]．

Section 15.6 [Intentionally Omitted]

5.5 契約書の準備段階における条項の削除

契約書の起案から締結に至るまでの過程においては契約当事者間でさまざまな条項について交渉が重ねられることも少なくなく，結果として一部の条項についてそのすべてを削除することとなるといった事態も予想される．しかし，契約書においては他の条項が(条項番号を用いて)削除対象となった条項を引用するなどしていることもあるため[387]，あらためて条項番号のすべてについて再度見直しを要するといった事態となりかねない．もっとも，そのような作業は煩雑なばかりでなく，作業の誤りによって契約書の解釈に関する問題を生じさせる原因ともなりうるから，可能であれば回避したいという場合もある．

そこで，削除対象となる条項の本文は削除しつつ，条項番号については，[Intentionally Omitted][388] と添えたうえでそのまま維持する方法[389]をとることが選択肢のひとつとなるのである[390]．

---

[385] *Id.*

[386] この場合，次のような規定を設けることになる．「All Confidential Information shall be safeguarded by Reciving Party as required by this Agreement for a period of three (3) years from the date of disclosure to Receiving Party. All Trade Secret information shall be safeguarded by Receiving Party as required by this Agreement in perpetuity or for so long as such information remains a Trade Secret under applicable law, whichever occurs first.」．

[387] 例えば 15.5 条においては 14.4(b)(i) 条を引用している．

[388] Kenneth A. Adams, "*Intentionally Omitted*", Adams on Contract Drafting (Sep. 27, 2007), http://www.adamsdrafting.com/intentionally-omitted/ (last visited Sep. 13, 2018); Adams, *supra* note 4, at 147.

[389] *E.g.*, $7,072,488,605 Secured Credit Agreement among General Motors Company, as the borrower, Guarantors, and The United States Department of the Treasury, as the Lender Dated as of July 10, 2009, Sec. 2.2., https://www.treasury.gov/initiatives/financial-stability/TARP-Programs/automotive-programs/Documents/New_GM_Company_090909.pdf (last visited Sep. 13, 2018).

[390] そのほか，[Intentionally Omitted]に代えて[Reserved]と記載する方法も見受けられる．*See* Dana H.

ARTICLE 16
LIMITATION OF LIABILITY

Section 16 No Liability for Consequential or Indirect Damages.

EXCEPT FOR LIABILITY FOR INDEMNIFICATION, LIABILITY FOR BREACH OF CONFIDENTIALITY, OR LIABILITY FOR INFRINGEMENT OR MISAPPROPRIATION OF INTELLECTUAL PROPERTY RIGHTS, NEITHER PARTY NOR ITS REPRESENTATIVES IS LIABLE FOR CONSEQUENTIAL, INDIRECT, INCIDENTAL, SPECIAL, EXEMPLARY, PUNITIVE, OR ENHANCED DAMAGES, ARISING OUT OF OR RELATING TO ANY BREACH OF THIS AGREEMENT, WHETHER OR NOT SUCH DAMAGES WERE FORESEEABLE OR SUCH PARTY WAS ADVISED OF THE POSSIBILITY OF SUCH DAMAGES, REGARDLESS OF THE LEGAL OR EQUITABLE THEORY (CONTRACT, TORT OR OTHERWISE) UPON WHICH THE CLAIM IS BASED, AND NOTWITHSTANDING THE FAILURE OF ANY AGREED OR OTHER REMEDY OF ITS ESSENTIAL PURPOSE.

5.6 Limitation of Liability Clause

　Limitation of Liability Clause は契約責任の制限を目的とするところ，これは責任対象となる「Damage」の範囲を制限すること，または，責任金額を制限することによって達成できる[391]．前者については，例えば，責任範囲を Direct Damages の範囲に限るものとし，Incidental Damages または Consequential Damages といった損害に対する責任を否定するのである．16条はこの責任対象の制限に関する規定である．後者については，例えば，自己の責任金額につい

Shultz, *What Does "Reserved" mean in a Contract?* (Oct. 12, 2018), The High-touch Legal Services, https://danashultz.com/2018/10/12/what-does-reserved-mean-in-a-contract/ (last visited Oct. 20, 2018).

[391] Kenneth M. Gorenberg et al., *Cite a Drafting Enforceable Limitation of Liability Clauses in Business Contracts Limiting Potential Damages and Avoiding Enforceability Pitfalls With Carefully Negotiated Provisions*, Media.straffordpub.com. (Mar. 3, 2015), 10, http://media.straffordpub.com/products/drafting-enforceable-limitation-of-liability-clauses-in-business-contracts-2015-03-03/presentation.pdf (last visited Jan. 29, 2018).

ては，対象取引の金額[392]または特定の金額を上限とするといったものがある．

・Limitation of Liability Clause に関する制約
契約当事者が Limitation of Liability Clause に基づく自己の責任の制限を主張するためには，以下の事項に該当しないことが求められる．また，それら制約との兼ね合いも考慮して，Limitation of Liability Clause は大文字または太文字など明示の方法で規定することが推奨される[393]．

i.「Unconscionable」ではないこと
Limitation of Liability Clause を設けること自体は，U.C.C.においても認められている[394]．しかし，それが Consequential Damages を責任対象から除外することになる場合，または，Consequential Damages に関する責任金額を制限することに場合においては，そのような責任の制限が「Unconscionable ではない」といえる必要がある[395]．

例えば，一般消費者向けの契約において人身損害に関する Consequential Damages を制限する契約は，「Unconscionable」であるとの推定が働く[396]．また，取引などに基づく力関係に差があると認められる契約当事者間におい

---

[392] この場合，次のような規定を設けることになる．「To the extent permitted by applicable law, in no event shall the liability for damages of Seller exceed the amounts actually paid to Seller by Buyer.」
[393] TermsFeed, *Draft Limitation or Exclusion of Liability clauses* (Oct. 23, 2016), https://termsfeed.com/blog/draft-limitation-exclusion-liability-clauses/#How_to_draft_the_clauses (last visited Jan. 31, 2018) (California 州においては Construction Contract に関する Limitation of Liability Clause の規定は契約当事者間の「negotiating and expressly agreeing」に基づくものである場合にはじめて許容される (Cal. Civ. § 2782.5). この「negotiating」は契約当事者が Limitation of Liability Clause に同意，拒否，または変更の申し入れを行う「適切な機会」があったことをいう (Markborough Cal. v. Superior Court, 227 Cal. App. 3d 705 (Ct. App. Cal. 1991)). そして，この「適切な機会」の存在を裏付ける意味で Limitation of Liability Clause の書体自体を変えることが推奨される旨を指摘する); *see, e.g.*, Nat'l Info. Solutions, Inc. v. Cord Moving & Storage Co., 475 S.W.3d 690, 692 (Ct. App. Miss. 2015) (自己の過失に基づく行為に関する責任についても Limitation of Liability Clause の対象とするためには，その旨を明確に規定する必要がある旨を示した) ("In general, for a party to effectively release itself from or limit liability for its own negligence, the language of the contract must be clear, unequivocal, conspicuous and include the word 'negligence' or its equivalent."); *cf.* Moving & Storage Co., 475 S.W.3d 690, 692 (Ct. App. Miss. 2015) (両契約当事者が同程度の契約交渉能力を持った事業者であるような場合においては，不明瞭な部分を有する Limitation of Liability Clause も有効であると理解される旨を示唆した).
[394] U.C.C. § 2-719 (Am. Law Inst. & Unif. Law Comm'n 2002).
[395] *Id.* § 2-719(3); *see, e.g.*, Gladden v. Boykin, 402 S.C. 140, 144 (Sup. Ct. Cal. 2013) ("[U]nconscionability is defined as the absence of meaningful choice on the part of one party due to one-sided contract provisions, together with terms that are so oppressive that no reasonable person would make them and no fair and honest person would accept them.").
[396] U.C.C. § 2-719(3) (Am. Law Inst. & Unif. Law Comm'n 2002).

て規定された Limitation of Liability Clause は,「Unconscionable」であるとして, その効果を認められない場合がある[397].

ii. Willful Misconduct, Gross Negligence, または Fraud に基づく責任を対象とするものではないこと

一方契約当事者が自己の故意, 重過失, または詐欺的行為によって相手方契約当事者に損害を生じさせた場合[398], Limitation of Liability Clause に基づく自己の責任の制限を主張することは認められない場合がある[399].

iii. Public Policy に反するものではないこと

Construction Contract のような専門的サービスの提供に関する契約において, 専門的サービス提供業者が Limitation of Liability Clause に基づく責任制限を主張することは, Public Policy の観点から認められない場合もある[400].

ARTICLE 17
INSURANCE OBLIGATIONS

Section 17.1 Insurance.

Without limiting Seller's indemnification obligations under this

---

[397] *But see* Keis George LLP, *Liquidated Damages and Limitation of Liability Clauses*, (Jul. 27, 2016), https://www.keisgeorge.com/news/2016/07/27/liquidated-damages-and-limitation-of-liability-clauses/ (last visited Feb.23, 2018) (両契約当事者が事業者である場合, 契約当事者間における取引関係などに基づく力関係の差を根拠として, Limitation of Liability Clause が「Unconscionable」であるとの主張が認められる可能性はかなり低い旨を指摘する).

[398] Jeremy P. Brummond & Chloe Mickel, *Limitation of Liability Provisions*, http://apps.americanbar.org/dch/thedl.cfm?.../LimitationofLiabilityProvisions111819.pdf (last visited Jan. 30, 2018).

[399] *See, e.g.*, Sale v. Slitz, 998 S.W.2d 159, 164 (Ct. App. Miss. 1999) ("A limitation of liability provision within a contract is ineffective in a cause of action where the conduct is willful and wanton.").

[400] *See, e.g.*, Lucier v. Williams, 366 N.J. Super. 485, 491 (Sup. Ct. N.J. 2003) ("[C]ourts have not hesitated to strike limited liability clauses that are unconscionable or in violation of public policy."; *see also e.g.*, Core-Mark Midcontinent, Inc. v. Sonitrol Corp., 300 P.3d 963, 970 (internal citation omitted) (Limitation of Liability を主張する者の行為の性質に着目しつつも, その適用を否定する直接の理由を Public Policy においた) ("Because of the egregiously wrongful nature of the conduct, enforcing a limitation of liability provision to shield a party from the consequences of such conduct is deemed to be contrary to public policy. Moreover, limiting liability for '[a] willful failure to monitor th[e] system or a deliberate disregard of a contractual duty would not be consistent with the intended protection service set forth in the contract.").

> Agreement, during the Term and for a period of five (5) years thereafter, Seller shall, at its own expense, maintain and carry in full force and effect, at least the following types and amounts of insurance coverage, subject to the requirements set forth in Section 17.2:
>
> (a) Commercial General Liability Insurance with limits no less than one million (US$1,000,000) for each occurrence and two million (US$2,000,000) in the aggregate, including bodily injury and property damage and products and completed operations and advertising liability, which policy will include contractual liability coverage insuring the activities of Seller under this Agreement;
>
> (b) Worker's Compensation and Employer's Liability Insurance with limits no less than the greater of (i) one million (US$1,000,000); or (ii) the minimum amount required by applicable law; and
>
> (c) Commercial Automobile Liability Insurance with limits no less than one million (US$1,000,000), combined single limit for each occurrence involving personal injuries and/or property damage; and
>
> (d) Excess Liability Insurance for the coverage in Section 17.1(a) and Section 17.1(c), with limits no less than five million (US$5,000,000).

5.7 Insurance Clause

　Insurance Clause は，一方契約当事者が他方契約当事者に対して負う責任を担保することを目的とする[401]．したがって，本契約のような製品売買契約においては，Buyer から Seller に対して保険の付保が要求されることが多い．

　Insurance Clause において付保が要求される保険品目の例としては，以下が挙げられる[402]．これらについてはすでに加入済である企業も多いかと思われる

---

[401] McNees Wallace & Nurik LLC, *Is that Covered? Insurance and Indemnity Clauses*, LexisNexis (Jan. 26, 2015), https://www.lexisnexis.com/legalnewsroom/insurance/b/insurancelaw/archive/2015/01/26/is-that-covered-insurance-and-indemnity-clauses.aspx?Redirected=true (last visited Oct. 23, 2017).

[402] 例えば California 州 San Bernardino County は，San Bernardino County と契約関係に入る事業者に対して，Commercial General Liability Insurance, Worker's Compensation Insurance, Employer's Liability Insurance, Automobile Liability Insurance, および Umbrella Liability Insurance の加入を要求する．*Indemnification and Insurance Requirements*, https://www.sbcounty.gov/uploads/drm/main/content/insurance/AllContracts.pdf (last visited Feb. 23, 2018).

が，要求されている付保金額を満たすかなどについては確認を要する[403]．

a. Commercial General Liability Insurance
基礎的なビジネス保険であり，事業に関して発生した人身事故，物品損害，医療費，および弁護士または裁判費用などを全般にわたって填補する保険契約である[404]．

b. Worker's Compensation Insurance
業務に関連して従業員が疾病または傷害などを負った場合に医療費および逸失利益を填補する保険契約である[405]．

c. Employer's Liability Insurance
事業者と従業員との雇用関係に関して生じた法的紛争（不当解雇，差別，またはハラスメント）などに関して生じる費用を填補する保険契約である[406]．

d. Automobile Liability Insurance
業務に関連して発生した自動車事故から生じた物的損害または人身損害などを填補する保険契約である[407]．

e. Excess Liability Insurance および Umbrella Liability Insurance
例えば，Seller が$1 million を保険金額とする Commercial General Liability Insurance を付保しているところ，Buyer から新たに借り受けた$5 million の価値を有する専用の製品製造設備を誤って毀損してしまったとする．この場合，Commercial General Liability Insurance の保険金額では填補しきれないため，Seller は自らその差額の$4 million を調達しなければならないことになる．

---

[403] 相手方契約当事者に保険の付保を要求する場合において，付保金額の設定は Insurance Clause を実効的なものとするうえで必要不可欠なものであるが，実際にはその設定のない契約も散見される．Chris Cox, *Tips for Drafting Effective Contractual Insurance Clauses* (Jan. 10, 2014), https://www.americanbar.org/groups/gpsolo/publications/gpsolo_ereport/2014/january_2014/tips_drafting_effective_contractual_insurance_claims.html (last visited Oct. 23, 2017).

[404] Nationwide Mutual Insurance Company, *Business Liability Insurance from Nationwide*, https://www.nationwide.com/small-business-liability-insurance.jsp (last visited Feb. 23, 2018).

[405] Nationwide Mutual Insurance Company, *Workers' Compensation Insurance – Nationwide*, https://www.nationwide.com/compensation-insurance.jsp (last visited Feb. 23, 2018).

[406] Nationwide Mutual Insurance Company, *Employment Practices Liability Insurance - Nationwide*, https://www.nationwide.com/employment-practices-liability-insurance.jsp (last visited Feb. 23, 2018).

[407] Nationwide Mutual Insurance Company, *Get Commercial Auto Insurance from Nationwide*, https://www.nationwide.com/commercial-auto-insurance.jsp (last visited Feb. 23, 2018).

Excess Liability Insurance および Umbrella Liability Insurance[408]は，被保険者が他に有する保険契約によっては填補できないような大きな事故にあった場合において，その不足部分（上記の例の場合における$4 million）を填補することを目的とする保険契約である．ただし，これらによる保険金額の交付を受ける前提として，被保険者が約定の金額を自ら負担することを要求される場合もある (Self Insured Retention という)．

Excess Liability Insurance および Umbrella Liability Insurance はその基本的特徴から混同されることも少なくないようであるが，次のような差異がある[409]．すなわち，Excess Liability Insurance は，被保険者が他に有する保険商品に追加の付保を提供する機能を持つにとどまる．したがって，被保険者が対象となる損害に関して基礎となる保険商品を有さない場合においては，Excess Liability Insurance も機能しない．これに対して，Umbrella Liability Insurance は，被保険者が対象となる損害に関して他に保険商品を有さない場合においても，その保険金額によって填補するという機能を持つ．ただし，Umbrella Liability Insurance の保険金額は，Excess Liability Insurance よりも高額になりがちである．

Section 17.2 Insurance Contract Requirements.

Seller shall ensure that all insurance policies required pursuant to Section 17.1:

(a) are issued by insurance companies reasonably acceptable to Buyer with a Best's Rating of no less than A-VIII RATING;

(b) provide that Seller gives Buyer at least thirty (30) Business Days' prior notice of cancellation or non-renewal of policy coverage, provided that, prior to such cancellation, Seller has new insurance policies in place that meet the requirements of this Article 17;

(c) provide that such insurance be primary insurance and any similar insurance in the name of and/or for the benefit of Seller shall be

---

[408] Nationwide Mutual Insurance Company, *Umbrella Insurance for Businesses – Nationwide*, https://www.nationwide.com/umbrella-insurance-policy.jsp (last visited Feb. 23, 2018).
[409] Emily Medinger, *Umbrella Coverage vs. Excess Liability*, Cottingham & Butler (Jun. 23, 2015), http://www.cottinghambutler.com/news/umbrella-coverage-vs-excess-liability/ (last visited Feb. 26, 2018).

excess and non-contributory;

(d) name Buyer and Buyer's Affiliates, including, in each case, all successors and permitted assigns, as additional insureds; and

(e) waive any right of subrogation of the insurers against Buyer.

Section 17.3 Insurance Certificates.

On Buyer's written request, Seller shall provide Buyer with copies of the certificates of insurance and policy endorsements for all insurance coverage required by this Article 17, and shall not do anything to invalidate such insurance. This Section 17.3 shall not be construed in any manner as waiving, restricting, or limiting the liability of either Party for any obligations imposed under this Agreement, including but not limited to, any provisions requiring a party hereto to indemnify, defend, and hold the other harmless under this Agreement.

5.8 Insurance Clause に関する制限

被保険者が Insurance Clause のもと，保険を付保するにあたって，以下のような制限を受けうる。

a. 保険契約による制限

保険会社の提示する保険契約においては，付保対象とならない事項が明示されていることが多い。例えば，Commercial General Liability Insurance において一般に付保対象とならない事項としては，被保険者が第三者と締結した契約に基づく責任であって，その責任はその契約なくしては発生しなかった場合[410]などが挙げられる。

---

[410] See, e.g., Insurance Service Office, Inc., Commercial General Liability Coverage Form CG 00 01 01 96 § 1-2 b, https://www.facworld.com/User%5Cgenstarforms.nsf/doc/CG%2000%2001%2001%2096/$File/CG%2000% 2001%2001%2096.pdf (last visited Jun. 1, 2018). したがって，契約上の規定の有無にかかわらず，被保険者が契約法上負うことになる責任については，保険の対象となる。

b. 州法による制限

いくつかの州の州法においては[411]，被保険者の損害が「Additional Insured」[412]の故意または過失などに起因する場合，Additional Insured は，被保険者と Additional Insured との間の契約内容にかかわらず，その保険金に関する権利を有さない旨を規定している．

c. 被保険者の義務

Insurance Clause に基づくか否かにかかわらず，保険に加入した被保険者については一般に保険契約のもと保険会社に対して，保険対象となる事象の調査に関する協力義務，および，訴訟の防御または和解などに関する協力義務を負うことになる．これら義務に違反したことをもって直ちに保険契約が失効する可能性は高くはないが[413]，保険金の給付を受けられない事態に陥ることもあるため留意が必要である[414]．

5.9 保険契約に関する要求

Insurance Clause の実効性を確保するうえでは以下の規定も重要となる．

a. Cancellation Notice

Insurance Clause のもと一方契約当事者が保険の付保を実行したとしても，その解約または付保金額の減額が断りなく行われたのではその意義を失いかねない．17.2(b)条は，保険購入者である Seller に対して，保険契約を解約または減額する際には Buyer に向けて事前の通知を行うこと，および，別の保

---

[411] California 州，Colorado 州，Kansas 州，および New Mexico 州などが挙げられる．Joann M. Lytle, *Contractual Indemnity and Additional Insured Coverage*, McCarter & English, LLP (Dec. 10, 2014), 56, http://www.ctrims.org/CONTRACTUAL_INDEMNITY_AND_ADDITIONAL_INSURED_COVERAGE___Connecticut_Valley_RIMS___REVISED_c.pdf (last visited Jun. 2, 2018); *e.g.*, Kan. Stat. § 16-121 (一方契約当事者に対して，他方契約当事者の故意または過失に基づく損害に関しても他方契約当事者に一方契約当事者の保険が適用されるよう義務付ける契約は無効であり，執行力がない旨を規定する)．

[412] 「Additional Insured」とは，保険購入者そのものではなく，保険購入者と契約関係などにあることから別途保険契約に被保険者として追加された者をいう．Robyn Anderson, *"Certificates of Insurance" and "Additional Insured" Coverage: Maximize Value and Avoid Pitfalls*, 22 The John Liner Rev. 87, 87-91 (2008). Additional Insured はあくまで保険契約購入者ではないため，保険金の支払い義務は負わない一方，保険契約の維持または更新を決定できる立場にもない．Additional Insured については後述する．

[413] J. Stephen Berry, *Eleventh Circuit affirms ruling of no coverage based on insured's failure to cooperate*, Globe Business Media Group (Aug. 24, 2016), https://www.lexology.com/library/detail.aspx?g=5586f92c-4c64-4db7-8a8d-1ce8250084db (last visited Feb. 28, 2018).

[414] *See, e.g.*, Piedmont Office Realty Trust, Inc. v. XL Specialty Ins. Co., 297 Ga. 38 (Sup. Ct. Ga. 2015) (被保険者が，自身が被告である訴訟の和解契約を締結するに先立って保険会社の同意を得ることを怠ったため，保険会社から和解金相当額の給付を受けることができなかった事案)．

険会社において同等の保険を新たに購入することを義務付けることで Insurance Clause の意義の維持を図るものである．

なお，Insurance Clause においては，被保険者たる契約当事者に対して，被保険者が保険契約の解約を試みた場合などには，保険会社が相手方契約当事者にその旨の連絡を直接行うような手当てを義務付ける規定を見受けることもできる[415]．しかし，保険会社も簡単にはこのような手当てには応じないようである[416]．

b. Additional Insured の設定

本契約の場合，保険契約を購入するのは Seller であるから，保険契約に関する請求は Seller と保険会社との間の問題として取り扱われるはずである．しかし，例えば Seller が Buyer のために発送した製品を積んだ船が座礁し，製品が滅失してしまった場合，Buyer が最終的な損害を被ることともなりかねない．その場合，Buyer としては，保険会社に直接保険金の給付に関する請求を行いたいと思うこともあろう．

そこで，17.2(d)条のように，一方契約当事者が他方契約当事者に対して保険の付保を要求するにあたっては，同時に自己を「Additional Insured」として指定することも要求する場合が多い．

i. 「Additional Insured」としての地位

契約当事者が Additional Insured として指定される場合においても，その立場が「Primary」であるか否かは実際の保険金の受領に大きな影響を及ぼしうる．つまり，Additional Insured が「Primary」の地位を有する場合，Additional Insured の損害についてはその保険契約が優先的な原資となって填補される．これに対して Additional insured が「Excess」の地位を有する場合，Additional Insured の損害は Additional Insured 自身が付保している保険では填補しきれない場合においてはじめて，その保険契約によって填補されることになる[417]．

---

[415] 例えば，次のような規定を設けることになる．「The certificate of insurance will provide that Buyer will receive thirty (30) days' prior written notice from the insurer of any termination or reduction in the amount or scope of coverage.」．

[416] 特に被保険者による保険料の不払いの場合においては，保険会社は，少なくとも，10日前の事前の連絡をもって保険契約を解約できる権利については譲らない傾向にあるとされる．Cox, *supra* note 403.

[417] この場合における Additional Insured の地位は，「an additional insured on an excess basis only」などと表現する．

ii. Certificates of Insurance および Additional Insured Endorsement

相手方契約当事者が自己を「Additional Insured」として適切に指定したかの確認を行うことができるよう，契約上，相手方契約当事者に「Certificates of Insurance」(または Acord Certificate という)[418]の発行を義務付ける場合がある．

ここで注意すべきは，Certificates of Insurance は Additional Insured が保険会社に対して保険契約の履行を直接請求できる権利を創出するものではないことである[419]．Additional Insured が保険会社に対して保険契約の履行を直接請求するためには，保険契約自体に被保険者として自己が追加されたことを示す裏書（Additional Insured Endorsement という）が行われる必要がある[420]．裏書には Additional Insured の権利および義務に関する規定が設けられる．

したがって，保険の付保が特に大きな意味を持つ取引においては，Additional Insured となる予定の契約当事者は，相手方契約当事者に対して，Certificates of Insurance の発行のほか，保険契約とその裏書のコピーも要求すべきである[421]．

iii. Additional Insured の義務

Additional Insured は保険会社に直接保険金の交付を請求できるといった利益を享受する一方，被保険者として一定の義務も負うことになる．

Additional Insured の義務の一つとして，保険対象事象が発生した場合の通知義務がある．例えば，Buyer が Additional Insured である場合においては，Buyer の製品で怪我をした消費者から法的措置を講じる旨の連絡を受けた場合，Seller の保険会社に対してその旨を通知する明示または黙示[422]の義務を負うことになる．

もっとも，このような義務は Additional Insured が保険契約の内容を知っ

---

[418]「Certificate of Insurance」は，Additional Insured が被保険者であることを証明する証書である．Anderson, *supra* note 412, at 90.

[419] *Id.*, 90-91.

[420] Cox, *supra* note 403.

[421] *Id.*

[422] *See, e.g.*, Liberty Ins. Underwriters, Inc. v. Great Am. Ins. Co., 2010 U.S. Dist. LEXIS 97722, 16 (internal citation omitted) (Additional Insured は，保険会社に対して，保険金請求に発展するような事実が発生次第，その旨を通知する義務を黙示に負っている旨を示した) ("Under New York law, even if an insurance policy does not require that an additional insured provide notice to the insurer from whom it seeks coverage, an additional insured nonetheless has an implied duty, independent of the named insured, to provide the insurer with the notice required under the policy. 'The fact that an insurer may have received notice of the claim from the primary insured, or from another source, does not excuse an additional insured's failure to provide notice.'").

ていてこそ履行可能なものともいえる．したがってこの点も Additional Insured となる契約当事者が相手方契約当事者に対して保険契約とその裏書のコピーを請求する根拠となりうるであろう．

CHAPTER 6 / GENERAL PROVISIONS

　General Provisions は，一般的な契約の取り扱い事項を規定したものであり，Boilerplate Provisions とも呼ばれる．General Provisions に向けられる契約当事者の関心は Action Provisions と比べると高くはないが，取引の実態に応じて重要な意味を持つ場合もある．

ARTICLE 18
GENERAL PROVISIONS

Section 18.1 Further Assurances.

Upon Buyer's reasonable request, Seller shall, at its sole cost and expense, execute and deliver all such further documents and instruments, and take all such further acts, necessary to give full effect to this Agreement.

6.1 Further Assurance Clause
　Further Assurance Clause も一方契約当事者が他方契約当事者に対して Covenant を提供するものである．しかし，例えば本契約の場合，13条において提供されている Covenants は契約締結時点においてすでに具体化している事項に関するものであるのに対して，18.1 条において提供される Covenant は契約締結時点においては具体化してはいないものの将来発生しうる事項に関するものである．

　本契約においては Seller のみが Further Assurance を提供している．しかし，例えば安全保障貿易管理との関係で Seller が日本国の経済産業省からある製品の輸出許可を得るにあたっては，Buyer から製品用途に関する誓約書をとりつける必要があるなど[423]，Further Assurance は Seller のみでなく Buyer との関係においても必要となりうる．したがって，Further Assurance Clause の適用は両契約当事者に及ぶものとすべきではないかを検討する必要がある．また，契約当

---

[423] Keizaisangyoshō, Jyuyosha no seiyakusho no kisaijikou, http://www.meti.go.jp/policy/anpo/kanri/shinseisho/tenpu24fy/seiyakusho_yoshiki_kisaiyouryou.html (last visited Mar. 5, 2018).

事者としては Further Assurance のような将来の発生が未確定の事項について絶対的な履行義務を負ってよいのかという問題もある．そこで例えば，Further Assurance Clause 所定の義務については，その義務の履行に向けて努力を尽くすことの確約にとどめるものとする（Efforts Clause という）ことも検討に値する[424]．

・Efforts Clause

Efforts Clause は，契約当事者が対象事項を実現するため一定の努力を尽くす旨を確約するものであり，Covenants の一つといえるが[425]，Covenant 提供者が果たしてどの程度の努力を尽くす義務を負っているのかという点が問題となりうる．これは契約上頻繁に用いられる「best efforts」，「reasonable efforts」，または「commercially reasonable efforts」といった表現の間で Covenants 提供者の負う義務の程度に違いがあるのかという問題と関係してくる．

この点については，各表現の間にある程度の差異を見いだした例もあるが[426]必ずしも整合がとれていないほか[427]，契約対象の業界の慣行を含む総合

---

[424] 18.1 条に Efforts Clause を取り入れた場合，次のような規定を設けることになる．「Upon Buyer's request, Seller agrees, at its sole cost and expense, to use commercially reasonable efforts to execute and deliver all such further documents and instruments, and take all such further acts, necessary to give full effect to this Agreement.」．

[425] ContractStandards, *Best Efforts*, https://www.contractstandards.com/public/clauses/best-efforts (last visited Mar. 5, 2018) ((Best) Efforts Clause は「implied covenant to act in good faith」を具体化したものである旨指摘する）．なお，「implied covenant to act in good faith」は U.C.C. などにおいても規定されている (U.C.C. § 1-304 (Am. Law Inst. & Unif. Law Comm'n 2001)) (Good faith による契約の義務または契約の遂行を要求する); Restatement (Second) of Contracts § 205 (Am. Law Inst. 1981); *see also* Ken Weinberg, Implied Covenant of Good Faith and Fair Dealing, Baker, Donelson, Bearman, Caldwell & Berkowitz, PC (Sep. 1, 2008), https://www.bakerdonelson.com/Implied-Covenant-of-Good-Faith-and-Fair-Dealing-09-01-2008 (last visited Jun. 19, 2018).

[426] *See, e.g.*, LTV Aerospace & Defense Co. v. Thomson-CSF, S.A. (In re Chateaugay Corp.), 198 B.R. 848, 854 (S.D.N.Y. 1996) (Best efforts は reasonable efforts よりも厳格な義務である旨を示した) ("The standard imposed by a 'reasonable efforts' clause such as that contained in section 7.01 of the Agreement is indisputably less stringent than that imposed by the 'best efforts' clauses contained elsewhere in the Agreement.").

[427] Soroof Trading Dev. Co. v. GE Fuel Cell Sys. LLC, 842 F. Supp. 2d 502, 511 (S.D.N.Y. 2012) (quoting Monex Fin. Servs. Ltd. v. Nova Info. Sys., Inc., 657 F. Supp. 2d 447, 454) (Best efforts は reasonable efforts と同義である旨を示した) ("When interpreting the meaning of a 'reasonable efforts' clause, 'New York courts use the term "reasonable efforts" interchangeably with "best efforts" . . . [and] a "best efforts" clause imposes an obligation to act with good faith in light of one's own capabilities.'"); California Pines Prop. Owners Ass'n v. Pedotti, 206 Cal. App. 4th 384, 394 (Ct. App. Cal. 2012) (Best efforts と reasonable efforts との間に明確な違いを示さなかった) ("Courts from other jurisdictions have held that when a contract does not define the phrase 'best efforts,' the promisor must use the diligence of a reasonable person under comparable circumstances ….We agree with these authorities."); U.C.C. § 2-306(2) cmt. 5 (Am. Law Inst. & Unif. Law Comm'n 2002) (Best efforts は「reasonable diligence as well as good faith」と同義であるとする）．

的な判断によるとした例も見受けられる[428]。
　したがって，これらの表現のうちのいずれを用いたかによってその Covenants 提供者が負う努力義務の程度に決定的な差異が直ちに導かれるとはいいがたい[429]。Efforts Clause を規定するにあたっては，むしろ Covenants 提供者による努力義務の履行手段を具体的に明示することの方が重要と思われる[430]。

Section 18.2 Cumulative Remedies.

All rights and remedies provided in this Agreement are cumulative and not exclusive, and the exercise by either Party of any right or remedy does not preclude the exercise of any other rights or remedies that may now or subsequently be available at law, in equity, by statute, in any other agreement between the Parties or otherwise. Notwithstanding the previous sentence, the Parties intend that a Party's rights under Article 11 are that Party's exclusive remedies for the events specified therein.

6.2 Cumulative Remedies Clause

　Cumulative Remedies Clause は，相手方契約当事者に法律上の責任を問う場合において，ある責任追及手段の行使が別途他の責任追及手段を行使することを

---

[428] Practical Law Commercial Transactions, *Efforts Provisions in Commercial Contracts: Best Efforts, Reasonable Efforts, and Commercially Reasonable Efforts*, Thomson Routers, https://uk.practicallaw.thomsonreuters.com/7-518-0907?transitionType=Default&contextData=(sc.Default)&firstPage=true&bhcp=1 (last visited Jun. 2, 2018) (first citing Citri-Lite Co. v. Cott Beverages, Inc., 2011 U.S. Dist. LEXIS 112901 (E.D. Cal. 2011); and then citing WaveDivision Holdings, LLC v. Millennium Digital Media Sys., L.L.C., 2010 Del. C. LEXIS 194 (Ch. Del. 2010)) ("The hierarchy of standards used for best efforts, reasonable efforts, and commercially reasonable efforts, if there is one, is unclear and may depend on the industry in which the term is used").

[429] なお，いずれの努力義務を規定した場合であっても，それは義務を負担する者に，その者の利益を犠牲にして，あらゆる手段をとってでも義務を履行することまでを要求するものではないと思われる。Practical Law Commercial Transactions, *supra* note 428; *see, e.g., Citri-Lite Co*, 721 F.Supp.2d, at 927 (Commercially reasonable efforts に関して，自己の利益を考慮したうえで努力義務を履行することが許容されている旨を示した) ("There is no settled or universally accepted definition of the term 'commercially reasonable efforts.' These cases are consistent with the principle that 'commercially reasonable efforts' permits the performing party to consider its economic business interests.").

[430] *See generally* Eric Fishman & Aubrey Charette, *Drafting a Better "Best Efforts" Clause*, Pillsbury Winthrop Shaw Pittman LLP (Jul. 23, 2013), https://www.pillsburylaw.com/images/content/4/3/v2/4368/DraftingaBetterBestEffortsClause-CorporateCounsel072313.pdf (last visited Mar. 5, 2018) (New York 州の裁判所は，契約上において努力義務が履行されたかどうかに関する客観的な判断基準が見当たらない限り Efforts Clause の執行を躊躇する傾向にある旨を指摘する)。

否定するものではない旨を明確にする規定である．なお，契約法は本来的にCumulative Remediesの立場を採っている[431]．

・Cumulative RemediesとExclusive Remedyとが混在する場合
一つの契約内においてCumulative Remedies ClauseとExclusive Remedy Clauseの双方を含む場合，契約内で矛盾が生じかねない．なぜなら，Exclusive Remedy Clauseに従う限り，ある契約上の責任については特定の救済方法がExclusive Remedyである旨解釈される一方，Cumulative Remedies Clauseに従う限りExclusive Remedyの追求は別途そのほかの責任追及手段を行使することを否定するものではない旨解釈されることにもなるためである[432]．

したがって，ある契約において，一部の契約責任については特定の救済方法をExclusive Remedyとし，その他の契約責任についてはCumulative Remediesとする場合，11.5条および18.2条のように，Exclusive Remedy Clauseの対象となる契約責任を明示し，その実効性を確保する必要がある．

Section 18.3 Equitable Remedies.

Seller acknowledges and agrees that (a) a breach or threatened breach by Seller of any of its obligations under Section 15 would give rise to irreparable harm to the other Party for which monetary damages would not be an adequate remedy and (b) in the event of a breach or a threatened breach by Seller of any such obligations, Buyer shall, in addition to any and all other rights and remedies that may be available to Buyer at law, at equity, or otherwise in respect of such breach, be entitled to equitable relief, including a temporary restraining order, an injunction, specific performance, and any other relief that may be available from a court of competent jurisdiction, without any requirement to post a bond or other

---

[431] *See, e.g.*, M.G.A., Inc. v. Amelia Station, Ltd., 2002-Ohio-5091, p13 ("The Ohio Supreme Court has also noted that HN6 while courts have upheld some contractual language as an adequate expression of the seller's intent to limit the buyer's remedies, the Uniform Commercial Code disfavors limitation of remedies and a presumption arises that a limiting clause provides a cumulative remedy rather than an exclusive one, unless it clearly states otherwise."); *see also* U.C.C. § 2-719 cmt.2 (Am. Law Inst. & Unif. Law Comm'n 2002) (There is "a presumption that clauses prescribing remedies are cumulative rather than exclusive. If the parties intend the term to describe the sole remedy under the contract, this must be clearly expressed.").
[432] Lawrence Hsieh, *Sandbagging Provisions; Cumulative vs. Exclusive Remedies* (Aug. 11, 2011), http://gcnewyork.com/columns11/081111hsieh.html (last visited Oct. 24, 2017).

> security, and without any requirement to prove actual damages or that monetary damages will not afford an adequate remedy. Seller agrees that Seller will not oppose or otherwise challenge the appropriateness of equitable relief or the entry by a court of competent jurisdiction of an order granting equitable relief, in either case, consistent with the terms of this Section 18.3.

6.3 Irreparable Harm Clause

相手方契約当事者による契約違反があった場合においては，金銭の賠償請求以外の手段を必要とする場合もある．例えば Buyer が Seller から得た秘密情報であるノウハウを利用して自社で製品の製造を始めたとする．これは本契約における Confidentiality Clause に違反する行為であるが，Seller としては損害賠償請求よりも，まずは Buyer による製品の製造および販売の差し止めを裁判所に対して請求し，損害の拡大を防ぎたいと考えることもあろう．

Irreparable Harm Clause は，差し止め請求に求められる要件のうち最も重要とされる「Irreparable Harm」の存在[433]についてあらかじめ契約当事者間で合意することで，差し止め請求が認められやすくなることを意図して設けられる[434]．

a. Injunction

Injunction とは，連邦裁判所，州裁判所，または郡裁判所によって発布される[435]作為または不作為に関する命令をいい[436]，差し止め請求もこれに含まれる．Injunction を求める者は，①Injunction が命令されない場合においては Injunction 請求者が重大な不利益（Irreparable Harm という）を被ることになること，②Injunction が発布されることによる Injunction 請求者の利益が Injunction が発布されることによる Injunction 被請求者の不利益よりも大きいこと，③実際の訴訟においては Injunction 請求者の主張が認められる可能性が高いこと，および④Injunction の発布が公共の福祉に適うものであることを

---

[433] *See, e.g.*, Faiveley Transp. Malmo AB v. Wabtec Corp., 559 F.3d 110, 118 (2d. Cir. 2009) (quoting Rodriguez v. DeBuono, 175 F.3d 227, 234 (2d. Cir. 1998) ("A showing of irreparable harm is 'the single most important prerequisite for the issuance of a preliminary injunction.'").

[434] Stephen J. Shapiro, *Contracting For Irreparable Harm May Not Be As Effective As You Think*, Mondaq Ltd. (Mar. 7, 2013), http://www.mondaq.com/unitedstates/x/225528/Financial+Services/Contracting+For+Irreparable+Harm+May+Not+Be+As+Effective+As+You+Think (last visited Jun. 3, 2018).

[435] A.B.A., *Understanding Injunctions*, 15, Insights on L. and Soc'y (2014), https://www.americanbar.org/publications/insights_on_law_andsociety/14/winter-2014/understanding-injunctions.html (last visited Oct. 24, 2017).

[436] *Black's Law Dictionary: Pocket Edition* 383 (4th ed. 2011).

示さなければならない[437]．

　Injunction は，Temporary Restraining Order，Preliminary Injunction，および Permanent Injunction に分類できる．Temporary Restraining Order は，一定の期間[438]に限り，効力を有する命令である．発効期間が短期である一方で，命令の発布に際して被請求者に向けての事前の通知を必要としない[439]．Preliminary Injunction は，対象事案が裁判によって解決されるまでの間，効力を有する命令であり[440]，被請求者に向けての事前の通知が必要となる[441]．これらに対して，Permanent Injunction は，無期限の効力を有する命令であり，裁判における請求の一つとして挙げられるのが通常である[442]．

b. Irreparable Harm Clause の有効性

　Irreparable Harm Clause の存在をもって Injunction に関する要件の一つである「Irreparable Harm」が認められるかについては，画一的な判断はされていない[443]．したがって，Irreparable Harm Clause を設ける場合，Irreparable Harm Clause の適用対象事象の明確化[444]および Choice of Law Clause における適用法

---

[437] *See, e.g.*, Winter v. NRDC, Inc., 129 S. Ct. 365, 376-77 (U.S. 2008) (quoting Weinberger v. Romero–Barcelo, 456 U.S. 305, 312 (U.S. 1982)) ("'In exercising their sound discretion, courts of equity should pay particular regard for the public consequences in employing the extraordinary remedy of injunction.'").

[438] Fed. R. Civ. P. 65(b)(2) (Temporary Restraining Order の有効期間は 14 日以内を原則とする).

[439] Fed. R. Civ. P. 65(b)(1). なお，このように相手方当事者を関与させずに実施される手続きを「ex parte」という．*Black's Law Dictionary: Pocket Edition* 291 (4th ed. 2011).

[440] A.B.A., *supra* note 435.

[441] Fed. R. Civ. P. 65(a).

[442] *See e.g.*, Apple Inc. v. Samsung Elecs. Co., 801 F.3d 1352 (Apple Inc.が Apple Inc.の iPhone に使用されたソフトウェアに関連する特許権などを Samsung Electronics Co., Ltd.が侵害しているとして，Samsung Electronics Co., Ltd.に対する Permanent Injunction を求めた事案).

[443] *See, e.g.*, AM Gen. Holdings LLC v. Renco Group, Inc., 2012 Del. Ch. LEXIS 289, 15 (first quoting Concord Steel, Inc. v. Wilmington Steel Processing Co., Inc., 2008 Del. Ch. LEXIS 44, 39 (Ch. Del. 2008); and then quoting Cirrus Holding Co. Ltd. v. Cirrus Industries, Inc. 794 A.2d 1191, 1209 (Ch. Del. 2001)) (Irreparable Harm Clause は Irreparable Harm の発生を証明するに足りる旨を示した) ("Under Delaware law, 'a contractual stipulation of irreparable harm may suffice to demonstrate irreparable harm.' Indeed, this Court has concluded 'that contractual stipulations as to irreparable harm alone suffice to establish that element for the purpose of issuing preliminary injunctive relief.'"); *cf.* Riverside Publ. Co. v. Mercer Publ. LLC, 2011 U.S. Dist. LEXIS 85853, 22 (W.D. Wash.) (Irreparable Harm Clause は契約当事者が Irreparable Harm の発生可能性を予見していたことの証拠とはなりうるものの，結果的に裁判所が Irreparable Harm の発生を否定することを妨げるものではない旨を示した) ("At best, the clause is evidence that at the time of the Settlement Agreement, the parties predicted that breaches of Paragraphs 1 and 2 would be of the sort that would cause irreparable harm. That prediction is perhaps entitled to some weight, but the court holds that it does not relieve Riverside of its obligation to demonstrate irreparable harm.").

[444] *See* Michael Frisch et al., *Contracting For Irreparable Harm*, Portfolio Media, Inc., https://www.mayerbrown.com/files/News/c7962a27-5d85-43fd-aba4-4ee7caf34be5/Presentation/NewsAttachment/79634f2e-b46f-4466-b4ec-5e4d4badb6f5/Contracting%20For%20Irreparable%20Harm.pdf (last visited Oct. 24, 2017); *see also*

の選択などによって Irreparable Harm Clause の実効性を高めておく必要がある。もちろん，Irreparable Harm を支える事実の存在自体が重要であることはいうまでもない。

Section 18.4 No Waiver.

Each Party acknowledges and agrees that (a) no waiver under this Agreement is effective unless it is in writing, and signed by an authorized representative of the Party waiving its right; (b) any waiver authorized on one occasion is effective only in that instance and only for the purpose stated, and does not operate as a waiver on any future occasion; and (c) none of the following constitutes a waiver or estoppel of any right, remedy, power, privilege, or condition arising from this Agreement: (i) any failure or delay in exercising any right, remedy, power, or privilege or in enforcing any condition under this Agreement; or (ii) any act, omission, or course of dealing between the Parties.

6.4 Non-Waiver Clause

「Waiver」とは，ある権利を有する旨を知った後，権利者によって行われる権利の意図的な放棄である[445]。Waiver は，当事者の明確な意思表示はなくともその行為などから認められる場合もあるほか[446]，他方当事者からの Consideration の提供がないとしても認められる[447]。

Non-Waiver Clause は，一方契約当事者が他方契約当事者による契約違反に対して，意図的にまたは不注意によって格別の行動をとらなかったとしても，そ

Shapiro, *supra* note 434 (Irreparable Harm Clause がいわゆる Boilerplate 条項として形式的に用意されたものであるかのような外観を持つ場合，その Irreparable Harm Clause としての効力はさらに低いものとなりかねない旨を指摘する).

[445] *See, e.g.*, City of Ukiah v. Fones, 48 Cal.Rptr. 865, 866–67 (Sup. Ct. Cal. 1966) (quoting Roesch v. De Mota, 24 Cal.2d 563, 572 (Sup. Ct. Cal. 1944)) ("'Waiver is the intentional relinquishment of known rights after knowledge of the facts.'").

[446] *See, e.g.*, Jernigan v. Langley, 111 S.W.3d 153, 156 (Sup. Ct. Tex. 2003) (Waiver is largely a matter of intent, and for implied waiver to be found through a party's actions, intent must be clearly demonstrated by the surrounding facts and circumstances.). なお，Waiver については，その放棄を主張する者が確固たる証拠に基づいてその存在を証明しなければならないとする。*See generally* DRG/Beverly Hills, Ltd. v. Chopstix Dim Sum Cafe & Takeout III, Ltd., 30 Cal.App.4th 54, 60 (Ct. App. Cal. 1994) ("The burden, moreover, is on the party claiming a waiver of a right to prove it by clear and convincing evidence that does not leave the matter to speculation, and 'doubtful cases will be decided against a waiver.'").

[447] 28 Am. Jur. 2d Estoppel and Waiver § 193.

れは契約違反に対する責任追及を放棄したことを意味しない旨を明らかにする規定である[448]．例えば，Buyer が Seller からの製品の発送が遅れたため，予定通りに製品を製造できず，損害を被ったとする．Buyer としては Seller に直ちに損害を請求したいところであるが，当面は Seller から製品を継続的に発送してもらう必要があるため，損害の賠償請求を躊躇するかもしれない．Non-Waiver Clause はそのような場合において，Buyer が Seller に対する損害賠償の請求に関する権利を放棄したとみなされることを防ぐ目的で用意される．

a. Non-Waiver Clause の非絶対性

　Non-Waiver Clause の最大の問題点は，Non-Waiver Clause 自体が Waiver の対象となるということである[449]．したがって，Non-Waiver Clause を規定するのみではなく，その後もなお権利を放棄したとみなされることのないよう注意深く振る舞う必要がある[450]．また，Non-Waiver Clause において Waiver を構成しない言動をとりわけ具体的に例示していた場合，実際にその言動が認められたとしても Non-Waiver Clause は依然として有効に機能し，Non-Waiver Clause の Waiver の成立を妨げることが可能となりうる[451]．

---

[448] Jonathan Bartley, *Beware the Non-waiver Clause*, World Service Group (Jul. 2009), https://www.worldservicesgroup.com/publications.asp?action=article&artid=2995 (last visited Mar. 9, 2018).

[449] *See, e.g.*, Bettelheim v. Hagstrom Food Stores, Inc. 113 Cal.App.2d 873, 878 (Ct. App. Cal. 1952) ("Even a waiver clause may be waived by conduct."); *see also, e.g.*, Lee v. Wright 485 N.Y.S.2d 543, 545 (Sup. Ct. N.Y. 1985) ("[I]t has long been the rule that parties may waive a 'no-waiver' clause"). もっとも，Waiver に関する証明責任が厳格であることを考慮すると，Non-Waiver Clause の意義は依然として認められるはずである．

[450] Greg Call et al., *Drafting Contract Provisions to Reduce Business Disputes* (Nov. 12, 2014), https://www.crowell.com/files/Drafting-Contract-Provisions-to-Reduce-Business-Disputes.pdf (last visited Mar. 9, 2018).

[451] *See, e.g.*, Shields Limited P'ship v. Bradberry, 526 S.W.3d 471 (Sup. Ct. Tex. 2017) (賃貸契約において，借主が賃料の支払いを遅延したのちに，家主が借主からその賃料を受領したことは，家主の借主に対して有する別途の請求権を放棄するものではない旨の Non-Waiver Clause が規定されていた場合において，その規定のとおりの効果を認めた．その賃貸契約における Non-Waiver Clause は次のとおりであった．「All waivers must be in writing and signed by the waiving party. Landlord's failure to enforce any provisions of this Lease or its acceptance of late installments of Rent shall not be a waiver and shall not estop Landlord from enforcing that provision or any other provision of this Lease in the future.」); *cf.* Kamco Supply Corp. v On the Right Track, LLC, 149 A.D.3d 275 (Sup. Ct. N.Y. 2017) (Supply Distribution 契約のもと，Distributor に一定数量の製品購入が義務付けられているにもかかわらず，Distributor がその義務を履行しない場合において，契約違反を主張しなかった相手方契約当事者については Distributor に対する製品購入義務の履行の請求権に関する Waiver があったものと評価した．Supply Distribution 契約における Non-Waiver Clause の規定は次のとおりであった．「No waiver of any provision of this Agreement or any rights or obligations of either party hereunder shall be effective, except pursuant to a written instrument signed by the party or parties waiving compliance. This waiver shall be effective only in the specific instance and the specific purpose stated.」).

b. Estoppel との関係

18.4 条においては，契約当事者のいかなる行為についても Estoppel の根拠となりえない旨を規定している．Estoppel[452]とは，一方当事者がとった行為の結果として事実関係が定まったといえる場合においては，その後その当事者がその事実関係に反する行為をとることを認めないという原則である[453]．したがって，Estoppel は一方当事者の行為に対して他方当事者が保護に値する信頼を寄せたことを根拠とした原則である点で Waiver とはその根拠が異なる[454]．

Section 18.5 Force Majeure.

Any delay or failure of either Party to perform its obligations under this Agreement will be excused to the extent that the delay or failure was caused directly by an event beyond such Party's control, without such Party's fault or negligence, and that by its nature could not have been foreseen by such Party or, if it could have been foreseen, was unavoidable (which events may include natural disasters, embargoes, explosions, riots, wars, or acts of terrorism) (each, a "Force Majeure Event"). Seller's financial inability to perform, changes in cost or availability of materials, components, or services, market conditions or supplier actions, or contract disputes will not excuse performance by Seller under this Section 18.5. Seller shall give Buyer prompt written notice of any event or circumstance that is reasonably likely to result in a Force Majeure Event, and the anticipated duration of such Force Majeure Event. Seller shall use all diligent efforts to end the Force Majeure Event, ensure that the effects of any Force Majeure Event are minimized and resume full performance under this Agreement.

If requested by Buyer, Seller shall, within ten (10) days of such request, provide adequate assurances that a Force Majeure Event will not exceed twenty (20) days. The rights granted to Seller with respect to excused

---

[452] Estoppel はさらに，(1) Equitable estoppel，(2) Promissory estoppel (Restatement (Second) of Contracts § 90 (Am. Law Inst. 1981))，および (3) Estoppel by silence に細分化できる．S & P Brake Supply, Inc. v. STEMCO LP 385 Mont. 488, 500 (Sup. Ct. Mont. 2016).
[453] 12 Ind. Law Encyc. Estoppel and Waiver § 1.
[454] 2 Cal. Affirmative Def. § 34:15 (2d ed.).

> delays under this Section 18.5 are intended to limit Seller's rights under any theories permitted by applicable law.

6.5 Force Majeure Clause

地震またはハリケーンといった災害が発生した結果，Seller が工場から製品を契約所定の期日までに出荷することができなかった場合，Seller はその出荷遅延について責任を負うことになるのであろうか．Force Majeure Clause は，歴史的大災害など[455]，契約当事者の責めによらない事由が発生した結果として，契約上の義務の履行が困難となった場合において，一定範囲でその履行に関する免責を規定するものである．

a. Common Law における取り扱い

Common Law においては，Force Majeure Event と類似した状況について Impossibility[456]，Impracticability[457]，または Frustration of Purpose[458]という概念によって対応する．

しかしながら，これらを根拠とした主張が認められる場合はかなりまれである．例えば，本契約の場合，Seller としてこれら Common Law の概念のもとでの免責を主張したい状況としては，ある災害が発生した結果，もはや通常のコストでその製品を製造することは不可能であるといった場合を想定することができる．ところが，Impossibility の主張は，Seller が（たとえより高いコストであったとしても）同種の製品を製造できる限り認められがたい．

また，Impracticability（このような場合における Impracticability を Commercial Impracticability という）の主張は，Seller がその製品を製造するた

---

[455] したがって，Force Majeure Clause は国際契約との関係で問題となることが多い．W. Laurence Craig et al., International Chamber of Commerce Arbitration 651 (3d ed. 2001) (Force Majeure Event をめぐる法制度は国際ビジネス社会の要求と慣習を受けて発達していると評価する).

[456] Impossibility とは，契約上の義務の履行対象が損壊した場合，または，履行手段が実行不可能となった場合などにおいて，契約当事者はその契約上の義務の履行を免れることができるとする原則をいう．Black's Law Dictionary: Pocket Edition 368 (4th ed. 2011).

[457] Impracticability とは，契約上の義務の履行が極度かつ不合理に困難となった場合において，契約当事者はその契約上の義務の履行を免れることができるとする原則をいう．See id. 368; see also, e.g., Restatement (Second) of Contracts § 261 (Am. Law Inst. 1981); see generally U.C.C. § 2-615 (Am. Law Inst. & Unif. Law Comm'n 2002).

[458] Frustration of Purpose とは，予期せぬ事情により契約の目的が実質的に損なわれたといえる場合において，契約当事者はその契約上の義務の履行を免れることができるとする原則をいう．Black's Law Dictionary: Pocket Edition 327 (4th ed. 2011); see, e.g., Restatement (Second) of Contracts § 265 (Am. Law Inst. 1981).

めに必要となるコストがあまりにも不合理といえる場合[459]でない限り認められない[460]。

さらに、一方契約当事者による Impossibility, Impracticability, または Frustration of Purpose に関する主張が認められる場合であっても、その効果は必ずしも契約履行義務者が他方契約当事者から、なんらの追加の行為[461]または補償[462]を要求されないことまでを意味しない。

b. Force Majeure Clause の適用

裁判所の Force Majeure Clause の適用に関する姿勢は慎重である[463]。したがって、契約上では、Force Majeure Event の定義(特に契約当事者がコントロールできるものではない、予見できない、および回避できない事情であることが重要である)、ならびに、Force Majeure Event に該当する事由の具体的な例示などに配慮し、Force Majeure Clause の適用の可能性を高めるよう試みる必要がある。

---

[459] See, e.g., Int'l Elecs. Corp. v. United States, 227 Ct. Cl. 208, 231 (quoting Natus Corp. v. United States, 178 Ct. Cl. 1, 11 (Ct. Cl. 1967)) ("[I]mpossibility may be established by proof of 'commercial impracticality.' This precept is based on the assumption that in legal contemplation a contractual duty is impracticable when it can be performed only at an excessive and unreasonable cost"); see also e.g., Jennie–O Foods, Inc. v. United States, 217 Ct.Cl. 314, 328 (Ct. Cl. 1978) (citing *Natus Corp.*, 178 Ct. Cl., at 11) ("There are other judicially imposed limits to the doctrine of commercial impracticability that suggest the Board was correct in labeling this case one of economic hardship. The doctrine may be utilized only when the promisor has exhausted all its alternatives, when in fact it is determined that all means of performance are commercially senseless.").

[460] See, e.g., *Natus Corp.*, 178 Ct. Cl., at 11 (Seller が製品に関する利益を確保できないことのみをもっては、その製品の製造コストが不合理とまではいえない旨を示した) ("[I]n neither case would it entitle a contractor to relief merely because he cannot obtain a productive level sufficient to sustain his anticipated profit margin. Plaintiff has not shown that the modified press-brake operation would be economically unrealistic.").

[461] E.g., U.C.C. § 2-616 (Am. Law Inst. & Unif. Law Comm'n 2002) (Seller が Buyer に対して Impracticability の通知を行った場合における Buyer の救済手段を規定する).

[462] E.g., Restatement (Second) of Contracts § 261 cmt. a (Am. Law Inst. 1981) (Impracticability は、契約上の義務履行者をその義務の履行自体からは免責するものの、すでに発生した契約違反に関する責任についてまでも免責するものではないとする).

[463] Mark Augenblick & Alison B. Rousseau, *Force Majeure in Tumultuous Times: Impracticability as the New Impossibility It's Not as Easy to Prove as You Might Believe*, Pillsbury Winthrop Shaw Pittman LLP (2012), https://www.pillsburylaw.com/images/content/3/9/v2/3990/BylinedArticleForceMajeureinTumultuousTimesJournalofWorldInvestm.pdf (last visited Jun. 4, 2018) (citing ICC Case No. 9978/1999 (Extract), 11 ICC Bull. 2000, 117) (Force Majeure Event を根拠とした免責の主張は、Force Majeure Clause に列挙された事象のうち、戦争、暴動、または通商停止といった極度の事由に限定されて認められる傾向にある旨を指摘する); see, e.g., GT&MC, Inc. v. Texas City Refining, Inc., 822 S.W.2d 252, 259 (Ct. App. Tex. 1991) (Act of God (地震、洪水、またはハリケーンなどを指す) の発生自体は契約当事者の履行義務を直ちに免除するものではない旨を示した) ("In contract cases, the rule is that an act of God does not relieve the parties of their obligations unless the parties expressly provide otherwise.").

> Section 18.6 Entire Agreement.
>
> Subject to Article 3, this Agreement, including and together with any related exhibits, schedules, attachments, and appendices, together with the Individual Transactions, constitutes the sole and entire agreement of the Parties with respect to the subject matter contained herein and therein, and supersedes all prior and contemporaneous understandings, agreements, representations, and warranties, both written and oral, regarding such subject matter.

6.6 Entire Agreement Clause

契約が締結に至るまでの間，契約当事者間では幾度にもわたっての交渉が重ねられることも少なくない．そしてそれらの交渉の結果として契約書が出来上がるわけであるから，締結した契約書の内容とそれまでの交渉内容との間には齟齬があることもある．そのような齟齬を理由とした契約の瑕疵に関する後日の主張を妨げ，その契約を唯一の合意内容である旨確定させるために用意されるのが Entire Agreement Clause (Integration Clause または Merger Clause ともいう) である．

　Entire Agreement Clause はいわゆる Parol Evidence Rule の適用を確認する趣旨を持つ[464]．Parol Evidence Rule とは，最終の合意内容として契約当事者間で用意された文書に関しては，その契約締結よりも以前または契約締結の時点において契約書外に存在する，契約書とは相反するまたは契約書に言及されていない契約条件を主張できないとする Common Law 上の原則である[465]．

　もっとも，Parol Evidence Rule は，例えば，(1) 契約内容の解釈の補助 (例えば契約書において使用されているある単語は特定の業界で用いられるものであることの証明)，(2) 契約が詐欺または脅迫などによって成立したことの主張，(3) 契約条件について錯誤があったことの証明，(4) 契約上の義務の履行に前提

---

[464] See Restatement (Second) of Contracts § 213 (Am. Law Inst. 1981); see also U.C.C. § 2-202 (Am. Law Inst. & Unif. Law Comm'n 2002). すなわち，Parol Evidence Rule が適用されるためには，①契約書が最終的な合意であること，および，②契約書が「Total Integration」(その契約書が対象事項に関する契約当事者間の合意内容を示すものとして完全かつ唯一のものである場合をいう) についての当事者の意思が認められる必要がある．Entire Agreement Clause はこれらの要件を裏付けるものとなる．なお，当事者の意思が「Total Integration」ではなく「Partial Integration」(その契約書が Total Integration に該当しない場合全般をいう) である場合，契約書に規定されていない事項については (契約書の内容と矛盾しない範囲において) 契約書外の内容を利用することができる．See Blum, supra note 255.

[465] Black's Law Dictionary: Pocket Edition 554 (4th ed. 2011).

条件があったことの証明、または、(5) 契約上規定された Consideration が実際には提供されていないことの証明に関連する事実を主張することを妨げるものではない[466]。

Section 18.7 Notices.

All notices, requests, consents, claims, demands, waivers, and other communications under this Agreement (each, a "Notice") must be in writing and addressed to the other Party at its address set forth below (or to such other address that the receiving Party may designate from time to time in accordance with this Section 18.7). Unless otherwise agreed herein, all Notices must be delivered by personal delivery, nationally recognized overnight courier or certified or registered mail (in each case, return receipt requested, postage prepaid).

Except as otherwise provided in this Agreement, a Notice is effective only (a) on receipt by the receiving Party, and (b) if the Party giving the Notice has complied with the requirements of this Section 18.7.

 Notice to Buyer:

 Address:
 Attention:
 E-mail:
 Facsimile:

 Notice to Seller:

 Address:
 Attention:
 E-mail:
 Facsimile:

---

[466] *See* Blum, *supra* note 255, at 404-10.

6.7 Notices Clause

18.7 条は，例えば対象製品による事故が発生した場合など，重要な事項に関する各契約当事者の連絡先をあらかじめ決定しておくことで，契約当事者間の適切な連絡，および，その後の適切な対応を可能とするものである[467]．

a. Return Receipt の必要性

「Notice」は，通常 Letter の送付によって行われることが期待されている．Letter が到着したか否かに関する後日の争いを避ける意味では，送付者が送付状況を確認できる U.S. Postal Service の Registered Mail[468]などによることが望ましい．これに対して，U.S. Postal Service の First-Class Mail[469]などはそのような確認ができず信頼性に欠けるとして，Notice の手段としては適切ではないと考えられているようである[470]．

b. E-mail または Facsimile の利用

Notice を実施するうえでは E-mail または Facsimile のほうが Letter よりも簡易かつ便利な手段である．しかし，これらについては連絡先側が気づかない可能性も比較的高いため，Notice の手段から除外する場合も少なくない．もっとも，例えば E-mail の受信確認機能を用いることなどによってこれを補完し，連絡手段として許容することもできると思われる．

c. 契約違反に関する Notice

契約当事者は，相手方契約当事者に契約違反が認められる場合，その旨の Notice を相手方契約当事者に向けて行うことによってその事実などを指摘することとなる．

この場合，Notice の発行にあたっては，その後紛争解決手続きに至る可能性もふまえ，(1) Notice が Notice Clause に沿った内容および手続きとなって

---

[467] *See generally* Steven R. Berger, Negotiating and Drafting Contract Boilerplate 464 (Tina L. Stark, 2003) (Notices Clause は契約法における Mail Box Rule を踏襲し，いったん Notice を発行したのちは Notice が他方契約当事者に到達したかどうかにかかわらず，その Notice の効果を主張できるようにした Notice の到達に関するリスクの配分に関する規定であるとする)．しかし，契約書をビジネスの円滑な遂行に貢献させたいと考える場合には Notices Clause はそのようなリスクの配分よりも両契約当事者のコミュニケーションの円滑化に向けて有用に活用すべきである．そこで，本契約においては Notice の効果を主張するための要件に相手方契約当事者への到達を加えている．

[468] USPS, *Shipping Insurance, Certified Mail &amp Extra Services*, https://www.usps.com/ship/insurance-extra-services.htm (last visited Mar. 26, 2018).

[469] USPS, *First-Class Mail*, https://www.usps.com/ship/first-class-mail.htm (last visited Mar. 26, 2018).

[470] Stark, *supra* note 1, at 230.

いるか，(2) Notice の発行日を（相手方契約当事者が自己の契約違反の事実を了知した日を推察できるよう）明確にしているか，(3) 相手方契約当事者がどの契約条項に違反しているのかを明確にしているか，(4) 相手方契約当事者にどのような対応を要求しているのかを明確にしているか，および (5) 事実の叙述に終始することに努めており，誇張表現などが用いられていないかを中心とした確認を行うべきである[471]．

Section 18.8 Headings.

The headings in this Agreement are for reference only and do not affect the interpretation of this Agreement.

6.8 Headings Clause

各条に添えられる表題（Heading）はその内容を一目で推察できるものとして有用である．また，Heading は，Limitation of Warranty Clause または Waiver of Jury Trial Clause のようにその規定を「Conspicuous」とすることが求められる場合においてそれを補助する機能を有する[472]．

もっとも Heading の記載が契約本文との間に齟齬を生じさせる場合には契約内容の解釈に疑義を生じさせかねない[473]．Headings Clause は，対象契約の解釈との関係において Headings が実質的な意味を持たない旨を明らかにすることで，そのような疑義の発生を予防するものである[474]．

---

[471] *See* Richard Stim, *Breach of Contract: The Notice of Breach If your contract has fallen through, take the first step toward resolving the problem*, Nolo, https://www.nolo.com/legal-encyclopedia/breach-of-contract-notice-of-32649.html (last visited Apr. 11, 2018).

[472] Anderson Kill P.C., *Enforceability of Jury Waiver Provisions in Federal Court* (Dec. 16, 2016), https://www.andersonkill.com/Publication-Details/PublicationID/1486 (last visited Oct. 18, 2017).

[473] *See, e.g.*, Nahra v. Honeywell, Inc., 892 F. Supp. 962, 967 (N.D. Ohio 1995) (「Liquidated Damages and Honeywell's Limits of Liability」との Heading のもと，同項の一文目に契約当事者の責任を否定する旨を規定し，二文目以降で Limitation of Liability について規定していた場合において，Limitation of Liability に関する部分のみに大文字の記載があること，および，Limitation of Liability については詳細な規定があることを理由として，同項全体が Limitation of Liability に関する規定であり，一文目の免責に関する部分は Limitation of Liability の必要性を強調したものにすぎないと判断した）．

[474] *See, e.g.*, Sunoco, Inc. (R&M) v. Toledo Edison Co., 129 Ohio St. 3d 397 (Sup. Ct. Ohio 2011) (ある条項の Heading と本文の内容が合致しないことを根拠として本文の内容に関する義務を負わない旨の被告の主張に関して，対象契約においてはいわゆる Headings Clause が規定されていることを根拠にその主張を退けた事案）．

> Section 18.9 Severability.
>
> If any term or provision of this Agreement is invalid, illegal, or unenforceable in any jurisdiction, such invalidity, illegality, or unenforceability shall not affect any other term or provision of this Agreement or invalidate or render unenforceable such term or provision in any other jurisdiction. Upon a determination that any term or provision is invalid, illegal, or unenforceable, the Parties shall negotiate in good faith to modify this Agreement to effect the original intent of the Parties as closely as possible in order that the transactions contemplated hereby be consummated as originally contemplated to the greatest extent possible.

6.9 Severability Clause

Severability Clause は，ある規定が無効であったとしてもその他の規定の効力までは否定しないものとすることで，契約の有効性をできる限り維持する機能を有する．契約法においても，次のとおり，同趣旨の規定を設けている．

　a. Common Law における取り扱い

契約中のある条項が無効であると判断された場合であっても，①その無効と判断された条項が契約の本質的な部分ではなく，かつ，②その他の条項について執行を求める契約当事者が著しく不適切な行為を行ったものではない限り，その他の条項についての有効性は妨げられないとする[475]．

　b. U.C.C.における取り扱い

Liquidated Damages Clause がペナルティであるとして無効と判断された場合[476]であっても，Actual Damages の請求は可能であるとされるほか[477]，Exclusive Remedy Clause が契約の本質を損なうものとして無効と判断された場合[478]にはその他の救済手段の行使を許容する[479]．

---

[475] *See* Restatement (Second) of Contracts § 184(1) (Am. Law Inst. 1981).
[476] U.C.C. § 2-718 (Am. Law Inst. & Unif. Law Comm'n 2002).
[477] Eric Fishman & Robert James, Drafting A Better Severability Clause, Pillsbury Winthrop Shaw Pittman LLP (Oct. 1, 2013), https://www.pillsburylaw.com/images/content/4/4/v2/4483/Article20131001DraftingaBetterSeverabilityClause.pdf (last visited Mar. 28, 2018).
[478] 例えば，Seller の保証内容を製品の修補のみに限定していたところ，その製品は修補できないものであった場合，その他の救済 (代替品の請求など) が許容されうる．
[479] U.C.C. § 2-719(2) (Am. Law Inst. & Unif. Law Comm'n 2002).

したがって，Severability Clause は上記の対象とならない場面との関係において特に重要となる．

c. ある規定が無効であると判断された場合の取り扱い
Severability Clause との関係で大きな関心事となるのは，ある規定が無効と判断された場合，以降，その規定の対象事項についてはどのような契約条件となるのかという点である．まれではあるが，Severability Clause において，この場合の契約条件の決定方法について規定する例も見受けられる．
この点，何らの指針なく両契約当事者の協議によって新たな契約条件を決定するのでは，解決に多大な時間および労力を要することとなり，得策とは思われない．一方で裁判所または仲裁機関を介して新たな契約条件を決定するとした場合も，解決に多大な時間および労力を要する点においては大きな違いはないほか，その手続きの実効性にも疑問がある[480]．
したがって，両契約当事者間の協議によって新たな契約条件を決定するものの，無効となった契約規定に最大限類似したものとする旨の規定を Severability Clause において規定しておくことが考えられる[481]．

Section 18.10 Amendment and Modification.

No amendment to or modification of this Agreement or any Purchase Order is effective unless it is in writing and signed by an authorized Representative of each Party.

6.10 Non-Modification Clause
交渉の結果として契約がいったん成立したといえる場合であっても，その契約内容は書面のみならず口頭によっても変更することができる[482]．18.10 条の

---

[480] Fishman, *supra* note 477 (例えば無効と判断した規定に対して，新たな規定を設けることまではせず無効部分を削除するのみにとどめる (Blue Pencil Doctrine という) という方針をとる裁判所との関係においては，実質的に意義のある新たな規定を望めない場合も想定される旨を指摘する).
[481] この場合，次のような規定を設けることになる．「If any term of this Agreement is to any extent illegal, otherwise invalid, or incapable of being enforced, such term shall be excluded to the extent of such invalidity or unenforceability; all other terms hereof shall remain in full force and effect; and, to the extent permitted and possible, the invalid or unenforceable term shall be deemed replaced by a term that is valid and enforceable and that comes closest to expressing the intention of such invalid or unenforceable term.」. *Id.*.
[482] Mark G. Matuschak & Kenneth Slade, *Subsequent Oral Agreements and Conduct Can Modify a Contract,*

規定する Non-Modification Clause は，契約内容の変更を契約当事者の署名のある書面によってのみ認めることで契約内容の安定を図るものである[483]．

a. Modification
契約の Modification が有効に認められるための要件は契約の成立要件と同じであるが，U.C.C.の適用対象となる本契約については，Consideration は不要である[484]．

b. Modification の書面化
Modification の内容を明確化するため，および，Non-Modification Clause との関係から，Modification の内容を規定した新たな契約書（Amendment Agreement などという）が用意されることが多い．

c. Non-Modification Clause の非絶対性
Non-Modification Clause についても Non-Waiver Clause と同じく[485]，契約当事者のとった行為の結果として Non-Modification Clause の適用が放棄されたと認められる場合がある[486]．その場合においては，例えば口頭による Modification

---

Despite Explicit Contractual Clause to the Contrary, Wilmer Cutler Pickering Hale and Dorr LLP (Jul. 24, 2002), https://www.wilmerhale.com/pages/publicationsandNewsDetail.aspx?NewsPubId=94555 (last visited Mar. 29, 2018). 法律上格別に対象契約の modification は書面によってのみ許容される旨規定されている場合でない限り，契約の modification は口頭によっても可能である (これはたとえ対象契約が modification は書面にのみによって可能である旨を規定している場合にも妥当する．この点については Non-Modification Clause の非絶対性と関係してくるものであるため後述する). *See, e.g.*, S & M Rotogravure Service, Inc. v. Baer, 252 N.W.2d 913, 919-20 (first citing 4 Williston on Contracts § 591 (3d ed. Jaeger 1961); and then citing 6 Corbin on Contracts § 1295 (1962)) ("It is universally accepted that, unless a contract is one required by law to be in writing, the contract can be modified orally although it provides that it can be modified only in writing.").
[483] いくつかの州の州法および U.C.C.において Non-Modification Clause と同趣旨の規定をおいている．Cal. Civ. § 1698; N.Y. Gen. Oblig. § 15-301; U.C.C. § 2-209(2) (Am. Law Inst. & Unif. Law Comm'n 2002).
[484] 詳細については 3.9 (Purchase Orders の変更) において紹介した．
[485] Glenn West, *What is the Deal with No Oral Modification/Waiver Clauses?*, Weil, Gotshal & Manges LLP (Jul. 17, 2017), https://privateequity.weil.com/insights/no-oral-modificationwaiver-clauses/ (last visited Apr. 2, 2018) (Shields Limited P'ship v. Bradberry, 526 S.W.3d 471 をふまえ，Non-Waiver Clause に関しては契約上の規定によって Non-Waiver Clause の Waiver を予防できるが，Non-Modification Clause の Waiver に関してはそのような対応が認められていない旨を指摘する).
[486] *See, e.g.*, Quality Products and Concepts Co. v. Nagel Precision, Inc. 666 N.W.2d 251, 253 (Sup. Ct. Mich. 2003) ("We hold that parties to a contract are free to *mutually* waive or modify their contract notwithstanding a written modification or anti-waiver clause because of the freedom to contract."); *see generally Quality Products*, 666 N.W.2d, 257 (Modification に関する契約当事者間における合意があったことについては「Clear and Convincing Evidence」によって証明される必要がある旨を示した) ("[C]ontracting parties are at liberty to design their own guidelines for modification or waiver of the rights and duties established by the contract, but even despite such provisions, a modification or waiver can be established by clear and convincing evidence that

の合意であっても有効に Modification が成立したものと認められうる[487]。

> Section 18.11 Counterparts.
>
> This Agreement may be executed in counterparts, each of which is deemed an original, but all of which together are deemed to be one and the same agreement. Notwithstanding anything to the contrary in Section 18.7, a signed copy of this Agreement delivered by facsimile, email, or other means of electronic transmission is deemed to have the same legal effect as delivery of an original signed copy of this Agreement.

6.11 Counterparts Clause

　例えば Buyer が日本の会社であり，Seller が米国の会社であるとする．この場合，両社が一同に介して契約に署名することは難しいし，Buyer が署名した契約書の原本を国際郵便で Seller に送り，それに Seller が署名するといった手続きをとることも煩雑である．

　Counterparts Clause は，全契約当事者がひとつの書面に署名する以外の方法，例えば Buyer が契約書に署名したのち，その契約書のコピーを E-mail によって Seller に送付し，Seller はそのコピーに署名することをもって有効に契約を成立させるといった方法を許容することで，このような問題を解決するものである．ここに，「Counterparts」とは，ある書面に関する完全なコピーを指す．

　Counterparts Clause に基づく運用を行った場合，形式的には複数の Counterparts（本契約の場合，Seller が署名した契約書と Buyer が署名した契約書の 2 通）が存在することになる．そこで，18.11 条のように，契約当事者間の合意はあくまで一つの契約書に関して形成されたものである旨を明記し，万全を期することが望ましい[488]。

---

the parties mutually agreed to a modification or waiver of the contract.").

[487] Non-Modification Clause と同趣旨の規定をおく州法または U.C.C.のもとにおいても，その後契約当事者間で Modification を容認する行為が認められた場合，Non-Modification の Waiver があったものとして取り扱う場合がある．E.g., U.C.C. § 2-209(2) (Am. Law Inst. & Unif. Law Comm'n 2002).

[488] Stark, *supra* note 1, at 236; *but see*, Practical Law Commercial Transactions, *General Contract Clauses: Counterparts*, Thomson Reuters, https://1.next.westlaw.com/Document/I7bc56302e1aa11e398db8b09b4f043e0/View/FullText.html?transitionType=SearchItem&contextData=(sc.Search)#co_anchor_a994780 (last visited Jun. 20, 2018) (Counterparts Clause を含まない契約が Counterparts を利用して締結されたとしても，その契約の有効性自体が否定される可能性はそれほど高くはなく，むしろ Counterparts Clause は証拠能力との関係における意義（後述する）のほうが大きい旨を指摘する）．

・Counterparts の証拠能力

証拠法においては，訴訟における書面の証拠については原則として原本の提出が要求されており（Best Evidence Rule という）[489]，副本の提出は所定の要件を満たした場合に限り許容される[490]．

そのため，一方契約当事者が Counterparts を訴訟における証拠として提出した場合，対立する他の契約当事者は，Counterparts は全契約当事者の署名が直接付されたものではないため原本には該当せず，副本としての提出に関する要件を満たす必要がある旨主張することも理論上は可能かのように思われる[491]．しかし，当事者間においてある Counterparts が原本に該当する旨合意している場合，その合意は証拠法上も有効なものとして取り扱われるところ[492]，Counterparts Clause はまさしくこの「Counterparts が原本に該当する旨合意している場合」に該当するものである．

したがって，Counterparts Clause を含む契約書の「Counterparts」については，いわゆる原本としての提出が認められているといえる．

Section 18.12 Relationship of Parties.

Nothing in this Agreement creates any agency, joint venture, partnership, or other form of joint enterprise, employment, or fiduciary relationship between the Parties. Seller is an independent contractor under this Agreement. Neither Party has any express or implied right or authority to assume or create any obligations on behalf of or in the name of the other Party or to bind the other Party to any contract, agreement, or undertaking with any third party.

6.12 Independent Contractor Clause

18.12 条においては，両契約当事者は別個の独立した企業であって，本契約に関する取引以外には何らの関係を形成するわけではないことを表明している．これによって，例えば，他方契約当事者が自己の代理人[493]であると判断された

---

[489] Fed. R. Evid. 1002.
[490] Id. 1004.
[491] Practical Law Commercial Transactions, *supra* note 488.
[492] Fed. R. Evid. 1004 (d) ("An 'original' of a writing or recording means the writing or recording itself or any counterpart intended to have the same effect by the person who executed or issued it.").
[493] *See* Restatement (Third) of Agency § 1.01 (Am. Law Inst. 2006).

結果として代理権を持つこと，自己が他方契約当事者と Partnership 関係[494]にあるとして他方契約当事者に対する Fiduciary Duty[495]を負うこと，または自己が他方契約当事者と雇用関係にあるとして Vicarious Liability[496]を負うことなどをある程度予防することが期待できる[497]。

もっとも Independent Contractor Clause をもって他方契約当事者との関係を絶対的に遮断できるわけではなく，現実の両契約当事者の関係も重視されることを理解しておく必要がある[498]。

> Section 18.13 Assignment and Delegation.
>
> Seller may not assign this Agreement nor any of its rights or delegate any of its obligations under this Agreement, by operation of law or otherwise, without Buyer's prior written consent. Any purported assignment or delegation in violation of this Section 18.13 is null and void. No assignment or delegation relieves the assigning or delegating Party of any of its obligations under this Agreement.

---

[494] See Unif. P'ship Act § 102 (11) (Unif. Law Comm'n 1997).

[495] See generally id. § 409(b), § 409(c) (Fiduciary Duty について，Duty of Royalty（競業避止義務などを含む）と Duty of Care（故意による不法行為または重過失による行為を回避する義務を含む）とによって構成する)。

[496] Respondeat superior ともいう。例えば，雇用者などの監督者が従業員などの被監督者の行為に関して，その被監督者との関係を理由として負う責任をいう。特に不法行為上の監督者の責任を追及する際に用いられることが多い。Legal Info. Inst., *Respondeat Superior*, https://www.law.cornell.edu/wex/vicarious_liability (last visited Jun. 5, 2018).

[497] See, e.g., Farlow v. Harris Methodist Fort Worth Hosp., 284 S.W.3d 903, 911 (Ct. App. Tex. 2008) (first citing Newspapers, Inc. v. Love, 380 S.W.2d 582, 588-90 (Sup. Ct. Tex. 1964); then citing Bell v. VPSI, Inc., 205 S.W.3d 706, 713-14 (Ct. App. Tex. 2005), and then citing Weidner v. Sanchez, 14 S.W.3d 353, 373 (Ct. App. Tex. 2000)) (医師の治療行為に関する過失責任を問うに際してその病院の責任をも問うた事案において，医師と病院との間の契約にいわゆる Independent Contractor Clause が規定されていることを重視し，病院の責任を否定した) ("A contract expressly providing that a person is an independent contractor is determinative of the relationship absent evidence that the contract is a mere sham or subterfuge designed to conceal the true legal status of the parties or that the contract has been modified by a subsequent agreement between the parties.").

[498] See, e.g., S. G. Borello & Sons, Inc. v. Department of Industrial Relations 54 Cal. Comp. Cases 80, 84 (Sup. Ct. Cal. 1989) (契約当事者の関係を契約上どのように規定したかよりも実質的な関係を重視すべき旨を示した) ("The label placed by the parties on their relationship is not dispositive, and subterfuges are not countenanced.").

6.13 Assignment and Delegation Clause

Assignment and Delegation Clause においては，契約当事者が契約のもとで得た権利および義務を第三者に譲渡することの可否について規定する．

a. Assignment

「Assignment」とは，契約上の権利を第三者に譲渡することをいう[499]．契約当事者による別段の意思表示がない限り，契約上の権利は譲渡可能であるのが原則である．例外的に Assignment が認められない場合としては，Assignment が，(1) 他方契約当事者の義務の履行に影響を与えることになる場合[500]，(2) 他方契約当事者の負う契約上のリスクを大きく高めることになる場合[501]，(3) 他方契約当事者の契約上の権利に大きな影響を与えることになる場合[502]，および (4) 法律または公共の福祉に反することになる場合[503]が挙げられる．

b. Delegation

「Delegation」とは，契約上の義務を第三者に譲渡することをいう[504]．契約上の義務については譲渡可能であるのが原則であるが，Delegation の対象となる義務がもともとの契約当事者によって履行されることに大きな意味がある場合[505]，Delegation は認められない．なお，Delegation が有効に実行された場合であっても，もともとの契約当事者は，Delegation の対象である義務につ

---

[499] *Black's Law Dictionary: Pocket Edition* 52 (4th ed. 2011).
[500] *See, e.g.*, U.C.C. § 2-210(2) (Am. Law Inst. & Unif. Law Comm'n 2002).
[501] *See, e.g., id.* § 2-210(2); *see also, e.g.*, Rhone Poulenc Agro, S.A. v. DeKalb Genetics Corp. 284 F.3d 1323, 1328 (Fed. Cir. 2002) (特許権のライセンス契約については，Licensor にとって誰が Licensee であるのかは特に重要な問題であるとして，一般には Personal Contract (Assignment が認められない契約) であると理解できる旨を示した) ("In so holding, courts generally have acknowledged the need for a uniform national rule that patent licenses are personal and non-transferable in the absence of an agreement authorizing assignment, contrary to the state common law rule that contractual rights are assignable unless forbidden by an agreement.").
[502] *See, e.g.*, U.C.C. § 2-210(2) (Am. Law Inst. & Unif. Law Comm'n 2002); *see also, e.g.*, Kenneth D. Corwin, Ltd. v. Missouri Medical Service, 684 S.W.2d 598, 600 (Ct. App. Miss. 1085) ("It is well recognized that in a contract for personal services, which involves special knowledge, skill or a relation of personal confidence, the duty to perform is not assignable without the consent of both parties.").
[503] *See, e.g.*, Richard Stim, *What Is an Assignment of Contract? What happens when rights and duties under a contract are handed off to a third party?*, Nolo, https://www.nolo.com/legal-encyclopedia/assignment-of-contract-basics-32643.html (last visited Jun. 5, 2018) (例として，従業員による自己の将来の給与の譲渡，または，人身損害に関する請求権の譲渡を挙げる).
[504] *Black's Law Dictionary: Pocket Edition* 217 (4th ed. 2011).
[505] 例えば，Seller が有数の陶芸家であり，その陶芸品を Buyer に販売する契約を締結した場合，Seller は自己の義務を Delegation の対象とすることが認められない．これに対して Buyer は，陶芸家に対する代金支払い義務を Delegation の対象とすることが認められる．

いて引き続き責任を負う[506].

c. Anti-Assignment Clause と Anti-Delegation Clause
　他方契約当事者の同意がなければ契約上の権利または義務を譲渡することができない旨の規定を Anti-Assignment Clause または Anti-Delegation Clause という．これらは無関係の第三者が突然契約関係に入ってくることを防止する目的で設定される．
　Anti-Assignment Clause および Anti-Delegation Clause は一般に有効とされるが[507]，以下の事項との関係について留意すべきである．

i. Seller が Buyer に対する売掛債権を第三者に譲渡する場合
　ある契約のもと Seller が Buyer に対して有することになる売掛債権は契約上の権利であるから，その契約に Anti-Assignment Clause が存在する場合，Seller は Buyer の別途の承諾なくして自己の Buyer に対する売掛債権を第三者に譲渡することはできないようにも思われる．
　しかし，U.C.C.は当事者間の契約によって第三者への売掛債権の譲渡を制限することを禁止しており，そのような契約上の規定は無効であるとする[508]．したがって，Seller は Anti-Assignment Clause の存在にもかかわらず Buyer に対する売掛債権を第三者に譲渡しうる[509]．

ii. 他方契約当事者が第三者による M&A の対象となる場合
　例えばある企業（以下，実行会社という）が Buyer（以下，対象会社とも

---

[506] *See, e.g.*, U.C.C. § 2-210(1) (Am. Law Inst. & Unif. Law Comm'n 2002); *see also, e.g.*, Lonsdale v. Chesterfield 662 P.2d 385, 389 (Sup. Ct. Wash. 1983) (first citing Board of Regents v. Frederick & Nelson, 90 Wash.2d 82, 84–85 (Sup. Ct. Wash. 1978); then citing Crane Ice Cream Co. v. Terminal Freezing & Heating Co., 147 Md. 588, 598 (Ct. App. Md. 1925), and then citing Restatement (Second) of Contracts § 318(3) (1981)) (もともとの契約当事者が Delegation の対象となる義務に関して負う責任は，その義務の承継者の保証人的立場としての二次的責任である旨を示した) ("When a party contracts to perform a specified obligation, he cannot escape liability for nonperformance by delegating his duty to perform; he remains secondarily liable (as a surety) for performance of the duty promised.").

[507] *See, e.g.*, Mueller v. Northwestern University, 195 Ill. 236, 249 (Sup. Ct. Ill. 1902) ("[T]he parties to a contract may in terms prohibit its assignment, so that an assignee cannot succeed to any rights in the contract by virtue of the assignment thereof to him, and the rule thus announced is well supported by the authorities."); *but see, e.g.*, Fluor Corp. v. Superior Court, 61 Cal. 4th 1175 (保険契約のもと，保険購入者が有する権利を保険会社の許可なくしては譲渡できない旨を規定した Anti-Assignment Clause については無効である旨を示した).

[508] U.C.C. § 9-406(d)(1) (Am. Law Inst. & Unif. Law Comm'n 2010).

[509] *See* Neil B. Cohen & William H. Henning, *Freedom of Contract vs. Free Alienability: An Old Struggle Emerges in a New Context*, 46 Gonz. L. Rev. 353, 364-65 (2010-2011), https://papers.ssrn.com/sol3/papers.cfm?abstract_id=2722153 (last visited Apr. 9, 2018).

いう）の M&A (mergers and acquisitions)を試みる場合，Buyer としては 自己が Seller との間で有する本契約も実行会社に承継させることで売却額をより高いものとしたいと考えることも想定できる．
　しかし，この場合において，Seller は，Buyer に対して，M&A は（その結果として本契約が実行会社に譲渡されることになるので）Anti-Assignment Clause における「assignment」または Anti-Deligation Clause における「deligation」（以下，まとめて「Assignment」という）を伴うものであって，18.13 条により認められないと主張したい場合もあろう．
　このような主張の妥当性については，M&A がどのような形態で行われるのかによるところが大きい．

(a) 資産の買収による場合
　資産の買収 (Asset Acquisition) が実行された場合，その結果として，対象資産に関して対象会社の有する権利および責任が実行会社に譲渡されることになる．したがって，本契約が関連する Asset Acquisition の実行は，「Assignment」を伴うものである[510]．

(b) 株式の買い取りによる場合
　株式の買い取り (Stock Acquisition) は，実行会社が対象会社の株主から対象会社の株式を取得する方法によって行われるため，対象会社の権利および責任の実行会社への移転を伴うものではない．したがって，Stock Acquisition の実行は，「Assignment」を伴わない[511]．

(c) 企業結合による場合
　企業結合 (Merger) に関しては，法律の効果 (Operation of Law という) として，一方当事者の有する権利および責任を（格別の譲渡行為なくして）他方当事者が承継することになる[512]．もっとも Merger にもさまざま

---

[510] *See generally* Bart D. Dillashaw, *Anti-Assignment Provisions and Their Effect on Transaction Structures*, Koley Jessen (Aug. 5, 2013), https://www.koleyjessen.com/newsroom-publications-anti-assignment-provisions-and-their-effect-on-transaction-structures (Apr. 9, 2018) (Asset Acquisition を買収手段として選択した場合の問題点は，Asset Acquisition が Anti-Assignment Clause の対象となることである旨を指摘する).
[511] *See, e.g.*, Baxter Pharm. Prods., Inc. v. ESI Lederle Inc., 1999 Del. Ch. LEXIS 47, 19 n.19 (Ch. Del. 1999) (first citing Star Cellular Tel. Co. v. Baton Rouge CGSA, 1993 Del. Ch. LEXIS 158 (Ch. Del. 1993); then citing Nicolas M. Salgo Assocs. v. Continental Illinois Properties, D.D.C., 532 F. Supp. 279 (D.D.C. 1981); and then citing PPG Indus., Inc. v. Guardian Indus. Corp., 597 F.2d 1090 (6th Cir. 1979) ("The three cases to which Lederle refers the Court to support their proposition that a change in corporate control is a violation of an anti-assignment clause all involve mergers, not stock purchases.").
[512] Howard M. Berkower & Kristen Zook, *Mergers & Acquisitions: How to Avoid Unnecessary Surprises from*

な形態があるため，ある Merger の実行が「Assignment」を伴うものであるかどうかについては，Merger の形態ごとの検討を必要とするところ，一般的な理解[513]，各州の州法[514]および Common Law[515]からうかがえる結論はさまざまである。

したがって，Merger の実行に伴う契約の承継が「Assignment」に該当するかどうかについては 18.13 条「by operation of law or otherwise」の一節のように明示しておくことが得策といえる[516]。

Anti-Assignment and Change of Control Provisions, McCarter & English, LLP., https://www.mccarter.com/Mergers--Acquisitions-How-to-Avoid-Unnecessary-Surprises-from-Anti-Assignment-and-Change-of-Control-Provisions-06-08-2009/ (last visited Apr. 10, 2018)

[513] Merger を，(1) Direct Merger (実行会社が対象会社と結合したうえで実行会社が存続することになる)，(2) Forward Triangular Merger (実行会社の子会社が対象会社を吸収合併し，対象会社は実行会社の子会社として存続することになる)，および (3) Reverse Triangular Merger (対象会社が実行会社の子会社を吸収合併し，対象会社は実行会社の子会社として存続することになる) に分類した上で，Direct Merger および Forward Triangular Merger については対象会社と相手方契約当事者との間の契約が対象会社から実行会社または実行会社の子会社に承継されることになるため，「assignment」が生じているとする。これに対して，Reverse Triangular Merger については，対象会社自体は実行会社の子会社としてそのまま存続するため，対象会社と相手方契約当事者との間の契約もそのまま対象会社のもとにとどまり，「assignment」は生じていないとするのである。Dillashaw, *supra* note 510.

[514] 過半数の州においては ABA Model Business Corporation Act. と類似の内容の州法を有しているとされるところ，ABA Model Business Corporation Act. の公式解説では，契約において別段の規定がない限り，Merger は「assignment」を伴うものではないとする。Alan Haus et al., *Structuring Reverse and Forward Triangular Mergers: Anti-Assignment Triggers, Tax Implications, Employment Considerations*, Royse law Firm PC (Aug. 25, 2016), http://media.straffordpub.com/products/structuring-reverse-and-forward-triangular-mergers-anti-assignment-triggers-tax-implications-employment-considerations-2016-08-25/presentation.pdf (last visited Apr. 10, 2018) ("The official comment to the current MBCA provides that 'a merger is not a conveyance, transfer or assignment' and that 'it does not give rise to a claim that a contract with a party to the merger is no longer in effect on the ground of non-assignability, unless the contract specifically provides that it does not survive a merger;' but not all states have based their merger statutes on the current MBCA."). Georgia 州法および Texas 州法は，Merger は「assignment」を伴うものではない旨規定する。*Id.* 18.

[515] *See, e.g.*, SQL Solutions v. Oracle Corp., 1991 U.S. Dist. LEXIS 21097, 8-9 (N.D. Cal. 1991) (California 州においては，会社所有者の変更は権利の譲渡または移転を伴うものと一貫して認識されている旨を示した) ("California courts have consistently recognized that an assignment or transfer of rights *does* occur through a change in the legal form of ownership of a business."); *see also, e.g.*, Meso Scale Diagnostics, LLC v. Roche Diagnostics GmbH, 62 A.3d 62, 164 (Ch. Del. 2013) (Delaware 州において，*SQL Solutions*., 1991 U.S. Dist. LEXIS 21097 の適用を否定しつつ，Reverse Triangular Merger は「assignment」を伴うものではない旨を示した) ("Roche has provided a reasonable interpretation of Section 5.08 that is consistent with the general understanding that a reverse triangular merger is not an assignment by operation of law.").

[516] そのほか，Merger の全般について対応する目的で次のような規定 (Change of Control Clause という) を設ける場合もある。「Any Change in Control of either shall be deems an assignment or transfer for purposes of this Agreement that requires the prior consent of the other party. Change in Control means the sale of all or substantially all the assets of a Party; any merger, consolidation or acquisition of a Party with, by or into another

Section 18.14 No Third-Party Beneficiaries.

This Agreement benefits solely the Parties to this Agreement and their respective permitted successors and assigns and nothing in this Agreement, express or implied, confers on any other Person any legal or equitable right, benefit, or remedy of any nature whatsoever under or by reason of this Agreement.

6.14 Third Party Beneficiaries Clause

　Third Party Beneficiary とは，契約当事者ではないものの，契約内容が履行されることによって利益を享受する第三者をいい，Intended Third Party Beneficiary と Incidental Third Party Beneficiary とに分類される。

　a. Intended Third Party Beneficiary
　例えば Buyer がノイズキャンセリング機能付のヘッドフォンを$500 で Seller から購入する契約を締結したところ，Seller からその$500 は Seller の債権者である Bank に支払ってほしい旨打診され，Buyer がこれに同意したとする。この場合における Buyer を「Promisor」，Seller を「Promisee」，Bank を「Intended Third Party Beneficiary」[517]という。Intended Third Party Beneficiary[518]は，一定の条件が満たされた場合[519]，Promisee のみでなく Promisor に対しても直接

---

corporation, entity or person; or any change in the ownership of more than fifty percent (50%) of the voting capital stock of a Party in one or more related transactions」.

[517] Restatement (Second) of Contracts § 302(1) (Am. Law Inst. 1981).

[518] Intended Third Party Beneficiary については，さらに，「Creditor Beneficiary」(自らも Promisee に対して Consideration を提供した結果として Intended Third Party Beneficiary の地位を得た者をいう）および「Donee Beneficiary」(自らは Promisee に対して何らの Consideration を提供していないにもかかわらず Intended Third Party Beneficiary の地位を得た者をいう）に細分化して理解される場合もある．Creditor Beneficiary については，Promisor のみならず，Promisee に対しても直接 Promisor と Promisee との間の契約上の義務の履行を求めることができるが，Donee Beneficiary については，Promisor に対してのみその義務の履行を求めることができる．Restatement (First) of Contracts § 133(2) (1932); see David M. Summers, *Third Party Beneficiaries and the Restatement (Second) of Contracts*, 67 Cornell L. Rev. 880, 883-86 (1982), https://scholarship.law.cornell.edu/cgi/viewcontent.cgi?article=4291&context=clr (last visited Jun. 6, 2018).

[519] Intended Third Party Beneficiary がその権利を行使するためには，Intended Third Party Beneficiary としての権利が授与 (Vesting という) されたといえる状況が必要となる．Vesting は，例えば，Intended Third Party Beneficiary としての指定を受けた第三者がその権利の存在を信頼し，自己の立場を大きく変更した場合などに認められる．*See, e.g.*, Restatement (Second) of Contracts 311(3) (Am. Law Inst. 1981).

Promisor と Promisee との間の契約上の義務の履行を要求することができる[520]。

b. Incidental Third Party Beneficiary
契約上特定の第三者に対して利益を与えるような格別の取り扱いは行われていなかったにもかかわらず，結果的に利益を受けることになった者を Incidental Third Party Beneficiary[521] という。例えば Buyer が Seller に対し，Seller がノイズキャンセリング機能付のヘッドフォンを製造するうえで必要となるゴム材料を自ら購入し支給する旨約束した場合，ゴム材料の供給業者は「Incidental Third Party Beneficiary」に該当する。

Incidental Third Party Beneficiary は，Promisor または Promisee のいずれに対しても，Promisor と Promisee との間の契約上の義務の履行を求めることはできない。

18.14 条においては，Third Party Beneficiary の存在を否定することで本契約に関する問題解決を複雑化させないことを意図している。これに対して特定の第三者に (Intended) Third Party Beneficiary としての権利を確保したい場合にはその旨を明示することになる[522]。

Section 18.15 Dispute Resolution.

In the event of any dispute, claim, question, or disagreement arising from or relating to this agreement or the breach thereof, the Parties hereto shall use their best efforts to settle the dispute, claim, question, or disagreement. To this effect, the Parties shall consult and negotiate with each other in good faith and, recognizing their mutual interests, attempt to reach a just and equitable solution satisfactory to both Parties. If the Parties do not reach such solution within a period of sixty (60) days, then, either Party may file suit in a court of competent jurisdiction in accordance with the provisions of Section 18.16 and Section 18.17 hereunder.

---

[520] Id. § 302(1).
[521] Id. § 302(2).
[522] この場合，次のような規定を設けることになる。「[Terrapins Inc.] is third party beneficiary to this Agreement and is entitled to the rights and benefits hereunder and may enforce the provisions as if it was the party hereto.」。

6.15 Dispute Resolution Clause

18.15条においては，本契約に関して契約当事者間で争いが生じた場合の解決策について，まずは契約当事者間で解決の途を探ったうえで，それでも解決ができない場合は裁判所におけるLitigationにより解決を図るものとしている．

もっとも，契約当事者以外の第三者が関与する紛争解決手続きには，Litigationを含め，以下のとおりいくつかの選択肢がある．

a. Litigation

Litigationとは，裁判所において，当事者が対立関係にたったうえで行われる訴訟手続きである[523]．すべての訴訟手続きは厳格な規則に従って行われる．なお，例えばビジネスと密接に関連するものなど，特定の事項に関する争いについては，専門能力を有する裁判官による裁判（Business CourtsまたはCommercial Courtsという）を用意する州もある[524]．Business Courtsにおいては裁判官による訴訟への積極的関与および代替的紛争解決手続き（Alternative Dispute Resolutionという）の利用などを導入することで公平かつ早期の紛争解決を図っている[525]．

b. Arbitration

Arbitrationは，紛争当事者が紛争解決を第三者たる仲裁人に委ねることに合意した場合に用いられる私的な解決手続きであり[526]，当事者の合意によっ

---

[523] もっとも，訴訟がTrial（証拠調べ手続きおよび法律上の請求に関する司法判断手続きが実施される）の段階まで進捗することはまれであり，90％以上の訴訟については和解によって解決されている．Judith Stilz Ogden & Nikki McIntyre Finlay, *Strategies for Choosing a Dispute Resolution Method*, https://csbweb01.uncw.edu/people/eversp/classes/BLA361/General%20Info/Trial%20Process%20&%20Legal%20Analysis/STRATEGIES%20FOR%20CHOOSING%20A%20DISPUTE%20RESOLUTION%20METHOD.pdf (last visited Apr. 11, 2018).

[524] Anne Tucker, *Making a Case for Business Courts: A Survey of and Proposed Framework to Evaluate Business Courts*, 24 Ga. St. U. L. Rev. (2012), http://readingroom.law.gsu.edu/gsulr/vol24/iss2/4 (last visited Jun. 7, 2018). なお，Business Courtsは2015年10月時点で27州において用意されている．Jenni Bergal, *Business Courts' Take on Complex Corporate Conflicts*, The Pew Charitable Trusts (Oct. 28, 2015), http://www.pewtrusts.org/en/research-and-analysis/blogs/stateline/2015/10/28/business-courts-take-on-complex-corporate-conflicts (last visited Apr. 11, 2018).

[525] *See generally* Hon. John C. Foster et al., *Business Courts, Arbitration, and Pre-Suit Mediation: A Modest Proposal for the Strategic Resolution of Business Disputes*, 35 The Mich. Bus. L. J., 21, 23-30, https://higherlogicdownload.s3.amazonaws.com/MICHBAR/ebd9d274-5344-4c99-8e26-d13f998c7236/UploadedImages/pdfs/journal/Fall2015.pdf (last visited Apr. 11, 2018) (2015年6月に実施されたMichigan州におけるアンケートでは，68％の訴訟当事者がBusiness Courtsは通常の民事訴訟手続きよりも望ましい手続きである旨を回答し，また，63％の訴訟当事者が解決までの手続きが短縮された旨回答していることを指摘する).

[526] Arbitrationによる解決を望む場合，例えば次のような規定を設けることになる．「In the event of any

て法的拘束力のあるもの (Binding Arbitration という) とも, 法的拘束力のないもの (Nonbinding Arbitration という) ともすることができる[527]。

　Binding Arbitration を選択した場合, 仲裁人の裁定結果に不服のある当事者が不服申し立てできる場合はきわめて限定される[528]。これに対して, Nonbinding Arbitration を選択した場合, 仲裁人の裁定はあくまでアドバイス的な意味を持つにとどまり, 当事者の合意がない限りは最終合意としての意味をもたない。当事者間で合意に至らない場合は通常の訴訟手続きを利用することもできる。Nonbinding Arbitration は裁判手続きの一環としても頻繁に利用される[529]。

・American Arbitration Association Rules

　契約当事者が Arbitration を紛争解決手段として選択した場合, その Arbitration は, American Arbitration Association の規則に従って, American Arbitration Association により行われる旨規定されることが多い[530]。American Arbitration Association の規則においては, 例えば, 不服申し立て手続きについては契約当事者間で格別の合意がある場合に限って認められるとするなど特徴的な規定も見受けられるため[531], 適宜これらを確認のうえ, 契約上適切に対処しておくことが必要となりうる[532]。

---

dispute, claim, question, or disagreement arising from or relating to this Agreement or the breach thereof, the Parties hereto shall use their best efforts to settle the dispute, claim, question, or disagreement. To this effect, the Parties shall consult and negotiate with each other in good faith and, recognizing their mutual interests, attempt to reach a just and equitable solution satisfactory to the Parties. If the Parties do not reach such solution within a period of 60 days, then, upon notice by either party to the other, all disputes, claims, questions, or differences shall be finally settled by arbitration administered by the American Arbitration Association in accordance with the provisions of its Commercial Arbitration Rules.」. See A. B. A., *Drafting Dispute Resolution Clauses A Practical Guide*, 12, https://www.adr.org/sites/default/files/document_repository/Drafting%20Dispute%20Resolution%20Clauses%20A%20Practical%20Guide.pdf (last visited Apr. 11, 2018).

[527] A.B.A. Sec. of Disp. Resol., *What You Need to Know about Dispute Resolution" The Guide to Dispute Resolution Process*, https://www.americanbar.org/content/dam/aba/migrated/2011_build/dispute_resolution/draftbrochure.authcheckdam.pdf (last visited Jun. 7, 2018).

[528] See, e.g., Robert N. Rapp & Alexander B. Reich, *AAA shakes up ADR with new rules to permit appeals of arbitration awards*, Calfee, Halter & Griswold LLP (Nov. 6, 2013), https://s3.amazonaws.com/documents.lexology.com/1310983d-17ec-41cb-a547-cf7fe8a73348.pdf (last visited Jun. 7, 2018) (連邦法および州法ともに, 「fairness and integrity of the process」に問題がある場合にのみ不服申し立てを認める旨を指摘する).

[529] Ogden, *supra* note 523.

[530] Rapp, *supra* note 528.

[531] A.B.A., Optional Appellate Arbitration Rules (Nov. 1, 2013), 5, https://www.adr.org/sites/default/files/AAA%20ICDR%20Optional%20Appellate%20Arbitration%20Rules.pdf (last visited Apr. 12, 2018).

[532] 不服申し立て手続きに関する両契約当事者の合意を示すものとしては, 次の規定が参考となる。
「Notwithstanding any language to the contrary in the contract documents, the parties hereby agree: that the Underlying Award may be appealed pursuant to the AAA's Optional Appellate Arbitration Rules ("Appellate

c. Mediation

Mediation は，紛争当事者による和解を第三者が補助する私的な手続きである[533]．裁判所が裁判手続きの一環として Mediation の利用を義務付けることもあるが，その場合においても和解に至るかどうかについてはあくまで当事者の意思によっている．和解の合意に達した場合，Mediator は裁判所で執行可能な内容の和解契約書の準備に至るまでを補助する場合もある[534]．

一般に Mediation はその利用場面および利用回数に関する制約がない．すなわち，紛争当事者は訴訟の途中で並行して別途 Mediation を試みることもできるし，また，Mediation が一度不調に終わったとしてもあらためて Mediation を試みることもできる．

Litigation，Arbitration，または Mediation のうちいずれの紛争解決手続きによるかの選択は，紛争解決に要する期間および費用，紛争解決手続の内容（厳格性または柔軟性），ならびに，担当機関の役割および信頼性（中立義務または秘密保持義務などを負うのか）などさまざまな事情を考慮したうえで，その事案との関係をふまえつつ行うことになる[535]．

Rules"); that the Underlying Award rendered by the arbitrator(s) shall, at a minimum, be a reasoned award; and that the Underlying Award shall not be considered final Optional Appellate Arbitration Rules 4 ARBITRATION RULES American Arbitration Association until after the time for filing the notice of appeal pursuant to the Appellate Rules has expired. Appeals must be initiated within thirty (30) days of receipt of an Underlying Award, as defined by Rule A-3 of the Appellate Rules, by filing a Notice of Appeal with any AAA office. Following the appeal process the decision rendered by the appeal tribunal may be entered in any court having jurisdiction thereof.」. *Id.* at 3-4. なお，契約上，Arbitration に関する不服申し立て手続の利用自体について合意しているとしても，不服申し立て手続きが実際に認められる場面は Arbitration に著しい瑕疵が認められる場合に限定される．*Id.* at 8-9. ("A party may appeal on the grounds that the Underlying Award is based upon: (1) an error of law that is material and prejudicial; or (2) determinations of fact that are clearly erroneous.").

[533] Mediation による解決を望む場合，次のような規定を設けることになる．「If a dispute arises out of or relates to this Agreement, or the breach thereof, and if the dispute cannot be settled through negotiation, the parties agree first to try in good faith to settle the dispute by mediation administered by the American Arbitration Association under its Commercial Mediation Procedures before resorting to arbitration, litigation, or some other dispute resolution procedure.」. *See* A. B. A., *supra* note 526, at 12.

[534] *See generally* Ogden, *supra* note 523 (Mediation は Mediator の手続きへの関与の仕方によって，(1) Facilitative (完全に中立的な立場をとり，個人的な意見の表明は行わない)，(2) Evaluative (紛争内容について個人的見解を述べるほか，解決に向けた提案を行う)，(3) Transformative (直接的な紛争解決よりも紛争当事者による相互の主張の理解および紛争解決に向けた姿勢の形成を補助する) に分類できるとする).

[535] Arbitration および Mediation については，Litigation と比較して，紛争解決に要する期間が短いこと，および，その費用が低廉であることが利点であるとされることが多い．この点，紛争解決に要する期間については，Litigation の場合 Trial に進むまでに 18 か月から 3 年を要するとの統計もある．Arbitration は規則上一定期間内の解決が要求されている場合もあり，解決に至るまでの期間はおおよそ 475 日と

Section 18.16 Choice of Law.

This Agreement, including all Individual Transaction documents and exhibits, schedules, attachments, and appendices attached to this Agreement and thereto, and all matters arising out of or relating to this Agreement, are governed by, and construed in accordance with, the Laws of the State of Ohio, the United States of America, without regard to the conflict of laws provisions thereof to the extent such principles or rules would require or permit the application of the Laws of any jurisdiction other than those of the State of Ohio, the United States of America. The parties agree that the United Nations Convention on Contracts for the International Sale of Products does not apply to any contract made under this Agreement.

6.16 Choice of Law Clause

　Choice of Law Clause（Governing Law Clause ともいう）は契約に関する紛争が発生した場合の準拠法を明示するものである。

　　a. Choice of Law Clause を規定しない場合の取り扱い
　　　ある契約において Choice of Law Clause が存在しない場合、その契約に関する紛争解決基準としての適用法を決定する必要が生じうる。この点については、まず、適用法となる可能性を有する州法[536]のいずれを適用した場合であってもその契約に関する紛争の解決結果は異ならないといえるのかどうかの

の統計もある。Mediation は規則自体が複雑でないため、より早期の解決が期待できるとされる。費用については、紛争解決に至るまでの期間との兼ね合いによるところが大きく、また、Arbitration および Mediation においてはその実施自体にも$10,000 近い金額が必要となることに留意する必要がある。Ogden, supra note 523; Barbara Kate Repa, *Arbitration Pros and Cons Learn about the advantages and disadvantaged of arbitration*, Nolo, www.nolo.com. Available at: https://www.nolo.com/legal-encyclopedia/arbitration-pros-cons-29807.html (last visited Oct. 12, 2017). Mediation のほうが Arbitration よりも利用者の満足度が高いと評価し、その理由として、(1) Arbitrator は自分が将来再び Arbitration の依頼を受けることがあるように振る舞う可能性があること、(2) Arbitration は Discovery 手続きなど一部の裁判手続きを簡易化しているため真に公平な解決が期待できるか疑問もあること、および、(3) Arbitration Hearing は時間的な制約があることを挙げるものもある。*Id.*

[536] 例えば、契約の締結地のほか、契約の履行地となる州の州法などが挙げられる。*See, e.g.,* Mutual Life Ins. Co. v. Liebing, 259 U.S. 209 (U.S. 1922) ("the law of the place where a contract is made to determine the validity and the consequences of the act."); *see also., e.g.,* Restatement (Second) of Conflicts of Laws § 187 cmt. a illust. (Am. Law. Inst. 1971).

判断を行うことになる.

　いずれの州法を適用したとしても紛争の解決結果は異ならない場合，実質的な適用法に関する争いはないものいえるため，裁判所は適用法に関する判断を下さず[537]，適用法となる可能性のある州法を実質的にひとつのものとして適用することになる[538].

　これに対して，いずれの州法を適用するかによって紛争の解決結果が異なる場合[539]，抵触法[540]の原則にしたがって適用法が決定される．すなわち，ある取引に関する紛争は，その取引に最も重大な利害関係を有する州の法律[541]によって解決されることになる[542]．ところがどの州が最も重大な利害関係を有する州であるのかという判断にあたってはさまざまな事情が考慮されることもあり[543]，その結果の予見は容易ではない．

---

[537] *See, e.g.*, Underhill Inv. Corp. v. Fixed Income Disc. Advisory Co., 319 Fed. Appx. 137, 140 (3d. Cir. 2009) (first quoting Berg Chilling Sys. v. Hull Corp., 435 F.3d 455, 462 (3d. Cir. 2006); and then quoting Williams v. Stone, 109 F.3d 890, 893 (3d. Cir. 1997)) ("To resolve this issue, 'we must determine whether a true conflict exists' between the application of Delaware and New York law. Where the laws of the two jurisdictions would produce the same result on the particular issues presented, there is a 'false conflict,' and the Court should avoid the choice-of-law question.").

[538] *See, e.g.*, Lucker Mfg. v. Home Ins. Co., 23 F.3d 808, 813 (3d. Cir. 1994) (internal citation omitted) (Pennsylvania 州法と Wisconsin 州法のいずれを適用すべきかに関して，紛争の対象である保険会社の Duty to Indemnification および Duty to Defend との関係では Pennsylvania 州法と Wisconsin 州法の間に違いはないとして両州法をひとつのものとして適用する旨を示した) ("Neither party has pressed a choice of law question on this appeal because neither has been able to identify any differences between Wisconsin and Pennsylvania law on the questions of an insurer's duty to defend and indemnify. Our own research has not identified any relevant differences either. As far as we can tell, the outcome of this lawsuit should be the same under either Wisconsin or Pennsylvania law. Since there is no conflict of law under such circumstances, we will avoid the choice of law question. We therefore will interchangeably refer to the laws of Wisconsin and Pennsylvania in discussing the law governing The Home's duty to defend and indemnify.").

[539] 本書においては米国法が適用される場合を前提とし，どの国家の法律を適用すべきかという国際私法に関する問題については考慮していない．また，本書においては契約の対象が動産たる製品であることを前提としている．これに対して契約の対象が不動産である場合，その契約の適用法は一般に不動産の所在地を管轄する法律とされる．*See, e.g.*, In re Will of Haldeman, 143 N.Y.S.2d 396, 423 (Sur. Ct. N.Y. 1955).

[540] ある訴訟の原因が複数の州にまたがる場合で，かつ，その各州がおのおの異なった内容の法律を有する場合において，いずれの州法を適用するのかについて決する法律をいう．*Black's Law Dictionary: Pocket Edition* 147 (4th ed. 2011).

[541] ここでいう法律とはいわゆる実体法をいう．手続法については裁判の実施される州の規定が適用されるのが原則である．*See* Restatement (Second) of Conflict of Laws § 122, cmt. a. (Am. Law. Inst. 1971); *see, e.g.*, Alaska Rent-A-Car, Inc. v. Avis Budget Group, Inc. 738 F.3d 960, 974 (9th Cir. 2013) ("Alaska generally follows the Restatement (Second) of Conflict of Laws, which says that a court usually applies its own local law rules prescribing how litigation shall be conducted even when it applies the local law rules of another state to resolve other issues in the case.").

[542] *See* Restatement (Second) of Conflicts of Laws § 6(2) (Am. Law. Inst. 1971).

[543] *See id.* § 188(2); *see also id.* § 6(2).

したがって，契約当事者間であらかじめ準拠法を決定しておく Choice of Law Clause は適用法に関する予見性を確保するものとして意義がある．

b. Choice of Law Clause を規定する場合の取り扱い

Choice of Law Clause を規定する場合，その準拠法が契約に関する紛争を解決するうえで適切かつ予見可能性に優れているのか，および，紛争解決地はどことするのか[544]がその選択に関する重要な基準である．

また，Choice of Law Clause のもとで準拠法が選択されている場合であってもその選択は絶対ではなく[545]さまざまな制約を受ける[546]．特に以下の事項については留意すべきである．

i. Choice of Law Clause の適用範囲

18.16 条における「[A]ll matters arising out of or relating to this Agreement are governed by, and construed in accordance with, the Laws of the State of Ohio」のように，Choice of Law Clause には「arising out of or relating to」の一節が含まれている場合がある．この一節は，契約関係から派生する権利を幅広く網羅する意図を達成するひとつの有効な手段である[547]．

---

[544] Stark, *supra* note 1, at 227 (Choice of Law Clause における準拠法を管轄する州と Choice of Forum Clause における紛争解決地とを整合させることは，準拠法がその選択とおり執行される可能性を高めることにつながる旨を指摘する).

[545] *See, e.g.,* Restatement (Second) of Conflicts of Laws § 187(2)(a) (Am. Law. Inst. 1971); *see also, e.g.*, U.C.C. § 1-301 (Am. Law Inst. & Unif. Law Comm'n 2001) (準拠法を管轄する州と取引との間にある程度の関係を要求する); *see also* Stark, *supra* note 1, at 227. これに対して New York 州および Delaware 州においては，一定の要件を満たす取引に関しては，たとえ自州と対象取引自体との間に関係がないとしても，自州の州法を準拠法とすることを認める. Del. Code Ann. Tit. 6, Section 2708(c) (2013); N.Y. Gen. Oblig. Law Section 5-1402 (2013); *see, e.g.*, Tosapratt, LLC v Sunset Props., Inc., 86 A.D.3d 768, 770-71 (Sup. Ct. N.Y. 2011) ("[T]he parties' choice of law provision is enforceable, unless procured by fraud or overreaching, even if, under a traditional choice of law analysis, the application of the chosen law would violate a fundamental public policy of another, more interested jurisdiction.").

[546] *See, e.g.*, Pivotal Payments Direct Corp. v. Planet Payment, Inc., 2015 Del. Super. LEXIS 1058, 8 (Sup. Ct. Del. 2015) (Statute of Limitations については Choice of Law Clause の対象である旨を明示しない限りはその適用を受けない旨を示した) ("Under Delaware law, choice-of-law provisions in contracts do not apply to statutes of limitations, unless a provision expressly includes it. If no provision expressly includes it, then the law of the forum applies because the statute of limitations is a procedural matter."); *see also, e.g.*, Glenn West, *Making Sure Your "Choice-of-Law" Clause Chooses All of the Laws of the Chosen Jurisdiction*, Harvard Law School Forum on Corporate and Financial Regulation (Sep. 18, 2017), https://corpgov.law.harvard.edu/2017/09/18/making-sure-your-choice-of-law-clause-chooses-all-of-the-laws-of-the-chosen-jurisdiction/ (last visited Oct. 13, 2017) (Statute of Limitations についても Choice of Law Clause の対象としたい場合においては，次のように規定すべきであると推奨する．「All matters arising out or relating to this Agreement are governed by the Laws of the State of [Ohio], including its statutes of limitations.」).

[547] *See, e.g.*, Innovative BioDefense, Inc. v. VSP Techs., Inc., 2013 U.S. Dist. LEXIS 95429, 16 (S.D.N.Y. 2013)

ii. 抵触法との関係

Choice of Laws Clause においては適用法を明示した後に,「抵触法における規定にもかかわらず」の意味で,「without regard to conflict of laws provision」の一節を続けることがある.

これは各州それぞれが抵触法を有していることに関係する. すなわち, 例えば契約において Ohio 州法を準拠法として規定したとしても, Ohio 州の抵触法の適用が許容されているのであれば, その適用のもと, 結局, その契約は Michigan 州法によって判断されるべきである旨判断されるといった事態も生じうるのである. しかし, それでは Choice of Law Clause を設けた意味がなくなってしまう[548]. そこで, そのような各州の抵触法が適用されることはない旨を明示し, Choice of Law Clause の実効性を確保しようとするのである[549].

(first quoting Williams v. Deutsche Bank Sec., Inc., 2005 U.S. Dist. LEXIS 12121, 5 (S.D.N.Y. 2005); and then quoting Frazer Exton Dev., LP v. Kemper Envtl., Ltd., 2004 U.S. Dist. LEXIS 14602, 10 (S.D.N.Y. 2004) (New York 州においては Choice of Law Clause の対象となる紛争に契約上の請求権に基づく紛争以外のものをも包含する意図である場合においては,「arising out of or relating to the contract」または「arising directly or indirectly from the Agreement」とするべきである旨を示した) ("New York courts have consistently held that language that the 'agreement itself' is to be governed by a particular law is too narrow to cover non-contractual claims, and that in order to achieve broad coverage, parties should utilize choice-of-law provisions that 'employ expansive language such as 'arising out of or relating to' the contract or 'arising directly or indirectly from the Agreement.'"); see also, e.g., Shelley v. Trafalgar House Public Ltd. Co. 918 F.Supp. 515, 522 (D.P.R. 1996) (citing Consolidated Data Term. v. Applied Digital Data Sys., 708 F.2d 385, 390 n. 3.) (不法行為上の請求権に関する紛争については, Choice of Law Clause は本来的な適用対象とは理解されない旨を示した) ("This Court will adhere to the reasoning of many jurisdictions which have held that contractual choice of law clauses do not encompass tort causes of action.").

[548] Stark, supra note 1, at 227; see generally id. (「Without regard to conflict of laws provision」については, 「Renvoi」(ある紛争がどの州の州法によって解決されるのかの決定が準拠法を管轄する州の実体法のみならず抵触法をも考慮したうえで行われること) による不都合 (例えば, 準拠法を管轄する州が自州の抵触法を適用した結果, 他の州の州法の適用が適当である旨判断したところ, その他の州の抵触法を適用すると, 準拠法を管轄する州の州法によることが適当である旨判断され, 循環状態に陥ってしまうこと) を回避することを目的として規定される旨を説明する).

[549] But see Shearman & Sterling LLP, *Common Sense Trumps Extra Words in Governing Law Clause* (Jan. 2013), http://www.shearman.com/~/media/Files/NewsInsights/Publications/2013/01/Common-Sense-Trumps-Extra-Words-in-Governing-Law__/Files/View-full-memo-Common-Sense-Trumps-Extra-Words-i__/FileAttachment/CommonSenseTrumpsExtraWordsinGoverningLawClauseC__.pdf (last visited Jun. 8, 2018) (Choice of Law Clause のもとである州法が適用法として選択された場合, その州の抵触法が別途適用されるようなことはなく,「without regard to conflict of laws provision」の一節は, その意義よりも慣例的な面を重視して用いられているとする) (IRB-Brasil Resseguros, S.A. v. Inepar Investments, S.A. 20 N.Y.3d 310 (Ct. App. N.Y. 2012) "holding ensures a court will apply New York substantive law if the parties choose New York law pursuant to section 5-1401, even if a traditional analysis of conflict-of-laws rules would result in the application of another jurisdiction's substantive law. The IRB-Brasil decision thus does away with the need to

6.17 CISG Clause

　CISG は，国際的な物品取引に関して，現代的，統一的，および公平な契約条件の整備を図ったものであり，2016 年 5 月時点で米国を含む 85 カ国の批准を受けている[550]．CISG は州法に優先する[551]．

　a. CISG の適用

　CISG の適用があるのは，①物品の売買に関する契約が，② (a) 異なる CISG 批准国に「place of business」を置く当事者間において締結される場合，または，(b) 対象契約に適用される国際私法によると CISG 批准国の法律が適用されることとなる場合である[552]．

　ここに両契約当事者の「place of business」が「異なる CISG 批准国」に所在するかどうかについては，各契約当事者が対象契約との関係上最も密接な関係を有する場所がどこであるかに基づいて判断される[553]．したがって，両契約当事者が必ずしも異なる CISG 批准国の法律に基づいて設立された会社である必要はなく[554]，例えば一方契約当事者が契約対象製品の製造を他方契約当事者の所在地とは別の CISG 批准国において行っているといった事実があれば CISG の適用対象となりうる．

　b. CISG の適用除外

　CISG は契約当事者間の合意によってその適用を排除することができ

---

include "without regard to conflict-of-laws principles" in the governing law provision of a commercial contract.").

[550] Olga Larionova & Karen A. Monroe, *CISG: To Include or Exclude? That is the Question*, Wilk Auslander LLP, (Apr. 5, 2017), https://www.lexology.com/library/detail.aspx?g=7ae22d0a-2873-425a-962e-3b32a0701529 (last visited Apr. 20, 2018). 未批准の国としては England，India，および South Africa などが挙げられる．Pace Law School Inst. of Int'l Commercial Law, *CISG: participating countries*, https://www.cisg.law.pace.edu/cisg/countries/cntries.html (last visited Apr. 20, 2018).

[551] *See, e.g.*, Asante Techs. v. PMC-Sierra, Inc., 164 F. Supp. 2d 1142, 1152 (N.D. Cal. 2001) ("Although the CISG is plainly limited in its scope (15 U.S.C. App., Art. 4.), the CISG nevertheless can and does preempt state contract law to the extent that the state causes of action fall within the scope of the CISG.").

[552] CISG art. 1. *See generally* United Nations Treaty Collection, *International Trade and Development*, https://treaties.un.org/pages/ViewDetails.aspx?src=TREATY&mtdsg_no=X-10&chapter=10&clang=_en (last visited Jun. 8, 2018). CISG の批准国は批准する際に要件② (b) についての適用を排除する旨を宣言することができるところ，米国はその宣言を行っている．

[553] CISG art. 10(a).

[554] *See, e.g., Asante Techs.*, 164 F. Supp. 2d (Delaware 州で設立された会社の間における電子部品の売買契約に関して生じた対象製品の不良などに関する事案．被告の製品の設計活動などが CISG の批准国である Canada で行われていた点に着目し，被告の「place of business」は Canada であり，対象取引には CISG の適用がある旨を示した).

る[555]．そこで，米国の実務上は，ほとんどの契約においてCISGの適用が排除されているようであるが，それはCISGの適用排除に関する実質的な選択の結果というよりも，CISGに関する理解の不十分さによるところが大きいように思われる[556]．

このような状況をふまえつつ，通常の取引においてはBattle of the Forms[557]に関する議論が比較的重要な位置を占めることをふまえた指摘もある．つまり，CISGでは実質的にはLast Shot Rule[558]が採用されていると評価できる[559]ことに着目し，SellerはCISGの適用を受ける方向で[560]CISG Clauseを調整することを推奨するのである[561]．

Section 18.17 Choice of Forum.

Each Party irrevocably and unconditionally submits to the exclusive jurisdiction of such courts and agrees to bring any such action, litigation, or proceeding of any kind whatsoever against the other Party in any way arising from or relating to this Agreement, including all Individual Transactions and exhibits, schedules, attachments, and appendices attached to this Agreement and thereto, and all contemplated transactions, including contract, equity, tort, fraud, and statutory claims only in United States District Court Southern District of Ohio or, if such

---

[555] CISG art. 6.
[556] See Leonard Budow, *United States: The Law That Dare Not Speak Its Name In The USA: The CISG*, Mondaq Ltd. (Sep. 8, 2015) (米国の実務家においてはCISGの存在自体が浸透していない旨を指摘する).
[557] See supra note 73.
[558] See supra note 76.
[559] Offerに対するOfferee の回答がOfferのMaterialな変更を伴うものである場合，それはCounter-offerとして取り扱われるところ (CISG art. 19(1))，CISGにおける「Material」は広汎に定義されているため (CISG art. 19(3))，Offereeの回答はCounter-offerを構成すると理解されることが多いものと思われる．その後OfferorがOffereeから発送された物品を受領するとその受領行為はCounter-offerのAcceptanceを構成し，結果的にOffereeの提示条件に拘束されることとなるのである．Richard F. Paciaroni & Jason L. Richery, *Sales of Products – Battle of the Forms Under UCC and CISG A Practical Perspective*, K&L Gates LLP, 28, 36, http://www.klgates.com/files/Publication/b07fa188-05de-415d-92e5-0dd640432da3/Presentation/PublicationAttachment/64a24a21-ae6f-47a2-ab41-1c7f9ff91b61/Paciaroni_Richey_Battle_of_the_forms.pdf (last visited Oct. 13, 2017); see also Alicia Journey, *Who's Afraid of the CISG?– Contracts for the International Sale of Goods*, Smith Debnam Narron Drake Saintsing & Myers, LLP, https://www.smithdebnamlaw.com/2008/07/whos-afraid-of-the-cisg-contracts-for-the-international-sale-of-goods/ (last visited Apr. 23, 2018).
[560] この場合，CISGの適用対象となる契約についてはCISGが自動的に適用されるのが原則であるから，SellerはCISGの適用に関して契約上格別の対応をとる必要はない．
[561] Paciaroni, *supra* note 559.

> court does not have subject matter jurisdiction, the courts of the State of Ohio sitting in Franklin County.
>
> Each Party agrees that a final judgment in any such action, litigation, or proceeding is conclusive and may be enforced in other jurisdictions by suit on the judgment or in any other manner provided by Law.

6.18 Choice of Forum Clause

　Choice of Forum Clause は，契約に関する紛争の裁定地を事前に規定することで契約当事者の紛争処理に関する予見性を高めるものである[562]．Choice of Forum Clause は Choice of Law Clause と異なる意義を有するため，独立した条項を用意することが望ましい[563]．

　また，特段の理由がない限り，Choice of Forum Clause に関する文言は Choice of Law Clause に関する文言と調和させ，一方の適用範囲が他方より狭められるといった事態を避けなければならない[564]．

　a. Choice of Forum
　Choice of Forum Clause においては，次の事項に関する検討が必要である．

　i. 裁定地の選択
　裁定地は，契約当事者および関係者などの所在地と地理的に近接してい

---

[562] Choice of Forum Clause が設けられていない場合，複数の場所が裁定地の候補となりうる．*See, e.g.*, 28 U.S.C. § 1391(b) (2011).

[563] Hague Conference on Private Int'l Law, *Principles on Choice of Law in International Commercial Contracts* (2015), 23-24, https://assets.hcch.net/docs/5da3ed47-f54d-4c43-aaef-5eafc7c1f2a1.pdf (last visited Jun. 8, 2015).

[564] *See, e.g.*, Innovative BioDefense, Inc. v. VSP Techs., Inc., 2013 U.S. Dist. LEXIS 95429, 17-18 (S.D.N.Y. 2013) (Choice of Law Clause (適用対象を「this agreement」とする) と Choice of Forum Clause (適用対象を「any controversy, claim or dispute」とする) の文言の差異に着目し，Choice of Law Clause の適用範囲を Choice of Forum Clause よりも狭めて解釈した) ("The choice-of-law provision at issue here states that '*[t]his Agreement* shall be . . . construed in accordance with the laws of . . . New York as to all matters.' The Court holds that this language is not sufficiently expansive to achieve the broad coverage Defendants assert. This holding is supported by the fact that, as compared to the language employed by the parties in the choice-of-law provision, they chose to use broad language in the forum-selection clause, which provides that: In the event of *any controversy, claim or dispute* between the Parties hereto *arising out of or relating to* this Agreement, such controversy, claim or dispute may be tried exclusively in the courts of the State of New York, County of New York or in the United States Federal District Court, Southern District, as either Party may elect . . . . The Court therefore assumes that the inclusion of broad language in the forum-selection provision and omission of similarly broad language in the choice-of-law provision was intentional. Accordingly, the Court finds that the choice-of-law provision should be read to apply only to disputes arising from the Agreements.").

るか，または，その事案について有利な結果が期待できるか[565]といった事情を考慮して選定することになる．

ii. Mandatory Choice of Forum または Permissive Choice of Forum の選択

Choice of Forum Clause は，その趣旨からして，少なくとも対象契約に関する紛争については設定された裁定地で解決を図る旨の契約当事者間の合意を表したものといえそうである．

ところが，実際には Choice of Forum Clause の規定する裁定地が，対象契約に関する紛争について利用可能な唯一の裁定地（Mandatory Choice of Forum という）であるのか，または，利用可能な裁定地のうちのひとつ（Permissive Choice of Forum という）にすぎないのかについて争いが生じる場合がある[566]．

そこで Mandatory Choice of Forum を選択する場合においては，「exclusive」および「shall be」[567]といった語句を使用し，その意図が客観的に明示されるようにすべきである[568]．

iii. 連邦裁判所または州裁判所の選択

Choice of Forum Clause においてはその裁定がどの州で行われるかのみならず，どの地区で行われるか，または，連邦裁判所もしくは州裁判所のい

---

[565] See, e.g., Marks & Associates, P.C., *Choice of Law and Forum Selection Provisions*, http://www.leaselawyer.com/cases-and-articles/choice-of-law-and-forum-selection-provisions/ (last visited Oct. 16, 2017)（裁定地として選定する州によく知った弁護士がいるか，また，その州は対象事案について一方に有利な判断を下す傾向にあるのか（例えば原告に有利な判断を下す，または，会社側に有利な判断を下す）などを挙げる）．

[566] See, e.g., Phillips v. Audio Active Ltd., 494 F.3d 378, 386 (2d. Cir. 2007) (internal citation omitted) ("Forum selection clauses may serve two distinct purposes. Contracting parties may intend to agree on a *potential* situs for suit so as to guarantee that at least one forum will be available to hear their disputes. A so-called permissive forum clause only confers jurisdiction in the designated forum, but does not deny plaintiff his choice of forum, if jurisdiction there is otherwise appropriate. Alternatively, contracting parties may intend to agree in advance on a forum where any and all of their disputes must be brought to eliminate surprise of having to litigate in a hostile forum.").

[567] ALM Media Properties, LLC., *To Avoid Unintended Results, Forum Selection Clauses Must Be Precise; IN PRACTICE Daily Report (Fulton County GA)* (Feb. 3, 2015), https://www.mmmlaw.com/files/documents/publications/To-Avoid-Unintended-Results.pdf (last visited Jun. 8, 2018).

[568] See, e.g., Falconwood Fin. Corp. v. Griffin, 838 F. Supp. 836 (S.D.N.Y. 1993) (「The parties hereby agree that the exclusive venue for suit with respect to this Agreement shall be the courts of the State of New York or the federal courts of the Southern District of New York ....」との規定を Mandatory Choice of Forum を選択したものである旨示した); ASM Communications Inc. v. Allen, 656 F. Supp. 838, 839 (S.D.N.Y. 1987) (Choice of Forum Clause で用いられている「shall」を Mandatory Choice of Forum をうかがわせる語句として，「may」を Permissive Choice of Forum をうかがわせる語句として示した)．

ずれで行われるかといったことまでも規定される場合がある[569].

これは Choice of Forum Clause の趣旨を徹底するものであるが，かなり具体的な規定となることから，その条項に含まれた文言の解釈をめぐった争いが生じる場合も多く[570]，いっそうの注意が必要となる．

b. Choice of Forum Clause の非絶対性
Choice of Forum Clause は原則として有効であり，無効または執行力がないものと判断される場合は，以下のとおり，きわめて限定的である．

i. 不合理または公共の福祉に反する場合
Choice of Forum Clause は，不合理または公共の福祉に反するような場合においては無効である．もっとも，両契約当事者が契約書を推敲するに十分な能力を持った事業者であるような場合は Choice of Forum Clause の有効性が支持される可能性が高い[571]．

ii. Doctrine of Forum Non Conveniens が適用される場合
たとえ訴訟が適切な連邦地方裁判所に提起されたとしても，その連邦地方裁判所は審理を拒否する固有の権利を有し[572]，これを Doctrine of Forum

---

[569] 裁定地に関する規定はあるものの連邦裁判所または州裁判所のいずれによって裁定されるかについての明示はない場合，連邦裁判所および州裁判所のいずれによる裁定も許容する趣旨と理解される例が多いようである．See also, ALM Media Properties, LLC., supra note 566; see, e.g., Alliance Health Group, LLC v. Bridging Health Options, LLC 553 F.3d 397 (5th Cir. 2008) (「Exclusive venue for any litigation related hereto shall occur in Harrison County, Mississippi.」との規定がある場合において，連邦裁判所または州裁判所のいずれにも訴訟提起を認めた条項である旨を示した).

[570] See, e.g., Doe 1 v. AOL LLC, 552 F.3d 1077 (9th Cir. 2009) (「Courts of Virginia」との文言について，Virginia 州裁判所を指し，連邦裁判所を含まない旨を示した); see also, e.g., Alliance Health Group, LLC, 553 F.3d 397 (「The Courts of Texas, U.S.A.」との文言について，連邦裁判所は州に属するものではないことを理由としてその対象には含まれない旨を示した); see also, e.g., Sompo Japan Ins., Inc. v. Alarm Detection Systems, Inc., 2003 U.S. Dist. LEXIS 13689 (N.D. Ill. 2003) (「Venue shall be proper in Kane County, Illinois should any portion of this contract have to be legally enforced.」との規定について，州裁判所の裁判地を示すうえでは「County」の表記が適切である一方，連邦裁判所の裁判地を示すうえでは「Judicial District」の表記が適切であるとして，州裁判所のみに管轄を認めた).

[571] See, e.g., Frontier Leasing Corp. v. Shah, 2007 PA Super 225, 14 (citing Liberty Bank, F.S.B. v. Best Litho, Inc., 737 N.W.2d 312, 315) ("A forum selection clause should control absent a strong showing that it should be set aside. A choice of forum made inan arm's-length negotiation by experienced and sophisticated businessmen should be honored by the parties and enforced by the courts absent some compelling and countervailing reason.").

[572] See, e.g., Vanderham v. Brookfield Asset Mgmt., Inc., 102 F.Supp.3d 1315, 1318 (S.D.Fla. 2015) ("Under the doctrine of forum non conveniens, a district court has the inherent power to decline to exercise jurisdiction even when venue is proper.").

Non Conveniens という[573]．連邦裁判所によるこの権利の行使は，例えば Ohio 州で訴訟が提起されたものの，訴訟の原因も証人となる者もすべて Hawaii 州が関係しているといったように，その裁判所による審理を進めることが著しく公共の福祉に反するような場合[574]に認められる．

このように Doctrine of Forum Non Conveniens は公共の福祉をも理念においたものであるため，Choice of Forum Clause に優先して機能する[575]．

Section 18.18 Waiver of Jury Trial.

Each Party acknowledges and agrees that any controversy that may arise under this Agreement, including any Individual Transactions or exhibits, schedules, attachments, and appendices attached to this Agreement, is likely to involve complicated and difficult issues and, therefore, each such Party irrevocably and unconditionally waives any right it may have to a trial by jury in respect of any legal action arising out of or relating to this Agreement, including any Individual Transactions, exhibits, schedules, attachments, or appendices attached to this Agreement, or the transactions contemplated hereby. Each Party certifies and acknowledges

---

[573] 28 U.S.C. § 1404(a) (2011).その連邦地方裁判所は訴訟審理を棄却したうえで，適切だと思われる別の裁判所へ事件を移送することになる．もっとも，その適切だと思われる別の裁判所が米国外の裁判所である場合，連邦裁判所は事件を移送する権限を持たない．したがって，連邦裁判所は事件を却下するのみとなる．その場合，公平を期すべく，別途原告が米国外で訴訟提起できるよう，訴訟却下の条件として，被告に時効の主張を行わない旨の確約などをとりつける場合がある．Thomas O Main, *"Toward a Law of 'Lovely Parting Gifts': Conditioning Forum Non Conveniens Dismissals"* (2012), Scholarly Works, Paper 786, http://scholars.law.unlv.edu/cgi/viewcontent.cgi?article=1808&context=facpub (last visited Jun. 22, 2018).

[574] *See, e.g.,* GDG Acquisitions, LLC v. Government of Belize, 749 F.3d 1024, 1028 (11th Cir.2014). "To obtain dismissal for *forum non conveniens,* "[t]he moving party must demonstrate that (1) an adequate alternative forum is available, (2) the public and private factors weigh in favor of dismissal, and (3) the plaintiff can reinstate his suit in the alternative forum without undue inconvenience or prejudice."

[575] *See generally* Jiangsu Hongyuan Pharmaceutical Co., Ltd. v. DI Global Logistics Inc., 159 F.Supp.3d 1316, 1327 ("The existence of a valid, enforceable, mandatory, and applicable forum selection clause—like the clause contained in the Agreement—is not alone dispositive in the *forum non conveniens* analysis."). もっとも，Choice of Forum Clause は，Doctrine of Forum Non Conveniens の適用の判断要素の一つである「private factors」については「forum non conveniens」を肯定する方向では考慮されないという意義を持つようである．*See, e.g.,* GDG Acquisitions, LLC v. Gov't of Belize, 749 F.3d 1024, 1028 (Atl. Marine Constr. Co. v. United States Dist. Court, 571 U.S. 49, 134 S. Ct. 568) ("When parties agree to a forum-selection clause, they waive the right to challenge the preselected forum as inconvenient or less convenient for themselves or their witnesses, or for their pursuit of the litigation. A court accordingly must deem the private-interest factors to weigh entirely in favor of the preselected forum . . . .").

> that (a) no Representative of the other Party has represented, expressly or otherwise, that such other Party would not seek to enforce the foregoing waiver in the event of a legal action, (b) such Party has considered the implications of this waiver, (c) such Party makes this waiver voluntarily, and (d) such Party has been induced to enter into this Agreement by, among other things, the mutual waivers and certifications in this Section 18.18.

6.19 Waiver of Jury Trial Clause
　陪審員による裁判を受ける権利は憲法上の権利である[576]。しかし，陪審員による裁判については，(1) 時間および費用を要すること，(2) 陪審員は裁判官と比べて個人および中小企業に対して同情的な判断を下す傾向が見受けられること，および (3) 陪審員による評決は裁判官による判決と比べて上級審で覆されることが多いことなどが懸念事項として挙げられる[577]。そこで，Waiver of Jury Trial Clause のもと，契約当事者間で陪審員による裁判を利用しない旨あらかじめ合意しておくという選択を行う場合がある。
　このような陪審員による裁判を受ける権利の放棄が有効[578]といえるためにはその放棄が，「knowing, voluntary and intelligent」[579]に行われる必要がある。特に契約書の起案との関係においては，「knowing, voluntary and intelligent」を満たすための要件の一つである「conspicuous language」[580]を満たすよう，Waiver of Jury

---

[576] U.S. Const. amend. VII.

[577] See, e.g., Daniel Avery & Daniel Brody, *Trends in M&A Provisions: Waiver of Jury Trials*, The Bureau of National Affairs, Inc., https://www.goulstonstorrs.com/portalresource/jury_trials_waiver (last visited Oct. 18, 2017).

[578] ただし，California 州，Georgia 州，および North Carolina 州においては Waiver of Jury Trial Clause を認めていない。See, e.g., Grafton Partners v. Superior Court, 116 P.3d 479, 485 (Sup. Ct. Cal. 2005) ("We agree with the Court of Appeal in the present case that, '[a]s our recitation of California's constitutional history reveals, unless the Legislature prescribes a jury waiver method, we cannot enforce it.' To the extent *Trizec Properties, Inc. v. Superior Court, supra*, 229 Cal. App. 3d 1616, holds that the right to jury trial may be waived in a manner that is without statutory authorization, it is disapproved."); *see also, e.g.,* Bank South, N.A. v. Howard, 444 S.E. 2d 799, 800 (Sup. Ct. Ga. 1994) ("we hold, as stated above, that pre-litigation contractual waivers of the right to trial by jury are not enforceable in cases tried under the laws of Georgia."); NC Gen Stat § 22B-10.

[579] See, e.g., Leasing Service Corp. v. Crane, 804 F.2d 828, 833 (4th Cir. 1986) ("The seventh amendment right is of course a fundamental one, but it is one that can be knowingly and intentionally waived by contract.").

[580] See, e.g., Malan Realty Investors v. Harris, 953 S.W.2d 624, 627 (Sup. Ct. Mo. 1997) ("To effectively waive a jury trial by contract, clear, unambiguous, unmistakable, and conspicuous language is required. Such a waiver provision will never be implied but must be clearly and explicitly stated. Additionally, the courts have examined the following factors: negotiability of the contract terms, disparity in bargaining power between the parties, the business acumen of the party opposing the waiver, and the conspicuousness of

Trial Clause は，大文字または太文字を用いて設けることが望ましい[581]．そのほか，Waiver of Jury Trial Clause を 18.18 条のように独立した条項として設けることも有効である[582]．

> Section 18.19 Prevailing Language.
>
> The whole text of this Agreement, as well as the documents derived from it, including those in the Schedules and Exhibits, have been written in English and Japanese, both versions being deemed authentic, but for legal purposes the text in English is to be given priority of interpretation.

6.20 Language Clause
特に両契約当事者が異なる国の企業である場合においては，ひとつの契約が複数の言語で用意されることも少なくはないが，その場合，両言語版の間で矛盾が生じうる．Language Clause はそのような事態が生じた場合において，どの言語版が優先的な効力を有するかを明確にするものである．

Language Clause のもと，どの言語版を優先させるかについては契約当事者間の交渉事項となるが，一般には問題の複雑化および無用な追加コストの回避を目的として，その契約の適用法または裁定地において用いられる言語を選択することが望ましいとされる[583]．なお，国際的取引に関する契約書の参考として用意された UNIDROIT Principles においては，言語間で矛盾が生じた場合は，契約の起案に使用された言語が優先して効力を有するものとされている[584]．

---

the jury waiver provision.")．

[581] *See* Anderson Kill P.C., *Enforceability of Jury Waiver Provisions in Federal Court* (Dec. 16, 2016), https://www.andersonkill.com/Publication-Details/PublicationID/1486 (last visited Oct. 18, 2017)．ただし，契約書全体を見た場合に大文字または太文字を用いた条項が他にも多く存在する結果として Waiver of Jury Trial Clause が目立たなくなるような事態は避けるべきであるとされる．*Id.*

[582] *Id.*

[583] *Language Clause in International Contracts*, Internatinalcontracts.net, http://www.internationalcontracts.net/Clauses/Language-Clause-in-International-Contracts.pdf (last visited Apr. 11, 2018).

[584] UNIDROIT Principles (2016) art. 4.7.

CHAPTER 7 / SIGNATURE LINES

契約は，①Offer，②Acceptance，および③Consideration の存在をもって成立し，書面または署名は必要とされないのが原則である[585]．しかし，両契約当事者による契約への合意の事実を明らかにする，または，契約に関する紛争が生じた際の証拠として有用であるといった理由から，契約書を用意したうえで，署名欄に署名を行うことはごく通常のこととして行われている．

[Sample Clause 1]

IN WITNESS WHEREOF, the Parties hereto have executed and delivered this Agreement as of the Effective Date.

[Sample Clause 2]

To evidence the Parties' agreement to this Agreement, the Parties hereto have executed and delivered this Agreement as of the Effective Date.

[Sample Clause 3]

To evidence the Parties' agreement to this Agreement, the Parties hereto have executed and delivered this Agreement on October 8, 2014, but it is effective as of the Effective Date stated in the preamble.

7.1 Testimonium Clause

Testimonium Clause は，契約当事者がその契約に署名し，契約の法的拘束力を受けることに合意したことを明示する機能を有する[586]．

　　a.「IN WITNESS WHEREOF」

Recitals において WITNESSETH Clause が用いられた場合，Testimonium Clause においては，Sample Clause 1 のように，「IN WITNESS WHEREOF」を

---

[585] *See, e.g.*, Schaller Tel. Co. v. Golden Sky Sys., 298 F.3d 736 (8th Cir. 2002) ("Iowa recognizes the validity of oral contracts, even in those cases in which the parties intend to commit their agreement to writing.").
[586] Stark, *supra* note 1, at 241.

含む一節が必要となることはすでに紹介したとおりである．これに対して，Recitals においては Background Clause を用い，Testimonium Clause においては Sample Clause 2 のように規定することも可能である．

b.「[E]xecuted and [D]elivered」
　Testimonium Clause においては，契約が成立したことの証明として，両契約当事者が契約書を「executed and delivered」した旨を規定することが多い．ここに「execution」とは，契約書への署名に代表される，契約を有効なものとする行為をいい[587]，「delivery」とは，署名済みの契約書を他方当事者に交付する行為をいう[588]．そこで，「executed」された契約書の「delivered」を要求する「executed and delivered」については，契約の成立要件に新たに「delivery」を追加したものであるとも評価できる[589]．

　契約に拘束されることに関する当事者の同意を明確化するという Testimonium Clause の趣旨をふまえると，「delivery」を契約の成立要件として加えることも理解できる．単に契約書に署名のみすることと，契約書に署名したうえで相手方に交付することでは，後者のほうが契約当事者の契約の拘束に関する認識は強いといえるからである[590]．

　これに対して，Testimonium Clause においては，契約当事者が対象契約を「executed」（または「signed」）したことのみをもって契約が成立したものとする[591]こともちろん可能である．ただし，この場合においても適用法における「execution」[592]または「signing」[593]の解釈について事前に確認しておくことが望ましい．

---

[587] *Black's Law Dictionary: Pocket Edition* 288 (4th ed. 2011).
[588] *Id.* at 217 (4th ed. 2011).
[589] Stark, *supra* note 1, at 240 (citing Midwest Mfg. Holding, L.L.C. v. Donnelly Corp., 1998 U.S. Dist. LEXIS 1398 (N.D. Ill. 1998)).
[590] Stark, *supra* note 1, at 241.
[591] つまり，この場合，次のように規定することになる．「IN WITNESS WHEREOF, the Parties hereto have executed ((または) signed) this Agreement as of the Effective Date.」．
[592] *See generally* Hayes v. Ammon, 1904 N.Y. App. Div. LEXIS 105, 3 (Sup. Ct. N.Y. 1904) (「Execution」について，「signing, sealing, and delivery」を意味する旨を示した) ("Execution implies complete execution -- signing, sealing and delivery; whereas signing implies only one of the steps towards execution.").
[593] *See generally* Hubbard v. Tobin, 15 Misc. 2d 65 (Sup. Ct. N.Y. 1958) (仲介手数料を「upon the signing of the leases」を条件として支払う旨規定した契約書の「signing」については，「signing, sealing, and delivery」の意味までも含む可能性と単に「signing」の意味のみを示す可能性とがあるものの，契約書が仲介手数料の受領予定者によって起案されたことも考慮すると単に「signing」の意味のみを示すとは解釈できない旨を示した).

c.「[A]s of the Effective Date」

「[A]s of the Effective Date」は，契約の効力発生日を示す機能を有するが，実際に「executed and delivered」が行われた日とは異なる場合もある[594]。そのような場合においては，契約の効力発生日と両契約当事者による契約書への署名日との関係を明確にするべく，Sample Clause 3 のような記載とすることも考えられる[595]。

```
                    [BUYER NAME]
                    By _____
                    Name:
                    Title:

                    [SELLER NAME]
                    By _____
                    Name:
                    Title:
```

7.2 Signature Block

署名は契約当事者の「Acceptance」を示す手段として非常に有力な方法であるが，以下のように，署名欄（Signature Block）の記載などによってその意義を失うような事態もおきかねない。

a. 署名者

契約当事者が個人である場合，その個人の法律上のフルネームを記載する[596]。これに対して，契約当事者が法人である場合，①契約当事者である

---

[594] Effective Date において両契約当事者が合意し，かつ，両契約当事者による署名が行われた場合，「the parties hereto have executed and delivered this Agreement dated the Effective Date」と表記することができる。これに対して，Effective Date において両契約当事者が合意したものの，両契約当事者による署名は別途行われるという場合においては，「the parties hereto have executed and delivered this Agreement dated as of the Effective Date」と表記することになる。Stark, *supra* note 1, at 68.
[595] *Id.* at 71.
[596] 「Acceptance」を示すという署名の趣旨からは，必ずしも契約当事者のフルネームでの署名は必要ないはずである。例えば，U.C.C.は，有価証券（negotiable instrument）との関係において，通称や記号であってもその契約当事者の契約への合意を示すに足りるものであれば署名として許容する。U.C.C. § 3-

会社の法律上の正式名称（Legal Name という[597]），および，②契約署名者の法律上のフルネームを記載することになる．会社名称の記載がなかった場合[598]，または，会社名称が不正確であった場合[599]においては署名者が個人としてその契約上の責任を問われる可能性もあることに留意しなければならない．

b. 署名者

相手方契約当事者との取引が初めてである場合などにおいては，署名者が適切な者であるかを確認する必要も生じうる[600]．また，法人が締結する契約の場合，その署名者による署名が Bylaws などの社内規則[601]によって許容されているかの確認が必要となる場合もある．例えば，契約締結の結果として会社が高額の金銭負担を負うこととなる場合，複数名の署名が会社規則によって要求されていることがある．

401(b) (Am. Law Inst. & Unif. Law Comm'n 2002).

[597] 例えば「Disneyland, Inc.」のように，「Inc.」，「LLC」，または「Corp.」といった会社種別を示す用語を含む名称をいう．Legal Name は会社の定款 (Articles of Incorporation) における明示が要求されている．

[598] See, e.g., Mahoney v. Pitman, 43 S.W.2d 143, 146 (Civ. App. Tex. 1931) (quoting 2 C. J. 816, §49) (代理人として行動する者は，その代理行為に関する個人責任を回避するためには，相手方当事者に対して，自己の代理人としての立場のみならず，本人の特定をも自発的に行う必要がある旨を示した) ("'It is the duty of the agent, if he would avoid personal liability on a contract entered into by him on behalf of the principal, to disclose not only the fact that he is acting in a representative capacity but also the identity of his principal, as the person dealt with is not bound to inquire whether or not the agent is acting as such for another.'").

[599] See, e.g., Lachmann v. Houston Chronicle Publishing Co., 375 S.W.2d 783, 785 (Civ. App. Tex. 1964) (会社の Trade Name (ビジネスで使用しているいわゆる通称．例えば「McDonald's」は一般消費者の間で認識されているファストフードチェーンの通称名たる Trade Name であるが，同社の Legal Name は「McDonald's Corporation」である．Trade Name は Fictitious Name または Doing Business As (DBA) ともいう) を示したことのみをもっては会社の代理人として契約に関与した個人をその契約に関わる責任から免責するには不十分である旨を示した) ("This case stands alone, and according to the annotation in 150 A.L.R. 1303, the majority of cases hold that the use of a trade name is not a sufficient disclosure of the identity of the principal and of the fact of agency.").

[600] 例えば Incumbency Certificate (法人が証明した文書であり，Officer の名称とそれらの署名サンプルなどが含まれている) の提出を依頼することが考えられる．

[601] そのほか，同一の契約当事者間で別に締結している契約によって契約署名者に関する制約が課されているような場合もあるので注意が必要である．See, e.g., Echo, Inc. v. Whitson Co., 121 F.3d 1099 (7th Cir. 1997) (原告と被告との間の設備売買に関する基本契約においては原告から被告に向けて発行された個別注文についての Acceptance は被告の本社によって行われる旨規定されていることを理由として，被告の地方事務所の営業責任者が署名した個別注文書の有効性を否定した).

c. 署名欄

署名欄はできる限り契約本文の最終条項と同じページ上に存在すべきである．署名欄が契約本文とまったく別のページに存在している場合，契約当事者が契約を確認したうえで署名したことが不明瞭になってしまい，結果として相手方契約当事者から契約に同意していない，または，契約内容について十分な説明を受けていないといった主張が行われかねない[602]．

もっとも，契約書の体裁上，署名欄がどうしても契約本文とは別のページになってしまう場合もある．その場合，契約本文が記載された最終ページのうち，区切りのよいところで記載を止めることになる．そのページには空白部分ができることになるため，最終文から数行の間隔をとった上で空白部分に，[INTENTIONALLY LEFT BLANK][603]と記載するか[604]，または，空白全体を「X」で覆い追記ができないようにする．契約本文の残りの部分の記載と署名欄は次ページに引き続いて記載することになる[605]．

7.3 電子署名

ある契約書が真正に成立したものであるかを判別するうえでは，自署が有力な手がかりとして機能する[606]．しかし，取引のグローバル化および迅速化ならびに電子機器の進化といった環境のもと，自署に変わって電子署名の方式がとられることも多い．一般に電子署名は契約書の署名として有効であるとされる[607]．ここに電子署名には，インターネット上で，「I Accept」などと表記され

---

[602] Stark, *supra* note 1, at 249.

[603] 大文字かつ太文字を用いることが推奨されている．*Id.* at 249.

[604] そのほか，[THE REMAINDER OF THIS PAGE INTENTIONALLY LEFT BLANK; SIGNATURE PAGE FOLLOWS]などと記載する例も見受けられる．

[605] Stark, *supra* note 1, at 249.

[606] Fed. R. Evi. 901(b)(2).

[607] 15 U.S.C. § 7001-7031 (The Electronic Signatures in Global and National Commerce Act という); Unif. Elecs. Transactions Act (UETA という) § 1-21 (2002) (2017 年 2 月時点で 47 州において採択されている); Kenneth Chase & Patrick J, Hatfield, *E-Signatures and Electronic Contracts: Complying With ESIGN and the UETA, Interplay With the UCC Navigating Issues of Enforceability, Authentication and Admissibility*, 16, http://media.straffordpub.com/products/e-signatures-and-electronic-contracts-complying-with-esign-and-the-ueta-interplay-with-the-ucc-2017-02-15/presentation.pdf (last visited Jun. 22, 2018). Illinois 州，New York 州，および Washington 州において UETA は採択されていないが，例えば New York 州も電子署名の有効性を肯定する旨を示している．*See, e.g.*, Naldi v Grunberg, 908 N.Y.S.2d 639, 646 (Sup. Ct. N.Y. 2010) (internal citation omitted) ("Thus, we conclude that E-SIGN's requirement that an electronically memorialized and subscribed contract be given the same legal effect as a contract memorialized and subscribed on paper is part of New York law, whether or not the transaction at issue is a matter 'in or affecting interstate or foreign commerce.'").

たボタンを押す場合も含む[608]。

7.4 イニシャルの利用

契約書においては，以下のような目的のもと，契約署名者の署名ではなく，イニシャルが利用される場面がある．

a. 契約内容の訂正または変更

契約書を用意したものの，署名手続きを実施する直前に誤記が発見されたり，または，契約内容の変更に合意するといったこともありうる．この場合，あらためて契約書を印刷して用意しなおす必要はなく，その訂正または変更箇所に契約署名者がイニシャルを添えることで足りる[609]．

b. 契約内容の改ざんの防止

契約書の各ページにイニシャルを記載することで契約書が勝手に改ざんされるような自体を防止することもできる．もっともあらゆる契約書においてこのような手続きをふむことは煩雑でもあるから，特に重要な契約に限るなどされているのが実状である[610]．

c. 契約内容に関する認識および同意の表明

特定の重要な条項については契約当事者の認識および同意を示す意味でイニシャルを添えることがある[611]．例えば，陪審員による裁判を受ける権利は契約当事者による「knowing, voluntary, intelligent」な権利の放棄が認められているが，そのような有効な権利の放棄を裏付ける目的のもとイニシャルを要求するのである．

---

[608] Stark, *supra* note 1, at 248.
[609] LegalNature, *Amending a Contract: When and Why*, http://help.legalnature.com/36446-articles/amending-a-contract-when-and-why (last visited Apr. 20, 2018).
[610] Kenneth A. Adams, *Initialing Each Page of a Contract*, Adams on Contract Drafting (May 9, 2009), http://www.adamsdrafting.com/intialing-each-page/ (last visited Apr. 20, 2018). ただし，特定の契約書について各ページへのイニシャルを要求する州法などもある．*E.g.*, Ohio Rev. Code § 1349.55 (法人が消費者との間で締結する和解契約に関しては，各ページにイニシャルを要求する).
[611] Stark, *supra* note 1, at 250.

CHAPTER 8 / ANCILLARY DOCUMENTS

契約書は，例えば製品の仕様書または開発スケジュールなどを内容の一部とすべき場合もあるが，そのような情報は契約本文において言及するよりも契約書の別紙として添付する方が適切な場合がある．

Schedule I

- Products (Section 1.22)
- Prices (Section 8.1)

Schedule II

- Specifications (Section 1.25)

8.1 Ancillary Documents

a. Definitive Agreement または Ancillary Documents

契約に関する基本的な内容を規定した契約書を Definitive Agreement という．これに対して，契約に関する補完的内容を規定した書面を Ancillary Documents といい，Schedules，Exhibits，および Addendums などを指す[612]．

b. Ancillary Documents

以下のとおり，Schedules，Exhibits，および Addendums は，それぞれ異なる目的で用意される．

i. Schedules

Schedules は，例えば，本契約の対象製品を一覧にして明確にする場合などに用いられるものであり，契約本文の一部そのものとなる[613]．

---

[612] J. Gerard Legagneur, *How to Effectively Use Schedules, Exhibits, and Addendums in Your Contracts*, Nolo, https://www.nolo.com/legal-encyclopedia/how-to-effectively-use-schedules-exhibits-and-addendums-in-your-contracts.html (last visited Mar. 20, 2018).
[613] 契約本文においては，例えば，次のように Schedules に関して規定することになる．「A true and complete list of the Products is set forth on Schedule I attached hereto.」．

ii. Exhibits

すでに存在する文書[614]、または、将来存在することになる文書は、参照目的で、「Exhibits」として契約に添付される場合がある[615]。例えば、契約当事者の存在を証明する目的で Certificate of Incorporation を添付する場合が挙げられる。Exhibit の内容は契約本文の一部そのものとはならない。

iii. Addendums

ある契約に依拠して締結される予定の別個の契約については Addendum[616] として契約に添付される場合がある[617]。例えば、開発契約においては開発に関する基本条件が規定され、それに基づいて個別の開発案件については別途詳細な事項に関する規定（Statements of Work などという）を設ける場合があるが、Statements of Work は開発契約の Addendums として添付されることが多い。Addendums の内容は契約本文の一部そのものとはならない。

このように Schedules、Exhibits、および Addendums はいずれも契約本文の後に添付される書面であるが、これらのうち Schedules は契約本文を構成するものとなるため、Exhibits および Addendums よりも先立って、契約本文の直後に添付されるべきである[618]。

---

[614] Legagneur, *supra* note 612.

[615] 契約本文においては、例えば、次のように Exhibits について規定することになる。「Within thirty (30) days of the Effective Date, each of the Buyer and the Seller shall execute a Service Agreement substantially in the form of Exhibit A attached hereto.」。

[616] Addendums は契約を改訂する趣旨で用意される Amendments とは別物である。Legagneur, *supra* note 612.

[617] 契約本文においては、例えば、次のように Addendums について規定することになる。「In the event the Parties mutually agree to any additional services to be provided by the Seller hereunder, the parties shall negotiate and execute a Statement of Work in connection therewith and attach each such Statement of Work to Addendum A hereto.」。

[618] *See* Kenneth A. Adams, *Which Come First, Schedules or Exhibits?*, Adams on Contract Drafting (Jan. 6, 2009), http://www.adamsdrafting.com/which-first-exhibits-or-schedules/ (last visited Mar. 21, 2018) (Schedule と Exhibit との間では Schedule を先立って契約本文の後に添付するべきとする)。

おわりに

　本書の構想に際して，書棚に積み重なった自己の研究，調査および検討に関する資料を融合させる作業に着手しはじめたのは，米国での生活も早 6 年に近づいたころであった．以降，同地で執筆を進めるわけであるが，完成も間近となったころには米国を離れることとなり，現在は新たな生活を開始している．したがって，本書は，筆者にとって，形式的にも実質的にも米国と強い関わりを持つ，非常に思い入れのある一冊である．

　本書の完成に至るまでの工程は，関係者の皆様のご協力によって，予想よりは困難を極めることなく進めることができた．この幸運を筆者が真の意味でうまく生かすことができたかどうかについては，読者の方々のご判断に委ねるほかないが，まずはここに，お世話になった皆様にお礼を申し上げる機会をいただきたい．

　まず，株式会社大学教育出版の佐藤守社長には，筆者のように無名かつ実績のない者による本書の原案に可能性を見いだしていただいた．次に，同じく株式会社大学教育出版の社彩香さんには，筆者のこだわりへのご対応を含め，本書の完成に至るまでを熱心にサポートしていただいた．そして，The Ohio State University Moritz College of Law の教授の皆様方には，本書のうち特に難解な部分についての確認作業のご快諾に加え，各専門分野ごとに適切かつ思慮深いアドバイスをもご提供いただいた．心よりお礼を申し上げたい．

最後に，筆者にとっての大きな挑戦をさまざまな形で支えてくれた妻の恵梨子と子の春真には，ただただ感謝するばかりである．ありがとう．

2019 年 2 月
米国中西部における日々を振り返りながら

瀬川　一真

■著者紹介

瀬川　一真（せがわ・かずま）

最終学歴：The Ohio State University Moritz College of Law
現　　職：アルプスアルパイン株式会社法務部法務2グループ
　　　　　グループマネージャー（米国弁護士（Washington, D.C.））
　　　　　The Ohio State University Moritz College of Law
　　　　　Office of International and Graduate Affairs 大使
学　　位：The Master of Laws（法学修士）
専門分野：米国契約法

米国法適用下における商取引契約書
Explanations of Commercial Contracts under U.S. law

2019年4月20日　初版第1刷発行

■著　者──瀬川一真
■発 行 者──佐藤　守
■発 行 所──株式会社 大学教育出版
　　　　　　〒700-0953　岡山市南区西市855-4
　　　　　　電話(086)244-1268㈹　FAX(086)246-0294
■印刷製本──モリモト印刷㈱
■ＤＴＰ──林　雅子

© Kazuma Segawa 2019, Printed in Japan
検印省略　　落丁・乱丁本はお取り替えいたします。
本書のコピー・スキャン・デジタル化等の無断複製は著作権法上での例外を除き禁じられています。本書を代行業者等の第三者に依頼してスキャンやデジタル化することは、たとえ個人や家庭内での利用でも著作権法違反です。

ISBN978-4-86692-003-0